Endorsed by
Cambridge International Examinations

Physics

Richard Woodside

www.pearsonglobalschools.com
Free online support
Useful weblinks
24 hour online ordering

ALWAYS LEARNING   PEARSON

Heinemann is an imprint of Pearson Education Limited, a company incorporated in England and Wales, having its registered office at Edinburgh Gate, Harlow, Essex, CM20 2JE. Registered company number: 872828

www.pearsonglobalschools.com
Heinemann is a registered trademark of Pearson Education Limited

Text © Pearson Education Limited 2009

First published 2009

20 19 18 17 16 15 14 13
IMP 10 9 8 7

British Library Cataloguing in Publication Data is available from the British Library on request.

ISBN 978 0 435966 81 2

Copyright notice
All rights reserved. No part of this publication may be reproduced in any form or by any means (including photocopying or storing it in any medium by electronic means and whether or not transiently or incidentally to some other use of this publication) without the written permission of the copyright owner, except in accordance with the provisions of the Copyright, Designs and Patents Act 1988 or under the terms of a licence issued by the Copyright Licensing Agency, Saffron House, 6–10 Kirby Street, London EC1N 8TS (www.cla.co.uk). Applications for the copyright owner's written permission should be addressed to the publisher.

Edited by Paul King and Saskia Besier
Designed by Tony Richardson
Typeset by Tech-Set Ltd
Original illustrations © Pearson Education Limited 2009
Illustrated by Tech-Set Ltd
Cover design by Creative Monkey
Picture research by Ginny Stroud-Lewis
Cover photo/illustration © Alamy/Andrew Patterson
Printed and bound in Malaysia (CTP-PPSB)

Acknowledgements
The author and publisher would like to thank the following individuals and organisations for permission to reproduce photographs:

Every effort has been made to contact copyright holders of material reproduced in this book. Any omissions will be rectified in subsequent printings if notice is given to the publishers.

There are links to relevant websites in this book. In order to ensure that the links are up-to-date, that the links work, and that the sites are not inadvertently linked to sites that could be considered offensive, we have made the links available on the Heinemann website at www.heinemann.co.uk/hotlinks. When you access the site, the express code is 6812S.

On the CD
Past paper questions are reproduced by permission of the University of Cambridge Local Examinations Syndicate.

The University of Cambridge Local Examinations Syndicate bears no responsibility for the example answers to questions taken from its past question papers which are contained on the CD contained within this publication.

IGCSE® is the registered trademark of Cambridge International Examinations.

Dedication
I would like to thank all those people who gave help and advice during the production of this book. I would particularly like to thank my wife, Cora, not only for proof reading the manuscript – but for the general support and help, without which I could not have completed the task.

Acknowledgements

The author and publisher would like to thank the following individuals and organisations for permission to reproduce photographs:

p.1 tl. © Science Photo Library / David Leah, tr. © Ginny Stroud-Lewis, bl. © Alamy / The Print Collector, br. © Shutterstock / Rod Beverley; p.5 l. © Shutterstock / Thomas Mounsey, c. © Shutterstock / Polina Lobanova, r. © Shutterstock / Simon Jenkins; p.6 tl. © Alamy / Leslie Garland Picture Library, tr. © Science Photo Library / Charles D Winters, bl. © Alamy / Leslie Garland Picture Library, br. © Alamy / David Martyn Hughes, p.9 t. © Alamy / The Print Collector, b. © Shutterstock / Rod Beverley; p. 12 © iStockphoto / Freddie Vargas; p.16 © Alamy / Jupiterimages / Pixland; p.21 tl. © Alamy / PhotoStock-Israel, br. © iStockphoto / Vinko Murko, c. © Shutterstock / rpixs; p.35 © Alamy / Photodisc / Stewart Charles Cohen; p.36 © Alamy / Bramwellslocker ; p.40 © Alamy / Mark Scheuern; p.43 tl. © Shutterstock / Debra James, tr. © Shutterstock / Kirsz Marcin; p.44 tl. © Shutterstock / Maksym Gorpenyuk, cl. © Art Directors and Trip / Helene Rogers, bl. © Shutterstock / niderlander; p.45 © Corbis / Miles / zefa; p.47 © Corbis / Miles / zefa; p.51 tr. © KPT Power Photos, br. © PhotoDisc; p.52© Alamy / James Nesterwitz; p.53 tl. © iStockphoto / Danny Warren, bl. © Digital Vision, br. © Shutterstock / argus; p.54 cl. © PhotoDisc, tc. © Art Directors and Trip / Helene Rogers, bc. © Pearson Education Ltd / Tudor Photography, cr. © iStockhphoto / Chris Crafter; p.55 tl. © Corbis / Schlegelmilch, tr. © PhotoDisc, bl. © PhotoDisc, br. © iStockphoto / Linda Kloosterhof; p.56 tl. © Science Photo Library / John Walsh, cl. © Shutterstock / ArchMan, bl. © Shutterstock / Terrance Emerson; p.57 © Getty Images / Photographer's Choice / Bengt Geijerstam; p.58 tl. © Shutterstock / Beth Van Trees, bl. © iStockphoto / Mark Evans, br. © Alamy / Paul Glendell; p.59 tl. © Shutterstock / Vera Tomankova, tr. © Shutterstock / Albert Lozano, br. © Shutterstock / Timothy Large; p.61 tl. © Science Photo Library / E. R. Degginger, bl. © Science Photo Library, br. © Science Photo Library / Philippe Plailly; p.62 tl. © Shutterstock / Sebastian Knight, cr. © iStockphoto / Leanne Kanowski, cl. © Science Photo Library / E. R. Degginger, cb © Science Photo Library / Eric Grave, br. © Shutterstock / Alexei Novikov; p.64 © Shutterstock / Mau Horng; p.70 tr. © Digital Vision, br. © NASA / HSTI / J. J. Hester, Arizona State University; p.72 © Peter Robinson; p.74 © Science Photo Library / Francoise Sauze; p.75 tl. © Shutterstock / Gina Sanders tr. © Alamy / sciencephotos; p.79 tl. © PhotoDisc, tr. © NOAA, bl. © Shutterstock / Claudio Givanni Columbo, br. © Shutterstock / Thierry Maffeis; p.80 © Shutterstock / Robert Soen; p.84 tl. © Shutterstock / Can Balcioglu, tr. © Shutterstock / Liga Lauzuma, br. © Shutterstock / Marika Eglite; p.87 © Shutterstock / Peter Elvidge; p.89 tr. © Shutterstock / WitR, bl. © Shutterstock / Timothy Large; p.90 tl. © Shutterstock / Dan Briški, tr. © iStockphoto / Brent Reeves; p.92 © Corbis / Javier Barbancho / Reuters; p.97 © Shutterstock / Henrique Daniel Araujo; p.101 © Science Photo Library / Martin Bond; p.103 tl. © Pearson Education Ltd / Tudor Photography, tr. © iStockphoto.com / Peeter Viisimaa, bl © Shutterstock / Andresr, br. © Alamy / Chris Howes / Wild Places Photography; p.104 © Shutterstock / Hiroshi Sato; p.111 t. © Shutterstock / Opla, b. © Shutterstock / Anson Hung; p.114 tr. © Alamy / Chris Howes / Wild Places Photography, cl. © Science Photo Library / Andrew Lambert Photography, bc. © Corbis / Owen Franken; p.120 © Science Photo Library / Deep Light Productions; p.126 tl. © Corbis / Bettmann, tr. © University of Manchester Jodrell Bank Observatory, br. © NASA / HSTI / J. J. Hester, Arizona State University; p.128 © Alamy / Scientifica / Visuals Unlimited; p.131 © UKAEA; p.132 © Science Photo Library / Andrew Lambert Photography; p.133© Shutterstock / Awe Inspiring Images; p.141 © NASA; p.143 l. © Shutterstocik / Stefano Tiraboschi, r. © Shutterstock / Thomas Mounsey; p.148 tr. © Digital Vision, bl. © Getty Images / Roger Viollet; p. 155 © Corbis / Car Culture; p.159 tl. © Science Photo Library / Andrew Lambert Photography, bl. © Alamy / sciencephotos; p.166 tl. © Alamy / Justin Kase zfourz, cl. © Shutterstock / Eimantas Buzas, cr. © iStockphoto / yanta, bl. © Shutterstock / Rafa Irusta, br. © Shutterstock / Anthony Berenyi; p.171 © Alamy / Keren Su / China Span; p.185 © Alamy / ClassicStock; p.192 tl. © IBM, cr. © IBM, bl. © Science Photo Library / Tek Image; p.193 © Science Photo Library / Adam Hart-Davies; p.199 l. © Shutterstock / Stefano Tiraboschi, r. © Shutterstock / Thomas Mounsey; p.207 © Science Photo Library / American Institute of Physics; p.210 © Alamy / The Print Collector; p.213 © Getty Images / Hulton Archive; p.214© Science Photo Library / Stevie Grand; p.215 tl. © Science Photo Library / Pascal Goetheluck, tr. © Getty Images / Time & Life Pictures / Jon Brenneis; p.216 l. © Science Photo Library / N. Feather, r. © Science Photo Library / C.T.R. Wilson; p.221 © Science Photo Library / Gianni Tortoli; p.222 tl. © Science Photo Library / David Hay Jones, br. © Science Photo Library / Patrick Landmann.

Contents

Introduction   viii

Chapter 1   Measurements in physics

1.1 SI units   2
1.2 Measurement   3

Chapter 2   Speed, velocity and acceleration

2.1 Speed   12
2.2 Velocity   16
2.3 Acceleration   16

Chapter 3   Forces and their effects

3.1 Force   21
3.2 Forces and motion   25
3.3 Measuring force   28

Chapter 4   Moments

4.1 Turning forces   35
4.2 Balancing and equilibrium   38

Chapter 5   Pressure

5.1 Measuring pressure   43
5.2 Pressure in liquids   45
5.3 Pressure in gases   47

Chapter 6   Work, energy and power

6.1 Work   51
6.2 Energy   52
6.3 Energy resources   57

Chapter 7   Kinetic molecular model of matter

7.1 What is matter made from?   62
7.2 The kinetic model of matter   64

Chapter 8 Expansion and temperature

| 8.1 Expansion of solids, liquids and gases | 71 |
| 8.2 Measuring temperature | 74 |

Chapter 9 Internal energy and changes of state

9.1 Thermal capacity	80
9.2 Change of state	82
9.3 Thermal energy transfer	88

Chapter 10 Waves and sound

| 10.1 Waves | 97 |
| 10.2 Sound | 103 |

Chapter 11 Light and lenses

11.1 Reflection of light	112
11.2 Refraction of light	115
11.3 Lenses	120

Chapter 12 The electromagnetic spectrum

12.1 Light	127
12.2 Further investigation of the spectrum	128
12.3 The complete electromagnetic spectrum	129

Chapter 13 Magnetism

13.1 Magnets	131
13.2 Magnetic fields	133
13.3 Electromagnets	137

Chapter 14 Electric current and simple circuits

| 14.1 Electric current | 141 |
| 14.2 Circuit diagrams | 142 |

Chapter 15 Electrostatics

| 15.1 Electric force | 149 |
| 15.2 Current and charge | 151 |

Chapter 16 Potential difference and more circuits

16.1 Potential difference	155
16.2 Cells and emf	157
16.3 Resistance	158
16.4 Series and parallel circuits	162
16.5 Energy and power	166

Chapter 17 Electromagnetism

| 17.1 The motor effect | 172 |
| 17.2 Electromagnetic induction | 175 |

Chapter 18 Cathode rays

18.1 Thermionic emission	185
18.2 The cathode ray oscilloscope	186

Chapter 19 Electronics

19.1 Electronic components	193
19.2 Digital electronics	199

Chapter 20 The atom

20.1 An exciting time in the development of physics	207
20.2 Nuclear structure	209

Chapter 21 Radioactivity

21.1 Background radiation	213
21.2 Types of radiation	215
21.3 Radioactive disintegration	218
21.4 Uses of radioactivity	220
21.5 Nuclear fission	222
21.6 Nuclear fusion	226

Appendix – Circuit symbols

226

Index

227

Introduction

This book includes many features which will help you during the course. Some of these features are described below.

Supplementary material

Sections marked with a letter S and a blue line like this

indicate supplementary material. You need to cover this material only if you are taking the extended syllabus.

Did you know?

The material at the start of each chapter, on a blue background, or in the 'Did you know' boxes is not specifically required by the syllabus, but is designed to widen your knowledge and deepen your understanding.

> **DID YOU KNOW?**
>
> When the word *specific* is used in science it means 'per unit mass'. So *specific volume* of a material would be the volume of a material that has a mass of 1 kg.

Hint Boxes

The 'Hint boxes' are designed to help you avoid common mistakes or to help you understand particular points.

> **Hint**
> The Boyle's law formula assumes that the temperature remains constant.

Links

The links show you where the activities on the CD fit in the course.

Activity 1.1
Measurement of length and volume

Worked examples

The worked examples show you how a problem is solved and demonstrates the way in which your answer should be set out.

WORKED EXAMPLES

An athlete runs at a steady speed and covers 60 m in 8.0 s. Calculate her speed.

$$\text{speed} = \frac{\text{distance}}{\text{time}}$$
$$= \frac{60}{8.0} \text{ m/s}$$
$$= 7.5 \text{ m/s}$$

Questions

There are questions throughout the book to check your understanding of each unit/topic.

QUESTIONS

1.8 Calculate the density of a steel door of mass 585 kg and dimensions 2.0 m × 0.75 m × 0.050 m.

1.9 Calculate the volume of a gold ring of mass 84 g. Density of gold = 19.3 g/cm³.

1.10 Calculate the mass of a cube of ice of side 2.0 cm. Density of ice = 0.92 g/cm³.

Chapter 1

Measurement

▲ Figure 1.1
What's the difference between mass and weight?

▲ Figure 1.2
How did early clocks measure time?

▲ Figure 1.3
Why does a block of iron sink but an iron ship floats?

▲ Figure 1.4
How does the balloon gain height?

Physics is a science that relies on accurate measurements. The scientific community throughout the world uses the same set of units, which are known as the SI (Système Internationale) units.

In this chapter we will look at the SI units, how the basic quantities of mass, length and time are defined and how they can be combined to form units for more complex quantities. Finally we will look at the concept of density, and investigate why things float.

1

1.1 SI units

SI units are based on seven basic quantities. In this course we will use five of these: length, mass, time, temperature and electric current. These are listed in Table 1.1.

Quantity	Unit	Symbol
Length	metre	m
Mass	kilogram	kg
Time	second	s
Thermodynamic temperature*	kelvin	K
Electric current	ampere	A

▶ Table 1.1 Basic SI uits.

*An alternative unit is the degree Celsius (°C). In this course we will use °C.

All other units are made up from these five basic units.

Sometimes the basic units are either too big or too small so we use prefixes to alter the size of the unit.

Table 1.2 shows some of the commonly used prefixes.

Prefix	Symbol	Meaning
Mega	M	× 1 000 000
Kilo	k	× 1000
Milli	m	÷ 1000
Micro	μ	÷ 1 000 000

▶ Table 1.2 Common prefixes.

DID YOU KNOW?
The prefix μ is the Greek letter mu, equivalent to our *m*.

For example:
1 kilometre (1 km) = 1000 m
1 milliampere (1 mA) = $\frac{1}{1000}$ A
1 microsecond (1 μs) = $\frac{1}{1000\,000}$ s

In the laboratory, when measuring length, the metre is often too large and the millimetre is too small, so we sometimes use the centimetre. So in addition to the common prefixes, you might also meet centi (c), which means ÷ 100.

DID YOU KNOW?
The metre was originally defined as a fraction of the Earth's circumference, but is now defined in terms of the distance travelled by light in a small fraction of a second.

The kilogram is defined as the mass of a standard kilogram held in a museum in Paris.

The second was originally defined as a fraction of the time it takes the Earth to orbit the Sun. It is now defined in terms of the time period of a particular frequency radiation.

QUESTIONS

1.1 Write down the following in the basic units.
   a) 32 km   b) 234 ms   c) 2400 mg
   d) 3500 μA   e) 3.5 Mm   f) 6400 g

1.2 Write down the following using the most appropriate prefix.
   a) 0.0048 m   b) 3540 g   c) 0.000 0032 s   d) 8900 m

Errors and uncertainties

No quantity can ever be measured precisely. Whenever a measurement is made there is an **uncertainty**. For example, a hand-held stopwatch can measure to the nearest one-tenth of a second. An athlete is timed as

Measurement

completing a 100 m race in 10.1 s. This means that, assuming the timing is done perfectly, his actual time lay between 10.05 s and 10.15 s, an uncertainty of 0.05 s either way. This is often written as 10.1 ± 0.05 s. This might be improved by using an electronic timer, which could measure to the nearest $\frac{1}{100}$ of a second; this might give a result of 10.12 s. The uncertainty is now reduced to 0.01 s — but still not eliminated.

The precision of a measurement can be shown by how the figures are written. A length written as 100 m means that the length is measured to the nearest metre. However, if this is written as 100.0 m, it indicates that it is measured to the nearest tenth of a metre.

Errors are quite different from uncertainties: they arise from poorly adjusted instruments or poor use of apparatus. This is explained in Figure 1.5, showing that care must be taken to ensure that the eye is at right angles to the ruler. A reading taken from point A would give an answer of 11 mm, instead of the correct length, 12 mm.

What would a reading taken from point B give?

Standard form

Another method of showing the precision of a measurement is to use standard form. For example, the distance of the Sun from the Earth is 150 000 000 km. In standard form this is written as 1.50×10^8 km. This method of displaying readings has two advantages:

1. It is much easier to read either very small or large numbers. For example, the mass of an electron is 9.1×10^{-31} kg, that means 9.1 divided by 1 followed by 31 zeros. Try writing that out in full!
2. It also clearly shows the precision to which the reading is taken. In the example above, the mass of the electron is shown to 2 significant figures, whereas a measurement of its mass taken to 5 significant figures is written as 9.1095×10^{-31} kg.

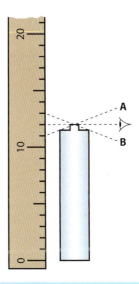

▲ **Figure 1.5**
When you use a rule it is important that the eye is placed so that you are looking at right angles to the rule. If the reading is taken from either position **A** or **B** an error is introduced. This type of error is called a **parallax error**.

WORKED EXAMPLE

1. Write 1.7×10^{12} m out in full.

    10^{12} m = 1 000 000 000 000 m
    1.7×10^{12} m = **1 700 000 000 000 m**

2. Write 0.000 04 s in standard form.

    $0.000\,04$ s = $\frac{4}{100\,000}$ s
    = 4×10^{-5} s

1.2 Measurement

Measurement of length

The basic SI unit of length is the metre, although kilometres (1000 m) are often used for long distances, and millimetres (0.001 m) are used for shorter distances. On some occasions the centimetre (0.01m) is also used. There are various instruments that can be used to measure length; the choice will be determined by the particular situation. In this course we shall only consider the use of rules.

QUESTIONS

1.3 Write the following in standard form.
   a) 21 500 m
   b) 0.031 s
   c) 299 000 000 m

1.4 Write the following in full.
   a) 3.0×10^8 m/s
   b) 1.7×10^{-4} m
   c) 5.12×10^{-3} s

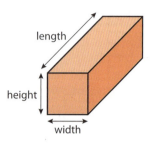

▲ Figure 1.6
Calculating volume.

Measurement of volume

The volume of an object is the space it takes up. Consider the box in Figure 1.6.

The volume of the box = width × height × length

The basic unit of length is the metre. If each of the sides is measured in metres, the unit of volume is metre × metre × metre, or the metre cubed. The short form for this is m^3. If the unit used for measuring the dimensions of the box is the centimetre, then the unit for the volume is cm^3.

The volume of liquids can be found using a measuring cylinder as shown in Figure 1.7. When using a measuring cylinder, you will see that the water curves up to the glass at the edges. This is called a **meniscus**. The reading should always be taken from the bottom of the meniscus. The measuring cylinder should be placed on the bench and the eye should be kept level with the line of the liquid, to avoid parallax errors.

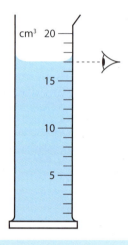

▲ Figure 1.7
Reading volume from a measuring cylinder

Measurement of the volume of an irregular object

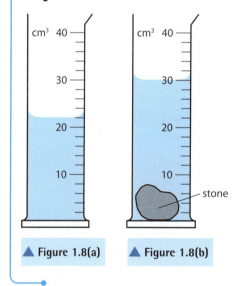

▲ Figure 1.8(a)   ▲ Figure 1.8(b)

First partly fill a measuring cylinder, Figure 1.8(a). Record the volume of water.

Then gently slide the stone into the measuring cylinder, Figure 1.8(b). Record the new volume.

The volume of the stone is the new volume minus the original volume of the water.

What is the volume of the stone in this example?

(Note that each division on the scale is $2\,cm^3$.)

Measurement of time

A stopwatch or stop clock may be used to measure time. The choice of which to use will depend on availability and the precision that is needed.

A stop clock, generally, will measure to the nearest second. If greater precision is needed, a stopwatch must be used. A hand-held stopwatch can be used to measure to the nearest one-tenth of a second. Even though a digital stopwatch may record to $\frac{1}{100}$ of a second, the uncertainty in the human reaction time is much more than this, consequently the hundredths must be used with caution. To measure to this level of precision, the stopwatch must be started and stopped electronically.

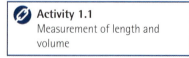

Activity 1.1
Measurement of length and volume

Measurement

QUESTIONS

▲ Figure 1.9(a)

▲ Figure 1.9(b)

▲ Figure 1.9(c)

1.5 What are the readings on the stop clock and stopwatches in Figures 1.9(a) to 1.9(c)? Give your answer to show the uncertainty in the reading.

The simple pendulum

Clocks must have a device that repeats at a regular interval. Early clocks used a pendulum.

A simple pendulum consists of a light string, clamped at the top and with a mass attached at the bottom. The mass is called a bob.

The time it takes for the pendulum to make one complete swing or oscillation is called its **period**. The period of a simple pendulum depends only on the length of the pendulum.

The period of a pendulum of length 25 mm is about 1s. To measure the time for a single oscillation with any reasonable degree of accuracy is difficult. Remember the uncertainty in the reading with a hand-held stopwatch is 0.1s, giving at best a 10% uncertainty.

To find the period accurately we time at least 10 oscillations and then divide the reading by the number of swings. This reduces the uncertainty in the time for one oscillation by a factor of 10, from 0.1s to 0.01s.

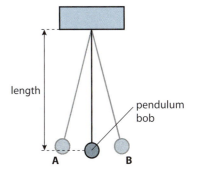
▲ Figure 1.10
One complete oscillation is from **A** to **B** and back to **A** once more.

Activity 1.2
The simple pendulum

Measurement of mass

Mass is one of the basic SI quantities. The basic unit of mass is the kilogram (kg). As with all units, multiples and submultiples may be used, so that small masses may be measured in grams, milligrams or even micrograms. Larger masses can be measured in megagrams, although for historical reasons one megagram is usually referred to as one tonne (t).

Mass is measured using a balance. The photographs in Figure 1.11 (see page 6) show various types of balances.

5

▲ Figure 1.11(a)
Beam balance.

▲ Figure 1.11(b)
Triple beam balance.

▲ Figure 1.11(c)
Lever arm balance.

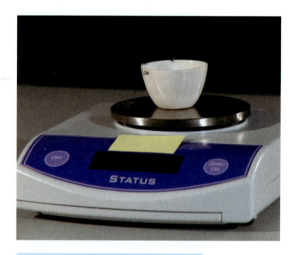

▲ Figure 1.11(d)
Top pan balance.

In everyday life we often use the term *weight* when we mean *mass*, and for this reason it is easy to confuse the terms.

Mass is the quantity of matter in an object, and it does not change with position.

Weight is the gravitational pull on the object. This means that the same object will have a greater weight on the Earth's surface than on the Moon's surface, because the Earth has a greater gravitational field strength than the Moon. The object will have no weight (be weightless) when in outer space . We will explore this in more detail in Chapter 3.

Activity 1.3
Measuring mass

Measuring masses of liquids

The mass of a sample of liquid cannot be measured directly. The liquid must be held in a container of some form. To measure the mass of a liquid, first measure the mass of the empty container, pour the liquid into the container, and then measure the mass again. The mass of the liquid is equal to the difference between the two readings.

Measurement

 WORKED EXAMPLE

An empty jug has a mass of 490 g. When it is filled with water its mass is 840 g.
Calculate the mass of water in the jug.

Mass of water = mass of jug and water − mass of empty jug
= 840 g − 490 g
= 350 g

 QUESTIONS

1.6 A beaker plus liquid has a mass of 695 g. The beaker has a mass of 110 g. What is the mass of liquid?

1.7 Convert the following:
a) 43 kg to grams
b) 475 g to kilograms
c) 2.46 g to milligrams
d) 387 kg to tonnes
e) 236 μg to grams

Density

We might say that 'lead is heavier than wood', but this is technically incorrect. A kilogram of lead has the same mass as a kilogram of wood, and therefore the same weight! The difference is that the wood has a much larger volume than the lead.

To compare materials we must look at equal volumes of material. We define **density** as the mass of 1 cm³ or 1 m³.

Density is defined as the mass per unit volume.

Density is a property of a material rather than a particular object. A given material always has the same density no matter what its size or shape.

To calculate density of an object we must measure both the mass and the volume of the object and then use the formula:

$$\text{density} = \frac{\text{mass}}{\text{volume}}$$

 Activity 1.4
Measuring density of regular objects

Units

The basic unit of mass is the kilogram (kg), and the basic unit of volume is the metre cubed (m³). The unit of density is formed by dividing kg by m³, giving kg/m³ or kgm⁻³. Alternatively, if the mass is measured in grams and the volume in centimetres cubed, the unit will be g/cm³ or gcm⁻³.

WORKED EXAMPLES

An aluminium cylinder has a volume of 250 cm³ and a mass of 675 g. Calculate the density of aluminium.

$$\text{density} = \frac{\text{mass}}{\text{volume}}$$

$$= \frac{675}{250} \text{ g/cm}^3$$

$$= 2.7 \text{ g/cm}^3$$

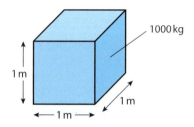

Figure 1.12 Cube of water.

A closer look at units

Water has a density of 1000 kg/m³.
Consider the cube of water of side 1 m shown in Figure 1.12. Its mass will be 1000 kg.

The volume of the cube is $1\,m \times 1\,m \times 1\,m = 1\,m^3$

$1\,kg = 1000\,g$

Therefore the mass of the cube is $1000 \times 1000\,g = 1\,000\,000\,g$

$1\,m = 100\,cm$

Therefore the volume of the cube $= 100\,cm \times 100\,cm \times 100\,cm$
$= 1\,000\,000\,cm^3$

$$\text{The density of the cube} = \frac{\text{mass}}{\text{volume}}$$
$$= \frac{1\,000\,000}{1\,000\,000}\,g/cm^3$$
$$= 1\,g/cm^3$$

So we see that a density of $1000\,kg/m^3 = 1\,g/cm^3$.

Measurement of density

To find the density of a material, you must measure both the volume and the mass of the material. The techniques used are the same as those met earlier in this chapter.

Figure 1.13 shows the stages of measuring the density of cooking oil.

QUESTIONS

1.8 Calculate the density of a steel door of mass 585 kg and dimensions $2.0\,m \times 0.75\,m \times 0.050\,m$.

1.9 Calculate the volume of a gold ring of mass 84 g. Density of gold = 19.3 g/cm³.

1.10 Calculate the mass of a cube of ice of side 2.0 cm. Density of ice = 0.92 g/cm³.

Figure 1.13 Measuring the density of cooking oil.

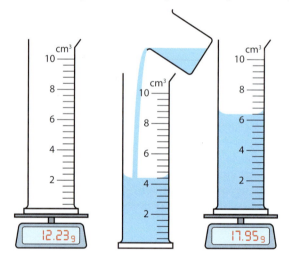

 Activity 1.5 Measuring the density of liquids

 Activity 1.6 Measuring the density of irregular objects

Mass of the measuring cylinder = 12.23 g
Mass of measuring cylinder and oil = 17.95 g
Volume of oil = 6.4 cm³
Mass of oil = 17.95 g − 12.23 g
= 5.72 g
Density of oil = $\frac{5.72}{6.4}$ g/cm³
= 0.89 g/cm³

The answer is given to two significant figures as the least accurate measurement (the volume) is only given to two significant figures.

Hint

Even though the problem is quite simple, each stage of the calculation is clearly shown. This is good practice, which you should follow. It will help you to avoid mistakes.

Measurement

Floating and sinking

Why do some objects float and others sink when placed in different liquids? If you look at Table 1.3, you will see that the substances that are less dense than water (cork, wood, wax, ice) will float in water. You will also observe that a helium-filled balloon, or a balloon filled with hot air will float in air. The general rule is that an object will float in a fluid if it is less dense than the fluid.

▼ Table 1.3
Densities.

Material	Density (kg/m^3)
Aluminium	2700
Copper	8940
Gold	19 300
Lead	11300
Platinum	21 450
Glass	2800
Perspex	1200
Cork	240
Wood	500–700
Wax	430
Water	1000
Brine	1200
Ice	920
Petrol	730
Air	1.26
Helium	0.22

▲ Figure 1.14
A steel boat floats because the average density of the steel and the air it contains is less than the density of water.

◀ Figure 1.15
Hot air is less dense than cool air, so the hot air balloon floats in air.

 Activity 1.7
Finding the density of margarine

 Activity 1.8
Investigating floating and sinking

QUESTIONS

(Use the values of density in Table 1.3.)

1.11 Calculate the density of a piece of wood measuring 30 cm × 20 cm × 5 cm and of mass 2.25 kg.
Give your answer a) in g/cm^3 and b) in kg/m^3.

1.12 A sheet of copper is used to make the roof a building. The copper sheet has dimensions 4.0 m × 3.2 m × 0.80 cm. Calculate the mass of the copper sheet.

1.13 Calculate the volume of 78 g of brine.

1.14 What are the lengths of the following items?

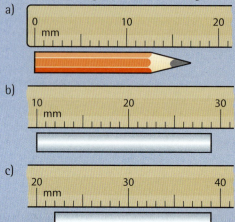

1.15 A student measures the length of a room five times. The readings are 4.85 m, 4.78 m, 4.90 m, 4.83 m and 4.79 m. What is the average reading? Explain the advantage of taking the reading more than once and taking an average.

1.16 Calculate the volume of the box.

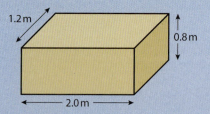

a) Calculate your answer in (i) m^3 and (ii) in cm^3 (remember that all the dimensions must be converted to cm).
b) Use your answer to find the number of cm^3 in a m^3.

1.17 What is the volume of liquid in each of the measuring cylinders?

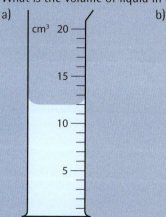

1.18 In an experiment a student makes the following measurements.
Mass of empty measuring cylinder = 134 g
Mass of measuring cylinder plus ethanol = 186 g
Calculate the mass of the ethanol.

1.19 List the stages needed to find the density of a stone.
A stone has a density of 2.70 g/cm³, and a mass of 62.1 g.
Calculate the volume of the stone.

1.20 A student needs to measure the diameter of a wire. She wraps the wire round a pencil, as shown in the diagram.

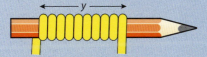

She measures the distance, y, as 12 mm.
a) Calculate the diameter of the wire.
b) Suggest one source of error in the measurement and state how it could be minimised.

Summary

Now that you have completed this chapter, you should be able to:

- use and recall the SI units of length, mass and time
- recognise prefixes to alter the size of units
- recognise that all units are made up from five basic units
- understand that there is always an uncertainty when taking a measurement
- understand the use of standard form
- use rulers and measuring cylinders to measure length and volume
- use a stopwatch to measure time
- measure mass of solids and liquids using a balance
- understand the meaning of density
- recall and use the equation density = $\frac{mass}{volume}$
- measure the density of regular solids and liquids
- recognise that objects will float in fluids if they have lower density than the fluid
- measure the volume of an irregular object
- measure the time period of a pendulum.

Chapter 2

Speed, velocity and acceleration

▶ Figure 2.1
What determines the maximum height that a pole-vaulter can reach?

In this chapter we look at moving bodies, how their speeds can be measured and how accelerations can be calculated. We also look at what happens when a body falls under the influence of gravity.

2.1 Speed

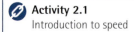
Activity 2.1
Introduction to speed

In everyday life we think of speed as how fast something is travelling. However, this is too vague for scientific purposes.

Speed is defined as the distance travelled in unit time.

It can be calculated from the formula:

$$\text{speed} = \frac{\text{distance}}{\text{time}}$$

Units

The base unit of distance is the metre and the base unit of time is the second. The unit of speed is formed by dividing metres by seconds, giving m/s.

An alternative unit is the kilometre per hour (km/h) often used when considering long distances.

Speed, velocity and acceleration

WORKED EXAMPLES

An athlete runs at a steady speed and covers 60 m in 8.0 s. Calculate her speed.

$$\text{speed} = \frac{\text{distance}}{\text{time}}$$
$$= \frac{60}{8.0} \text{ m/s}$$
$$= \mathbf{7.5 \text{ m/s}}$$

Measurement of speed

We can measure the speed of an object by measuring the time it takes to travel a set distance. If the speed varies during the journey, the calculation gives the average speed of the object. To get a better idea of the instantaneous speed we need to measure the distance travelled in a very short time.

One way of doing this is to take a multi-flash photograph. A light is set up to flash at a steady rate. A camera shutter is held open while the object passes in front of it. Figure 2.2 shows a toy car moving down a slope.

Successive images of the car are equal distances apart, showing that the car is travelling at a constant speed. To find the speed, we measure the distance between two images and divide by the time between each flash.

Acceleration

So far we have looked at objects travelling at constant speed. However, in real life this is quite unusual. When an object changes its speed it is said to **accelerate**. If the object slows down this is often described as a deceleration.

Figure 2.3 shows the toy car rolling down a steeper slope. This time its speed increases as it goes down the slope – it is accelerating.

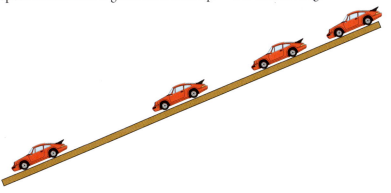

QUESTIONS

2.1 A car travels 200 m in 8.0 s. Calculate its speed.

2.2 A cricketer bowls a ball at 45 m/s at a batsman 18.0 m away from him. Calculate the time taken for the ball to reach the batsman.

◀ **Figure 2.2**
The car is moving at constant speed.

◀ **Figure 2.3**
Here, the car is accelerating.

Using graphs

Distance–time graphs

Activity 2.2
Understanding distance–time graphs

Graphs are used a lot in science and in other mathematical situations. They are like pictures in a storybook, giving a lot of information in a compact manner.

We can draw distance–time graphs for the two journeys of the car in Figures 2.2 and 2.3.

In Figure 2.2 the car travels equal distances between each flash, so the total distance travelled increases at a steady rate. This produces a straight line as shown in Figure 2.4. The greater the speed, the steeper the slope (or gradient) of the line.

In Figure 2.3 the car travels increasing distances in each time interval. This leads to the graph shown in Figure 2.5, which gradually curves upwards.

The graph in Figure 2.6 shows the story of a journey. The car starts at quite a high speed and gradually decelerates before coming to rest at point P.

Activity 2.3
Introduction to speed–time graphs

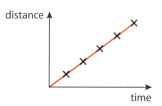

▲ **Figure 2.4**
Distance changing at a steady rate.

▲ **Figure 2.5**
Increasing distances with time travelled.

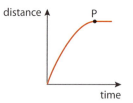

▲ **Figure 2.6**
Story of a car journey.

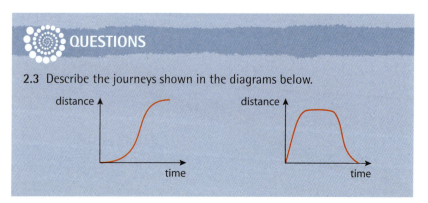

QUESTIONS

2.3 Describe the journeys shown in the diagrams below.

Speed, velocity and acceleration

Speed–time graphs

Instead of using a graph to look at the distance travelled over a period of time, we can look at how the speed changes.

Figure 2.7 appears similar to Figure 2.4. However closer inspection shows that it is the **speed** which is increasing at a constant rate, not the **distance**. This graph is typical for one in which there is a constant acceleration. In this case the gradient of the graph is equal to the acceleration. The greater the acceleration the larger the gradient.

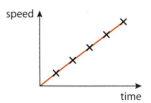

▲ Figure 2.7
Speed changing at steady rate.

The graph in Figure 2.8 shows the story of the speed on a journey.

This is a straight-line graph, sloping downwards from left to right (a negative gradient). This shows constant deceleration, sometimes described as negative acceleration.

Using a speed–time graph to calculate distance travelled

$$\text{speed} = \frac{\text{distance}}{\text{time}}$$

Rearrange the equation:

$$\text{distance} = \text{speed} \times \text{time}$$

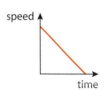

▲ Figure 2.8
Story of speed on a journey.

Look at Figure 2.9. The object is travelling at a constant speed v for time t.

The distance travelled $= v \times t$

We can see that it is the area of the rectangle formed.

Now look at Fig. 2.10, which shows a journey with constant acceleration from rest. The area under this graph is equal to the area under the triangle that is formed.

The distance travelled $= \frac{1}{2}v \times t$

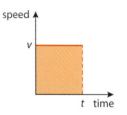

▲ Figure 2.9
Area under graph of constant speed.

$\frac{1}{2}v$ is the average speed of the object and distance travelled is given by average speed $\times$ time, so once again the distance travelled is equal to the area under the graph.

The general rule is that the **distance travelled is equal to the area under the speed–time graph**.

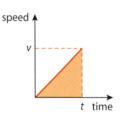

▲ Figure 2.10
Area under graph of constant acceleration.

WORKED EXAMPLES

Use the graph in Figure 2.11 to calculate the distance travelled by the car in the time interval from 0.5 s to 4.5 s.

Time passed $= (4.5 - 0.5)\,\text{s} = 4.0\,\text{s}$
Initial speed $= 0\,\text{m/s}$
Final speed $= 120\,\text{m/s}$

In this case, the area under the line forms a triangle and the area of a triangle is found from the formula:

$$\text{area} = \tfrac{1}{2}\,\text{base} \times \text{height}$$

area under the graph $=$ the distance travelled

$$= \tfrac{1}{2} \times 4.0\,\text{s} \times 120\,\text{m/s} = \mathbf{240\,m}$$

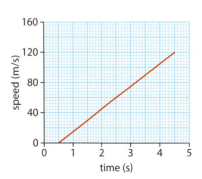

▲ Figure 2.11
Distance travelled by a car.

15

▲ Figure 2.12
The lap of the track is 3.0 m, and the car completes a full lap in 6.0 s.

The average speed of the car is 0.5 m/s. However its average velocity is zero! Velocity is a vector and the car finishes at the same point as it started, so there has been no net displacement in any direction.

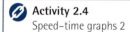
Activity 2.4
Speed–time graphs 2

2.2 Velocity

Velocity is very similar to speed. When we talk about speed we do not concern ourselves with direction. However, velocity does include direction. So an object travelling at 5 m/s due south has a different velocity from an object travelling at 5 m/s northwest.

It is worth observing that the velocity changes if the speed increases, or decreases, or if the direction of motion changes (even if the speed remains constant).

There are many quantities in physics which have direction as well as size. Such quantities are called **vectors**. Quantities, such as mass, which have only size but no direction are called **scalars**.

2.3 Acceleration

We have already introduced acceleration as occurring when an object changes speed. We now explore this idea in more detail.

If a body changes its speed rapidly then it is said to have a large acceleration, so clearly it has magnitude (or size). Acceleration can be found from the formula:

$$\text{acceleration} = \frac{\text{change in velocity}}{\text{time taken}}$$

Units

The base unit of speed is metres per second (m/s) and the base unit of time is the second. The unit of acceleration is formed by dividing m/s by seconds. This gives the unit m/s^2. This can be thought of as the change in velocity (in m/s) every second.

You will also notice that the formula uses change of velocity, rather than change of speed. It follows that acceleration can be not only an increase in speed, but also a decrease in speed or even a change in direction of the velocity. Like velocity, acceleration has direction, so it is a vector.

WORKED EXAMPLES

1. A car on a straight, level test track accelerates from rest to 34 m/s in 6.8 s. Calculate its acceleration.

$$\text{acceleration} = \frac{\text{change of velocity}}{\text{time}}$$
$$= \frac{(\text{final velocity} - \text{initial velocity})}{\text{time}}$$
$$= \frac{(34 - 0)}{6.8} \, m/s^2$$
$$= 5.0 \, m/s^2$$

It is important that the track is straight and level or it could be argued that there is a change of direction, and therefore an extra acceleration.

Speed, velocity and acceleration

2 A boy on a bicycle is travelling at a speed of 16 m/s. He applies his brakes and comes to rest in 2.5 s. Calculate his acceleration. You may assume the acceleration is constant.

$$\text{acceleration} = \frac{\text{change of velocity}}{\text{time}}$$
$$= \frac{(\text{final velocity} - \text{initial velocity})}{\text{time}}$$
$$= \frac{(0 - 16)}{2.5} \text{ m/s}^2$$
$$= -6.4 \text{ m/s}^2$$

Activity 2.5
Falling under gravity

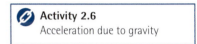

Activity 2.6
Acceleration due to gravity

Notice that the acceleration is negative, which shows that it is a deceleration.

Calculation of acceleration from a velocity–time graph

Look at the graph in Figure 2.13. We can see that between 1.0 s and 4.0 s the speed has increased from 5.0 m/s to 12.5 m/s.

$$\text{acceleration} = \frac{(12.5 - 5)}{(4 - 1)} \text{ m/s}^2$$
$$= \frac{7.5}{3} \text{ m/s}^2$$
$$= 2.5 \text{ m/s}^2$$

Mathematically this is known as the gradient of the graph.

$$\text{gradient} = \frac{\text{increase in } y}{\text{increase in } x}$$

We see that acceleration is equal to the gradient of the speed-time graph. It does not matter which two points on the graph line are chosen, the answer will be the same. Nevertheless, it is good practice to choose points that are well apart; this will improve the precision of your final answer.

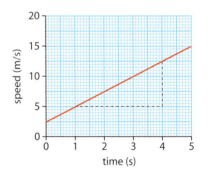

▲ Figure 2.13
Velocity–time graph.

QUESTIONS

2.4 Describe the motion of the object shown in the graph in Figure 2.14.

2.5 a) Describe the motion of the object shown in the graph in Figure 2.15.
b) Calculate the distance travelled by the object.
c) Calculate the acceleration of the object.

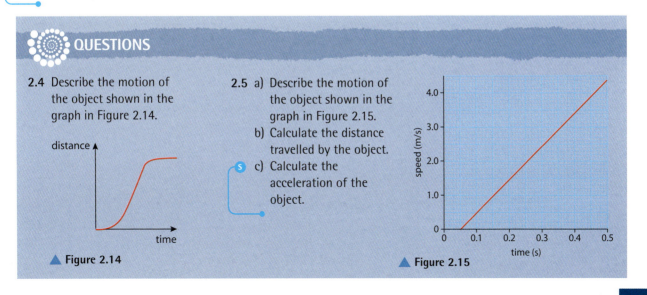

▲ Figure 2.14

▲ Figure 2.15

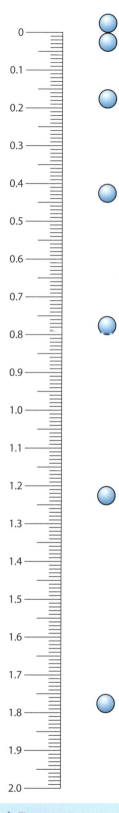

Figure 2.16
Falling steel ball.

Figure 2.16 shows a multi-flash photograph of a steel ball falling. The light flashes every 0.1 s.

We can see that the ball travels further in each time interval, so we know that it is accelerating. Figure 2.17 shows the speed–time graph of the ball.

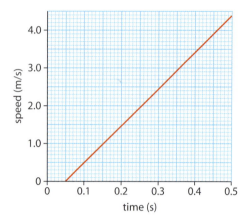

Figure 2.17
Speed–time graph of falling steel ball.

The graph is a straight line, which tells us that the acceleration is constant.

We can calculate the value of the acceleration by measuring the gradient.

Use the points (0.10, 0.50) and (0.45, 3.9).

$$\text{gradient} = \frac{(3.9 - 0.50)\ \text{m/s}}{(0.45 - 0.10)\ \text{s}}$$

$$= \frac{3.4}{0.35}\ \text{m/s}^2$$

$$= 9.7\ \text{m/s}^2$$

The acceleration measured in this experiment is 9.7 m/s².

All objects in free fall near the Earth's surface have the same acceleration.

The recognised value is 9.8 m/s², although it is quite common for this to be rounded to 10 m/s². The result in the above experiment lies well within the uncertainties in the experimental procedure.

This is sometimes called the acceleration of free fall, or acceleration due to gravity, and is given the symbol g.

In Chapter 3 we will look at gravity in more detail, including what happens if there is significant air resistance.

QUESTIONS

2.6 An aeroplane travels at a constant speed of 960 km/h. Calculate the time it will take to travel from London to Johannesburg, a distance of 9000 km.

2.7 Describe what happens to the speed in the two journeys described in the graphs

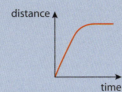

2.8 Describe how the speed changes in the two journeys described in the graphs.

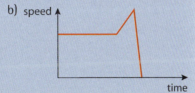

2.9 A motorist is travelling at 15 m/s when he sees a child run into the road. He brakes and the car comes to rest in 0.75 s. Draw a speed-time graph to show the deceleration, and use your graph to calculate
   a) the distance travelled once the brakes are applied
   b) the deceleration of the car.

2.10 A car accelerates from rest at 2 m/s^2 for 8 seconds.
   a) Draw a speed-time graph to show this motion.
   b) Use your graph to find
      (i) the final speed of the car
      (ii) the distance travelled by the car.

2.11 The graph shows how the speed of an aeroplane changes with time.

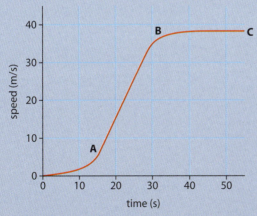

   a) Describe the motion of the aeroplane.
   b) Calculate the acceleration of the aeroplane during the period A to B.
   c) Suggest during which stage of the journey these readings were taken.

Summary

Now that you have completed this chapter, you should be able to:

- define speed
- recall and use the equation speed $= \dfrac{\text{distance}}{\text{time}}$
- understand that acceleration is a change of speed
- draw and interpret distance-time graphs
- draw and interpret speed-time graphs
- calculate distance travelled from a speed-time graph
- recognise that the steeper the gradient of a speed-time graph the greater the acceleration
- recognise that acceleration of free fall is the same for all objects
- understand that velocity and acceleration are vectors
- recall and use the equation acceleration $= \dfrac{\text{change in velocity}}{\text{time}}$
- calculate acceleration from the gradient of a speed-time graph
- describe an experiment to measure the acceleration of free fall.

Chapter 3

Forces and their effects

◀ **Figure 3.1**
What is a force? What effects can a force produce? What forces are at work on these sports people and on the owl as it flies and comes in to land? We will look at the effect of gravity on a mass and why weight is different from mass.

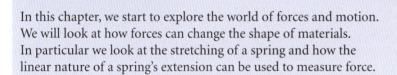

In this chapter, we start to explore the world of forces and motion. We will look at how forces can change the shape of materials. In particular we look at the stretching of a spring and how the linear nature of a spring's extension can be used to measure force.

3.1 Force

Think of different forces – a child pushing a toy car, stretching an elastic band, the force between two magnets when they are close to each other, the act of lifting a large mass. In all these examples we can think of force as being a push or a pull.

Units

The unit of force is the **newton (N)**. It is named after one of the most brilliant scientists of all time, Sir Isaac Newton.

We will see the relationship between the newton and SI units later in the chapter. To get an idea of the size of a newton, lift a 100 g mass. The force that you are applying is about 1 newton.

Force, mass and weight

We have already met force (push or pull) and mass (quantity of matter in an object) but how do they relate to **weight**?

When an object is near the Earth, it is pulled towards the surface of the Earth by gravity. This pull is the object's weight.

> **Weight is defined as the gravitational force on an object.**

Weight is a type of force, so like all forces it is measured in newtons.

In Figure 3.2, the astronaut has a mass of 80 kg, and this mass remains the same throughout the trip. His weight however, does change. On the Earth's surface it is about 800 N. On the Moon's surface (which has less gravity) his weight is only 130 N. There is a point on the way to the Moon where there is no resultant gravitational field. At this point his weight is zero – he is weightless!

▼ Figure 3.2
Weight of an astronaut.

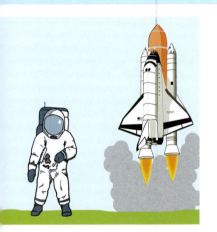
mass = 80 kg
weight = 800 N

mass = 80 kg
weight = 130 N

mass = 80 kg
weight = 0 N

Stretching of a steel spring

Fig. 3.3 shows the apparatus needed. With no masses on the holder, record the position of the pointer. A mass is added and the position is recorded. This is repeated for several masses.

The weight of the masses provides the force, or load, which stretches the spring.

The table shows typical results.

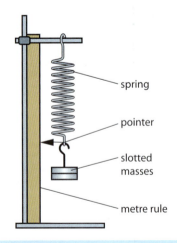

▲ Figure 3.3
Stretching a spring.

Load (N)	Position of pointer (cm)	Extension (cm)
0	12.3	0
1	19.6	7.6
2	27.0	14.7
3	34.8	22.5
4	42.5	30.2
5	49.9	37.6

Forces and their effects

Figure 3.4 shows the graph when the load is plotted against extension.

The graph is a straight line through the origin. This tells us that **the extension is proportional to the load**. This means that if we double the load, the extension doubles. If we triple the load, the extension triples and so on.

Whenever we get this type of graph, we can say that one variable is proportional to the other.

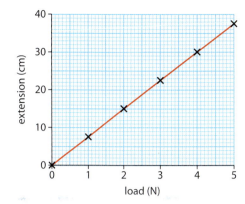

▲ Figure 3.4
Loading a spring.

More about proportionality

The mathematical way of expressing that the extension is proportional to load is:

$$\text{load} \propto \text{extension}$$

or in symbols:

$$F \propto x$$

or

$$F = kx$$

where k is a constant of proportionality.

In the example of the spring, k is called the spring constant and tells us how stiff the spring is.

The equation can now be used to calculate extensions from known loads.

WORKED EXAMPLE

A load of 4.5 N is added to a steel spring of length 9.6 cm. Its length increases to 27.6 cm.
Calculate the spring constant of the spring.

The extension of the spring = (27.6 − 9.6) cm
= 18.0 cm

using
$$F = kx$$
$$k = \frac{F}{x}$$
$$= \frac{4.5}{18.0} \text{ N/cm}$$
$$= 0.25 \text{ N/cm}$$

Activity 3.1
Extension of springs

Measurement of force

A spring balance (or newtonmeter) uses the proportionality of load and extension of a spring to measure force.

A typical spring balance is shown in Figure 3.5. A force is applied to the hook at the end and the size of the force can be read from the scale.

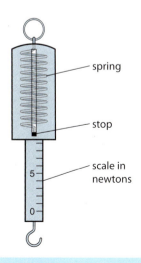

▲ Figure 3.5
Spring balance.

23

More about stretching

The apparatus used in the previous experiment, stretching a steel spring, can be used to investigate what happens if a larger load is added. If too great a load is added, the behaviour of the steel spring changes. For a small load, the spring goes back to its original length when the load is removed. The spring is said to be **elastic**.

When more load is added, the spring becomes easier to stretch, and when the load is removed, the spring does not go back to its original length. The point where the extension is no longer proportional to the load is called the **limit of proportionality**. This is shown on the graph in Figure 3.6.

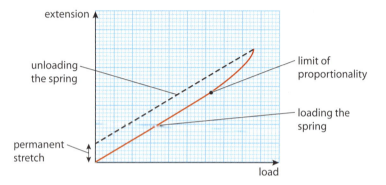

▶ **Figure 3.6**
Loading a spring, showing the limit of proportionality.

Hooke's Law

It is not only steel springs which change shape in this way – many materials also follow this pattern. Robert Hooke was an architect and scientist who lived and worked in the seventeenth century. He discovered this behaviour of materials and his law states

The extension of a material is proportional to the applied load provided the limit of proportionality is not exceeded.

QUESTIONS

3.1 Use the graph in Figure 3.4 to find
   a) the extension when a load of 3.5 N is placed on the spring
   b) the load required to produce an extension of 20 cm
   c) the spring constant of the spring.

3.2 An unstretched spring has a length of 12.4 cm. When a load of 4.8 N is added, it stretches to a length of 28.2 cm.
   a) Calculate
      (i) the spring constant
      (ii) the length of the spring when the load is 7.6 N.
   b) What assumption must be made to calculate the answer in (ii)?

3.2 Forces and motion

If you push an object across the floor, it soon comes to rest. If the floor is polished or covered in ice, it will continue to travel further, and if it is made to float on a cushion of air, it will continue almost indefinitely.

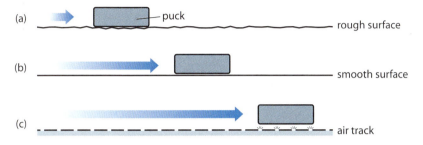

▶ Figure 3.7
Puck travelling across three differerent surfaces.
(a) Large frictional force – the puck slows down rapidly.
(b) The frictional force is much smaller – the puck takes longer to slow down.
(c) The frictional force is virtually zero – the puck travels at almost constant speed.

At one time it was believed that a force was required to keep an object moving. Sir Isaac Newton realised that this was not true. A force is *not* needed to keep a body moving, unless there is another force (such as friction) opposing the motion.

The effect of applying a force to a body is to either make the body accelerate from rest or to change its motion once it is moving. It should be recognised that the change in motion is always in the direction of the force.

This is summed up in Newton's First Law of Motion.

 Activity 3.2
Effect of friction on motion

A body will continue in its state of rest or uniform motion in a straight line unless it is acted upon by an external force.

When a force is applied to a moving object its motion may change in three ways:
- it may accelerate, i.e. go faster
- it may decelerate, i.e. slow down
- it may change direction.

 DID YOU KNOW?

Sir Isaac Newton 1643–1727

Sir Isaac Newton was born in Lincolnshire in 1643. He went to Cambridge University in 1661 with the aim of gaining a degree in law. It was while he was at Cambridge that he developed an interest in mathematics and natural philosophy (which we call physics). An outbreak of the plague in 1665 caused the closure of the university until 1667. Newton went back home and during these two years laid the foundations of the advanced mathematical techniques of differential and integral calculus. He also developed an interest in astronomy and in particular the motion of the planets. By 1666 he had formulated his ideas on motion and had recognised that it was gravity that not only caused objects to fall to Earth but was also the force that kept the planets in orbit about the Sun.

On his return to Cambridge in 1668 he took up a post in the astronomy department. His first real success was the invention of the reflecting telescope. He also showed that white light is a mixture of the colours of the rainbow.

Sir Isaac Newton was one of a handful of truly great scientists that the world has seen, and his ideas are as relevant today as they were when he developed them over 300 years ago.

Adding forces

If more than one force acts on an object, the resultant force is equal to the sum of the forces. If the forces are in opposite directions, one of them must be considered to be negative.

> **WORKED EXAMPLE**
>
> Figure 3.8 shows a tug-of-war competition.
>
>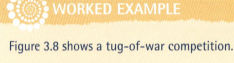
>
> Calculate the resultant force produced by the two teams and comment on the direction of the acceleration of the teams.
>
> Net force = (3.0 − 2.8) kN
> = **0.2 kN**
>
> The teams will accelerate towards the right of the page, in the direction of the larger force.

▶ **Figure 3.8** Forces in a tug-of-war.

Hint

It is essential to draw the arrows representing forces to scale. For example, use a scale of '1 cm represents 2 N', so that a 10 N force might be represented by an arrow 5 cm long, whilst a 6 N force would be represented by an arrow of length 3 cm.

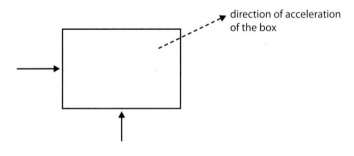

Figure 3.9 shows a box being pushed by two forces. The forces are at right angles to each other and the box will move in the direction shown.

▶ **Figure 3.9** Adding two non-parallel vectors.

The resultant of two forces acting in non-parallel directions can be found by drawing a **vector diagram**.

Draw arrows F_1 and F_2 to represent (in size and direction) the two forces in Figure 3.10. Then complete the rectangle (or parallelogram) as shown by the dashed lines. The resultant force is represented by the diagonal, F_R. This represents not only the size of the resultant force but also shows its direction.

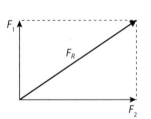

▲ **Figure 3.10** Vector diagram to find resultant vector F_R.

This method can be used with all vectors, not just forces.

26

Forces and their effects

WORKED EXAMPLE

Two tugboats are towing a ship. One tugboat applies a force on the ship of 750 kN, and the second tugboat applies a force of 500 kN at right angles to the first force. Find the size and the direction of the resultant vector.

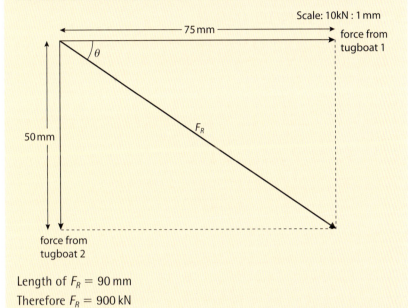

◀ Figure 3.11

Length of F_R = 90 mm
Therefore F_R = 900 kN
Angle θ = 34°
Therefore a force of **900 kN acts at 34°** to the force from the first tugboat.

QUESTIONS

3.3 Calculate the resultant force on the bodies in Figure 3.12 and state whether each body speeds up, slows down or maintains a constant speed.

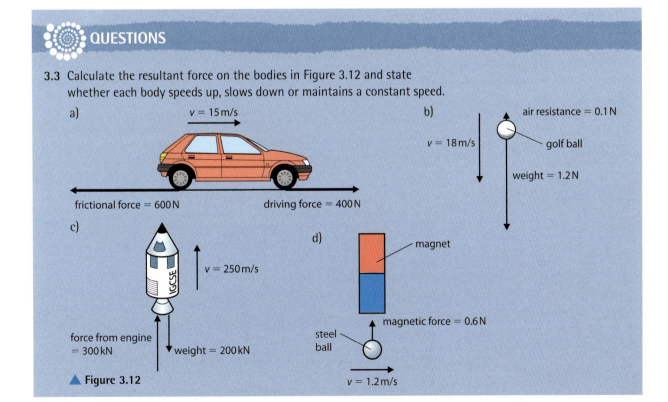

▲ Figure 3.12

3.4 Two tugboats pull an oil tanker into harbour. One tugboat pulls with a force of 200 kN, and the other with a force of 250 kN at right angles to the first tug.

Draw a vector diagram to a stated scale to show the forces involved and use it to calculate the resultant force on the oil tanker.

3.3 Measuring force

The greater the force applied to an object, the larger the acceleration produced. It can be shown experimentally that acceleration is proportional to the force.

It can also be shown that the greater the mass of an object, the smaller the acceleration for the same force. To produce the same acceleration, the force has to increase in proportion to the mass.

This can be summed up by the equation:

$$\text{force} = \text{mass} \times \text{acceleration}$$

$$F = ma$$

Units

To use this equation the mass must be in kg, the acceleration must be in m/s^2 and the force must be in N.

This equation actually defines the newton.

1 N is the force which will cause an object of mass 1 kg to accelerate at 1 m/s².

We see that $1\,N = 1\,kg \times 1\,m/s^2$.

Activity 3.3
Relationship between force and acceleration

WORKED EXAMPLES

A force of 4.9 N is applied to a mass of 1.4 kg.
Calculate the acceleration of the mass.

$$F = ma$$
$$a = \frac{F}{m}$$
$$= \frac{4.9\,N}{1.4\,kg}$$
$$= 3.5\,m/s^2$$

QUESTIONS

3.5 a) Calculate the force required to accelerate 4.5 kg at 6.0 m/s².
b) Calculate the acceleration when a force of 72 N is applied to a mass of 18 kg.
c) A force of 42 N causes an object to accelerate at 2.8 m/s². Calculate the mass of the object.
d) Calculate the acceleration of a mass of 48 g when a force of 7.2 N is applied to it.

28

3.6 A car of total mass of 1200 kg is travelling at 15 m/s. The brakes are applied and the car comes to rest with uniform acceleration in 8.0 s. Calculate the braking force.

DID YOU KNOW?

Mass has the property of 'resisting' a change to its state of motion. We call this property *inertia*. We experience this when standing on a bus that brakes suddenly – with the result that we tend to carry on at our original speed and feel ourselves move toward the front of the bus.

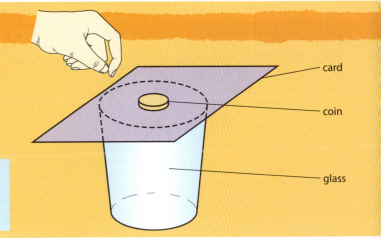

▶ Figure 3.13
When the card is flicked sharply away the coin falls into the glass. This is an example of inertia.

Acceleration due to gravity and gravitational field

We have already seen that all objects have the same acceleration in free fall. If we look at the equation linking force to acceleration:

$$F = ma$$

The acceleration due to gravity is g,

therefore $$F = mg$$

Force F is the object's own weight, which we have already defined as the gravitational pull on the body.

$$W = mg$$
or $$g = \frac{W}{m}$$

This means that g can be also considered as the gravitational pull per unit mass. This is referred to as the gravitational field. The units are N/kg.

▲ Figure 3.14
The force which is causing the acceleration is the object's own weight.

Effect of air resistance on falling bodies

Up to this stage, we have only looked at free fall and have not considered the effect of air resistance. In practice, air resistance is very important, particularly as this increases with increasing speed.

Figure 3.15 shows the forces on a sky diver.

◀ Figure 3.15
Forces on a skydiver.

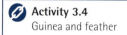
Activity 3.4
Guinea and feather

At the start of a parachute jump, the air resistance is small and the acceleration is close to *g*. As the skydiver gathers speed, the air resistance increases and the acceleration gets smaller. Eventually the air resistance will equal the weight of the skydiver and the net force will become zero – he will fall at a constant velocity. This velocity is known as the **terminal velocity**.

▶ Figure 3.16
A velocity–time graph for the sky diver.

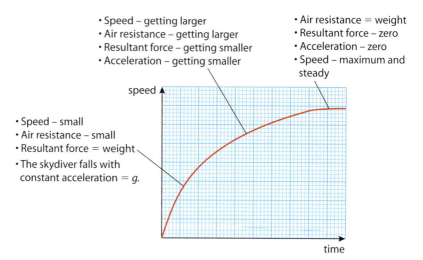

Forces not in the direction of motion

A ball is thrown horizontally. Figure 3.17(a) shows the only force acting on it is its weight. Fig. 3.17(b) shows the path it will take.

▶ Figure 3.17
Forces acting on a thrown ball, showing the resultant path.

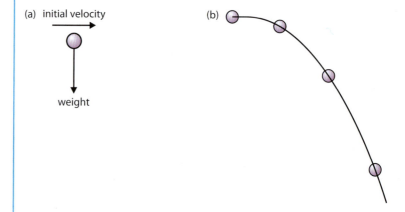

The force and the velocity are initially at right angles. The ball will continue at a constant speed in the horizontal direction (provided air resistance is negligible). However, it will accelerate downwards in the direction of the accelerating force (gravity), so its vertical speed increases. As a result the ball falls in the curved path shown.

Circular motion

Activity 3.5
Circular motion

Figure 3.18 shows a skater being spun round by her partner in a circle. In this example, the force is at right angles to the velocity and continuously changes direction as the velocity changes direction, so that it always remains at right angles to the velocity. The force is towards the centre of the circle and is called a **centripetal** force. In circular motion, the speed of the object remains constant, but the direction is continuously changing.

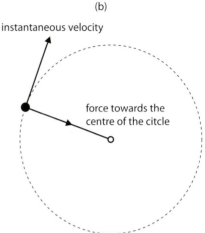

▼ Figure 3.18
The force on the female skater is towards the centre of the circle.

Centripetal acceleration

A force causes acceleration in the direction in which it is acting and the centripetal force in circular motion is no exception. This means that a body travelling in a circle has acceleration towards the centre of the circle. The force and the acceleration are both at right angles to the velocity, so the magnitude of the velocity does not change. It is only the direction of the velocity that changes, and it is this change that means the body is accelerating.

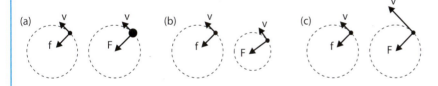

Figure 3.20 shows the velocity of the object and its position in successive time intervals. In each short time interval, the direction of velocity changes but the direction of the force also changes so that it remains at right angles to it. Consequently, the speed remains unchanged but the direction of the velocity continuously changes.

◀ Figure 3.19
(a) The size of the centripetal force needed depends on the mass of the rotating body. The larger the mass the larger the centripetal force.
(b) The size of the centripetal force needed depends on the radius of the circle. The smaller the radius the larger the centripetal force.
(c) The size of the centripetal force needed depends on speed of the rotating body. The larger the speed the larger the centripetal force.

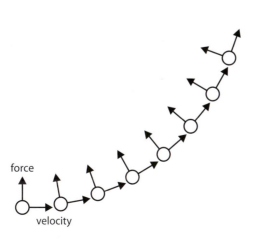

◀ Figure 3.20
Changes in force and velocity for circular motion.

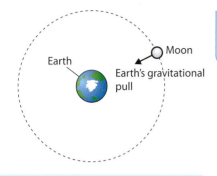

▲ **Figure 3.21**
The Earth pulls the Moon towards its centre.

▶ **Figure 3.22**

The motion of the Moon around the Earth and the planets around the Sun are further examples of circular motion. The centripetal force in these examples is provided by gravity.

QUESTIONS

3.7 a) Explain why, when a small coin and a larger coin are dropped at the same time, they also hit the ground at the same time.
b) Explain why, when a golf ball and a table tennis ball are dropped in a similar manner, the golf ball hits the ground first.

3.8 A car takes a corner at high speed. Figure 3.22 shows a plan view of this.

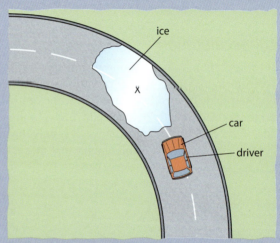

a) Copy the diagram and show the direction of the force the car applies on the driver.
b) At point X the car hits a patch of ice and the frictional force between the tyres and the road drops to nearly zero. Draw an arrow to show the path of the car when it hits the ice.

3.9 A student is given a spring and six unmarked masses. She is told to investigate the stretching of the spring under different loads.
a) State what additional apparatus the student will need to carry out the experiment.
b) Describe two precautions the student should take to get as precise an answer as possible.

3.10 A horse pulls a cart along a flat level track at a constant speed. The frictional force is 60 N.
a) What force does the horse apply to the cart?
b) State what will happen to the speed of the cart if the force applied by the horse is increased.

3.11 A car travels at a constant speed. Draw a diagram to show the forces acting on it and state the value of the resultant force on it.

3.12 A student is investigating the stretching of a spring. He records his readings in the table.

Load (N)	0	1.0	2.0	3.0	4.0	5.0	6.0
Length of spring (mm)	25	37	51	65	77	85	89
Extension (mm)	0	12					

a) Copy and complete the table.

b) Draw a graph to show the extension of the spring against the load.

c) What feature of the graph tells you that that the extension is *not* proportional to the load.

3.13 A cyclist of mass 55 kg is accelerating at 0.8 m/s^2 along a flat level road. The frictional force is 20 N. Calculate the total force that the cyclist must apply.

3.14 The spring used in a newtonmeter has a spring constant of 800 N/m. Each division on the scale is to represent 2 N. Calculate the spacing of the divisions.

Summary

Now that you have completed this chapter, you should be able to:

- understand the meaning of the term *force*
- state that the unit of force is the newton (N)
- understand the difference between mass and weight
- understand that weight is a force
- describe an experiment to investigate the stretching of a spring
- plot and use load-extension graphs
- recognise that forces cause a change in the motion of a mass
- recognise that a body will continue at rest or to move in a straight line at constant speed unless it is acted upon by a force
- recognise that frictional forces oppose motion
- add and subtract parallel forces
- recognise that all bodies fall with the same constant acceleration near the Earth's surface (in the absence of air resistance)
- recall and use the equation $F = kx$
- understand the meaning of the term *limit of proportionality*
- state Hooke's Law
- use suitable vector diagrams to add vectors acting at right angles to each other
- recognise that the newton is defined in terms of the acceleration a force produces on unit mass
- recognise that gravitational fields and acceleration due to gravity are different ways of looking at the same concept
- recognise that air resistance increases with increasing velocity
- recognise that when a body reaches a speed so that the air resistance is equal to gravitational pull on the body, it will fall at a constant speed
- understand the term *terminal velocity*
- understand that when a force acts at right angles to a body it causes a change in the direction of the motion but no change in the size of the speed
- understand that the change of direction is in the direction of the force
- understand that in circular motion the force is directed towards the centre of the circle.

Chapter 4

Moments

◀ **Figure 4.1**
Now that's what I call a spanner! Bet you could get some torque with that!

Turn a door handle, open a door, turn on a tap, take a screw-cap off a jar, tighten a nut with a spanner, or spin a cricket ball. Do any of these things and you are using another property of forces – their ability to cause rotation. In this chapter, we introduce the turning effect of a force and look at everyday examples.

4.1 Turning forces

Try opening a door by pushing close to the hinge. A very much larger force is required to open the door than would be needed if you were pushing near the handle.

The turning effect of a force about a point is called its **moment** about that point. The size of the moment depends on the size of the force and its distance from the pivot. Look at the diagram in Figure 4.2 and see how the turning effect is made bigger by applying the force as far from the hinge as possible.

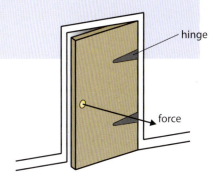

▲ **Figure 4.2**
Have you ever thought why a door handle is always placed at the edge of the door furthest from the hinge?

35

Using moments

We use the idea of moments all the time in everyday life. We have already looked at how we use moments when we open a door. Here are some more examples.

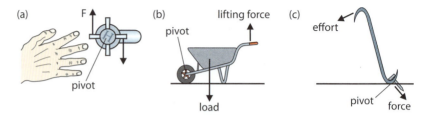

 Fig. 4.3
(a) Two forces in opposite directions cause a moment about the centre of the tap turning it on.
(b) The wheel acts as the pivot. The load is nearer to the wheel than the lifting force, so the man does not need to apply such a large force.
(c) The crowbar multiplies the force. The effort is a long way from the pivot. The pull on the nail is much closer, so for the moments to be balanced, the force on the nail is much larger than the effort force.

▶ **Figure 4.4**
Canals used to be a major method of transporting goods but now they are used for leisure purposes. The lock gate is being opened by pushing on the extended arm.

The moment of a force about a point is equal to the size of the force multiplied by the perpendicular distance from the force to the point.

Moment = force × perpendicular distance

$$M = F \times d$$

Units

Force is measured in newtons and distance in metres. Therefore the unit of the moment is newton metres (Nm).

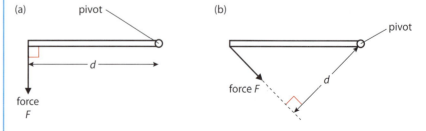

▶ **Figure 4.5**
In (b) the moment about the pivot is less than in (a). The force is the same size, but the perpendicular distance is smaller.

Note that it is the *perpendicular* distance from the force to the pivot that must be measured.

Moments

WORKED EXAMPLE

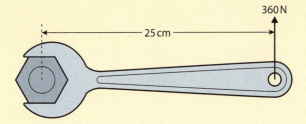

◀ Figure 4.6

Calculate the moment of the force about the centre of the nut produced by the force on the spanner in Figure 4.6.

Moment = force × perpendicular distance

= 360 N × 25 cm

= 360 N × 0.25 m

= **90 Nm**

This is the moment the spanner provides and it will be equal to the moment on the nut.

Hint

Change the distance to metres.
25 cm = 0.25 m

QUESTIONS

4.1 Calculate the moment produced about the pivot by the forces in the diagrams in Figure 4.7.

a)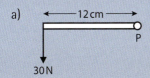

b)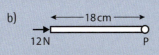

◀ Figure 4.7

c)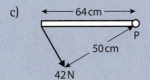

d)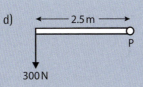

4.2 A force of 320 N is applied at one end of a beam of length 3.0 m. The other end of the beam remains on the ground and acts as a pivot. Calculate the moment produced about this end.

37

4.2 Balancing and equilibrium

Balancing – the seesaw problem

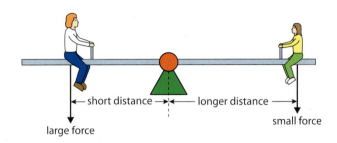

▶ **Figure 4.8**
This shows how two children of different sizes can balance a seesaw.

Activity 4.1
Balancing beams

The bigger child needs to be nearer the pivot than the small child. If she moves to exactly the right place this will equal the moment produced by the smaller child and the seesaw will balance.

The force produced by the larger child tries to turn the seesaw in an anticlockwise direction, whilst the force due to the smaller child tends to turn it in a clockwise direction. For the seesaw to balance, the moments produced by the two children must be equal, and turning the seesaw in opposite directions.

Conditions for equilibrium

We now have two conditions for a body to be in equilibrium.

1 **The resultant force on a body must be zero.** This is explained in Chapter 3. If there is a force on the body it will accelerate.

2 **The resultant moment on a body must be zero.** If there is a resultant moment the body will start to rotate.

The principle of moments states that for a body to be in equilibrium the net moment about any point is zero.

Hint

To calculate exactly where the two children must sit we need to know the masses of the two children and how far one of them is sitting from the pivot.

> **WORKED EXAMPLE**
>
> Two children of masses 32 kg and 40 kg sit on a seesaw so that it balances. The smaller child sits 1.5 m from the pivot. Calculate where the other child must sit.
> (Take g as 10 N/kg.)
>
> Weight of the small child = 32 × 10 N
> = 320 N
>
> Weight of the large child = 40 × 10 N
> = 400 N

Moments

Clockwise moment = weight of small child × distance from the pivot
= 320 × 1.5 Nm
= 480 Nm

Anticlockwise moment = weight of large child × distance from the pivot
= 400 N × y

For balance:
anticlockwise moment = clockwise moment
400 N × y = 480 Nm
$$y = \frac{480}{400} \text{ m}$$
= 1.2 m

The larger child must sit 1.2 m from the pivot and on the opposite side to the smaller child.

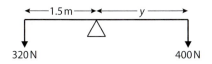

▲ Figure 4.9
It is a good idea to draw a simple diagram to help you visualise the situation.

QUESTIONS

4.3 The diagrams in Figure 4.10 show balanced rulers. Calculate the unknown quantity in each case.

a)

b)

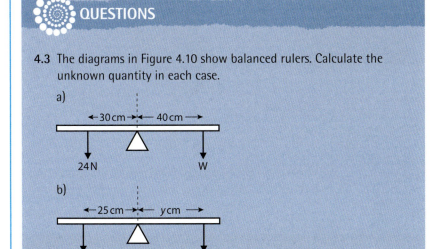

◀ Figure 4.10

The beam balance

The balancing principle is used in the beam balance, where an unknown mass is compared with that of known masses. In the balance shown, the two containers holding the masses are equal distances from the pivot – so the unknown mass is equal to the sum of the known masses.

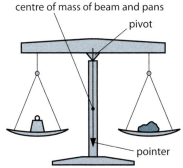

▲ Figure 4.11
The beam balance.

Centre of mass

Up to now we have ignored the mass (and weight) of the seesaw or metre rule. In reality, the mass of any body is distributed over the whole body but it can be considered to be concentrated at a single point. We call this point the **centre of mass**.

For a uniform beam, the centre of mass is at the centre of the beam. The beam balance illustrates this; it is designed so that its centre of mass is directly in line with the pivot. As a result, when balanced, it produces no turning effect about the pivot and does not affect the balancing. This can be seen in Figure 4.11.

Centre of mass and stability

Experiment to find the centre of mass of a plane lamina

The centre of mass of a flat sheet, or lamina, can be found by drilling two small holes in the lamina and then suspending it from one hole with a pin. This is shown in Figure 4.12. A plumb line is suspended from the pin and its position is marked with a cross (Figure 4.12(a)).

The lamina is then hung from a second hole and the position of the plumb line is marked again (Figure 4.12(b)). In each case the centre of mass must be vertically below the point of suspension, so the centre of mass must be where the two lines cross.

> **Activity 4.2**
> Locating the centre of mass of a plane lamina

▶ **Figure 4.12**
Finding the centre of mass for a lamina.

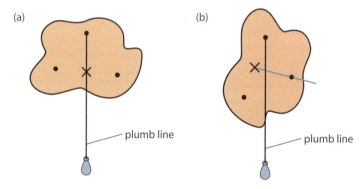

As a check, the lamina can now be suspended from a third hole, and the line made by the plumb line should cross the other two lines at their intersection.

▶ **Figure 4.13**
This racing car is designed so that the centre of mass is as close to the ground as possible. This means it is more **stable** and is less likely to turn over when it corners at high speed.

Stability

Figure 4.14 shows three balls in different states of equilibrium.

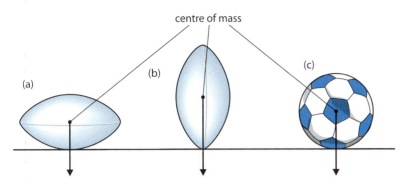

▲ Figure 4.14
(a) This rugby ball is in **stable** equilibrium. If there is a small movement of the ball, the line of action of its weight will remain inside the base on which it is balanced. This will cause it to fall back to its starting position.
(b) This rugby ball is in **unstable** equilibrium. A small movement of the ball will take the line of action of its weight outside the base on which it is balanced. This will cause it to rotate and topple over.
(c) This football is in **neutral** equilibrium. If there is a small movement of the ball, the line of action of its weight remains above its point of contact with the ground, so it will remain in its new position.

If we look at Figure 4.11 again, we will see that the centre of mass of the beam balance is well below the pivot. This makes it very stable.

QUESTIONS

4.4 Figure 4.15 shows a decanter designed for use at sea.
   a) State the two design features that make it stable so that it is unlikely to fall over in rough seas.
   b) Explain how these features make it stable.

◀ Figure 4.15

4.5 Figure 4.16 shows a snooker cue. A player attempts to balance the cue on his finger.

◀ Figure 4.16

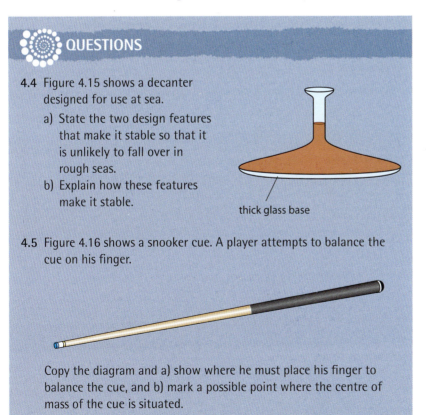

Copy the diagram and a) show where he must place his finger to balance the cue, and b) mark a possible point where the centre of mass of the cue is situated.

4.6 A door handle is 0.75 m from the hinge. The door is on a spring and a moment of 4.8 Nm is required to open the door. Calculate the force needed to open the door.

4.7 A student makes a simple balance by balancing a uniform metre rule at its centre. She places a cup of flour at the 75 cm mark. She balances the metre rule by placing a 2.0 N weight at the 10 cm mark. Calculate the weight of the cup of flour.

Summary

Now that you have completed this chapter, you should be able to:

- describe the moment of a force about a point as its turning effect about that point

- recognise that the moment of a force about a point depends on the size of the force and its perpendicular distance from the point

- recognise situations in everyday life where the moment of a force is used

- describe, qualitatively, the balancing of a pivoted beam

- understand that for a body to be in equilibrium there is no resultant force and no resultant moment on it

- understand the meaning of *centre of mass*, and describe an experiment to find the centre of mass of a plane lamina

- describe the effect of position of centre of mass on an object's stability

- know and use the formula: moment = force × perpendicular distance

- describe an experiment to verify that there is no net moment on a body when it is in equilibrium

- use the principle of moments in simple balancing problems.

Chapter 5

Pressure

▲ Figure 5.1
What happens to the pressure as the diver goes deeper?

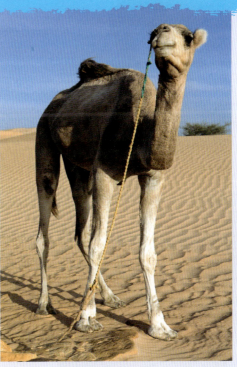

▲ Figure 5.2
Why do camels have such big feet?

What is pressure? How does it differ from force? In this chapter we explain the difference between the two ideas and explore how we measure pressures in liquids and in gases, including atmospheric pressure.

5.1 Measuring pressure

If you were going to push a drawing pin into a notice board, you would use the method in Fig. 5.3(a), not 5.3(b)! The same force might be applied in both examples, but in Figure 5.3(a), the force on the thumb is applied over a fairly large area with the force on the board concentrated on a very small area: the pin is easily pushed into the board. In Figure 5.3(b), it is the opposite way round – the tip of the pin would be pushed into the thumb.

> Activity 5.1
> Pins and plasticine

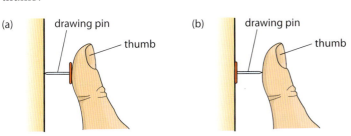

◀ Figure 5.3
Which method would you choose?

43

(a)

(b)

(c)

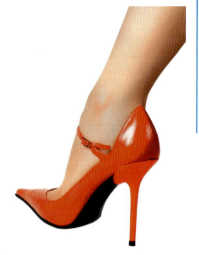

Calculating pressure

We call this idea of force acting on an area **pressure**. The explorer uses snowshoes and the farmer stands on a plank to reduce the pressure on the ground, whereas the lady using stiletto heels increases the pressure on the dance floor.

Pressure is calculated using the formula:

$$\text{pressure} = \frac{\text{force}}{\text{area}}$$

or in symbols:

$$P = \frac{F}{A}$$

Units

The unit of force is the newton (N) and the unit of area is metre squared (m^2).

So the unit of pressure is newtons per metres squared or N/m^2.

1 N/m^2 is given the special name, 1 pascal (Pa).

Sometimes the area might be measured in centimetres squared (cm^2). This unit of pressure is N/cm^2. 1 m^2 is 100 cm × 100 cm = 10 000 cm^2.

1 Pa or 1 $N/m^2 = \frac{1}{10\,000}$ N/cm^2

WORKED EXAMPLE

A skater has a mass of 54 kg. She is balancing on a single skate. An area of 2.5 cm^2 of the skate is in contact with the ice. Calculate the pressure exerted on the ice, giving your answer in N/cm^2 and Pa. (g = 10 N/kg)

Weight of the skater = mg
= 54 kg × 10 N/kg
= 540 N

Pressure = $\frac{\text{force}}{\text{area}}$ (In this case the force is the weight of the skater.)

= $\frac{540}{2.5}$ N/cm^2

= **216 N/cm^2**

1 N/cm^2 = 10 000 Pa

Therefore: 216 N/cm^2 = **2 160 000 Pa**   (This could be expressed as 2.16 × 10^6 Pa.)

◀ **Figure 5.4**
(a) Snow shoes are used to spread the load of a man walking on soft snow.
(b) A farmer stands on a plank to spread his load so he does not compress the soil.
(c) A stiletto heel has a very small area in contact with the floor, so it damages wooden floors.

Pressure

> ### QUESTIONS
>
> 5.1 Calculate the pressure, in Pa, exerted by a brick of mass 2.1 kg and dimensions 7 cm × 8 cm × 20 cm when it is placed on each of its three faces.
>
> 5.2 The safety valve in a boiler is designed to open when the pressure in the boiler reaches 80 000 Pa. The valve has a cross-sectional area of 3.2 cm^2. Calculate the force on the valve that opens it.

Activity 5.2
Pressure in fluids

5.2 Pressure in liquids

Jets of water from holes in a can show how pressure increases with increasing depth; the deeper you go the more powerful the jet.

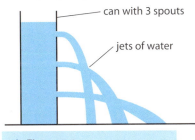

▲ **Figure 5.6**
This experiment shows that the pressure in a column of water increases with depth.

▼ **Figure 5.5**
When you dive under water you can feel that pressure on your ears increases as you go deeper.

Note that the pressure does not depend on the cross-sectional area of the container. It only depends on
- the depth below the surface of a liquid
- the density of the liquid.

We will look at this in more detail on the next page.

Pressure in fluids and direction

Pressure is a scalar quantity so it does not have direction. However, it will exert forces on any body in the fluid, and these forces will always be at right angles to the surfaces of the immersed body.

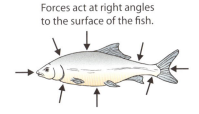

◀ **Figure 5.7**
Pressure on a fish.

The jets of water spray out at right angles to the surface of the balloon, showing that the forces produced by the pressure of the water are at right angles to the balloon surface.

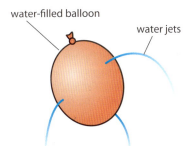

◀ **Figure 5.8**
Pressure on a balloon.

45

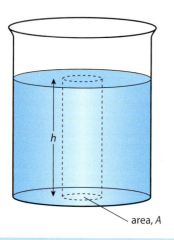

Figure 5.9
Pressure in a liquid.

Calculation of pressure in a liquid

Figure 5.9 shows a beaker containing a liquid of density, ρ.

The pressure on the area, A, is due to the weight of the column of water of height, h, above it.

> **DID YOU KNOW?**
>
> ρ is the Greek letter *rho*, equivalent to our r.

weight = mass × g (where g is the gravitational field)

mass of the column = density × volume (where the volume of the column of water = $A \times h$)

mass of the column = $\rho \times A \times h$

weight of the column = $\rho \times A \times h \times g$

$$\text{pressure on area } A = \frac{\text{force}}{\text{area}}$$

$$= \frac{\text{weight}}{\text{area}}$$

$$= \frac{\rho \times A \times h \times g}{A}$$

$$= \rho \times h \times g$$

or **pressure = $\rho h g$**

> **Hint**
>
> To use this formula, the density must be in kg/m³, the height must be in metres and g in N/kg.

You will notice that the pressure does not depend on the area chosen, only on the density of the liquid and the depth.

WORKED EXAMPLE

A diver dives to a depth of 8.0 m in seawater of density 1100 kg/m³. Calculate the pressure exerted on her by the water.

Pressure from the water = $\rho h g$
= 1100 × 8.0 × 10
= 88 000 Pa

QUESTIONS

5.3 Calculate the pressure at the bottom of an oil tank of depth 15 m. Density of oil = 0.85 kg/m³.

5.3 Pressure in gases

The atmosphere exerts a pressure

Above your head there is a column of air of height in excess of 10 km. In a similar way to a liquid column, this exerts a pressure on you!

Figure 5.11 shows the large forces that atmospheric pressure produces. In a demonstration a vacuum pump is attached to an old oil can. When the air is pumped out of the can, the pressure of the atmosphere will crush the can and it will collapse.

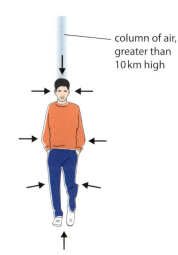

◀ **Figure 5.10**
The air around you presses inwards on all parts of your body.

Activity 5.3
Pressure due to the atmosphere

▼ **Figure 5.11**
The arrows show how the atmosphere pushes in to crush the can when there is no air inside it.

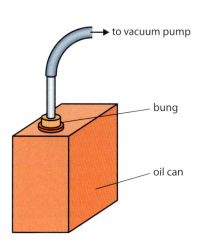

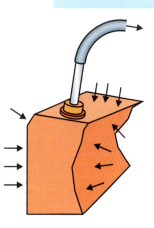

Measurement of gas pressure

The examples in Figure 5.12 show that gases exert pressure.

(a)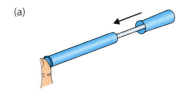
(b)
(c)

▲ **Figure 5.12**
(a) Put your finger over the end of a bicycle pump and try to push the piston in – feel the resistance.
(b) Blow up a balloon, hold it near to your face and then let the air out slowly.
(c) Push the valve on a cycle tyre – feel the air come out.

The manometer

Figure 5.13 shows a U-tube with water in the bottom.

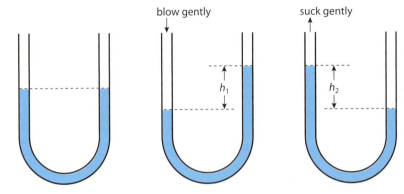

Figure 5.13
(a) When both sides of the U-tube are open, the pressure on each side is the same and the water levels in each arm are the same.
(b) When you gently blow in one side, the water level in that side goes down and the other side goes up. The harder you blow the greater the difference in height. The height difference (h_1) is a measure of the extra pressure produced by blowing.
(c) When you gently suck, the water level in that side goes up and the other side goes down. As before, the harder you suck the greater the difference in column height. The height difference (h_2) is a measure of the reduction in pressure produced by sucking.

This instrument is called a **manometer** and it measures the pressure difference above or below atmospheric pressure.

The pressure difference can be calculated by using the formula $P = \rho h g$.

A height difference of 90 mm would mean a pressure difference of $1000 \text{ kg/m}^3 \times \frac{90}{1000} \text{ m} \times 10 \text{ N/kg} = 900 \text{ N/m}^2$.

If you use mercury instead of water in the U-tube you will find it much more difficult to get a significant height difference. The density of mercury is much larger than water. The density of water is 1000 kg/m³, whereas the density of mercury is 13 600 kg/m³.

Measuring atmospheric pressure

A tube of length about 1 m has one end in a dish of mercury. The other end is attached to a 'trap' and a vacuum pump. When the air is pumped out of the tube, there is less pressure in the tube and the atmospheric pressure acting on the surface of the mercury in the dish pushes the mercury up the tube. When the mercury level gets to about 760 mm above the level of the mercury in the dish, it will not go any further. All the air has now been pumped out of the tube and the weight of the mercury in the column produces a pressure equal to the pressure exerted on the mercury surface in the dish.

This gives us a method of measuring atmospheric pressure. The measurement of atmospheric pressure is important in weather forecasting. When the pressure is high the weather is likely to be sunny and fine, whereas low pressure indicates that the weather will be cloudy and wet.

The simple mercury barometer

A device for measuring atmospheric pressure is pressure is called a **barometer**. The simple mercury barometer is based on the apparatus described above. A tube, of length about 1 metre, full of mercury, is sealed at both ends. One end is placed under the surface of mercury in a dish and that end unsealed. Some of the mercury flows out of the tube leaving a vacuum at the top of the tube. As in the previous experiment, the pressure of the atmosphere supports a column of mercury of height about 760 mm.

Activity 5.4 Measuring pressure

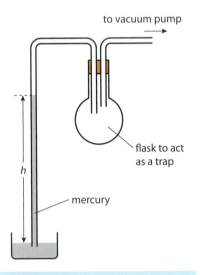

▲ Figure 5.14
Using mercury to measure atmospheric pressure.

Standard atmospheric pressure will support a mercury column of height 760 mm. We can calculate the value of atmospheric pressure using this information.

$$P = \rho h g$$
$$= 13\,600 \times 0.76 \times 10 \text{ Pa}$$
$$= \mathbf{1.03 \times 10^5 \text{ Pa}}$$

Hint

First convert all units to SI.
$\rho = 13\,600$ kg/m^3,
$h = 760/1000$ m,
$g = 10$ N/kg

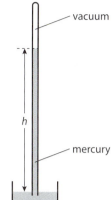

▲ Figure 5.15
A simple mercury barometer.

QUESTIONS

5.4 Explain why atmospheric pressure decreases with increasing height. (You will find it helpful to compare it with the pressure in a liquid.)

5.5 A student takes a sealed bag of crisps on a trip to a mountain. As he climbs the mountain the bag blows up as shown.
Explain why this happens.

packet at sea level

same packet high up the mountain

5.6 A manometer is used to measure the pressure of a gas supply. Explain which of the diagrams shows how the manometer should be set up and gives the correct result.

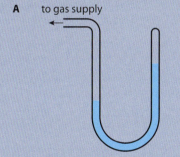

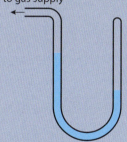

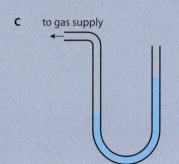

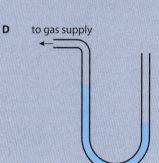

5.7 The pressure on a diver in a fresh water lake is 120 kPa.
Calculate the depth to which he has dived.

5.8 A gymnast of mass 45 kg is balancing on a beam of width 4 cm.
The length of her shoe in contact with the beam is 15 cm.
Calculate the pressure the gymnast exerts on the beam.

5.9 A car of mass 1200 kg rests on four tyres. The pressure in the tyres is
8.0×10^2 Pa.
Calculate the total area of tyre in contact with the ground.

Summary

Now that you have completed this chapter, you should be able to:

- understand that pressure is the force per unit area
- recall that pressure is measured in pascals (Pa)
- recall that $1\,\text{Pa} = 1\,\text{N/m}^2$
- understand that the pressure in a liquid increases with increasing depth
- understand how a simple mercury barometer can be used to measure atmospheric pressures
- understand how a manometer can be used to measure gas pressures
- recall and use the equation $P = \dfrac{F}{A}$
- recall and use the equation $P = h\rho g$.

Chapter 6

Work, energy and power

The modern world relies on the efficient transfer of raw fuels or energy sources into useful forms of energy. We burn fossil fuels to run industry, for transport, and for leisure purposes. We need to generate electricity, not only for industry but for comforts at home. Without electricity there would be no washing machines, no electric lighting, and no television.

We take our modern luxuries for granted but it comes at a cost. As more countries industrialise there will be increasing demand for fuel. What will this mean for the future? What are the effects of burning coal, gas and oil? Can we continue to rely on the car for personal transport? Can we expect to fly around the world? Are there better ways of generating electricity?

▲ Figure 6.1
We are addicted to our own personal transport. What effects does that have?

6.1 Work

The concept of energy is not simple. We may have a feeling for what it means: 'If we have energy we can run around a lot, or do tiring jobs', but as scientists we need to have a more precise idea of the meaning.

To understand energy, we need to look at forces.

A boy holding a book is doing no more than could be done by having the book on a desk. This job could be done without using any fuel, but to lift the book from the ground onto the desk, fuel is needed – we say work is done.

Whenever a force acts on an object to make it move, work is done. In the example in Figure 6.3, work is done against the pull of gravity.

The further the point of application of a force moves, or the larger the force that is used, the more work is done.

▲ Figure 6.2
Is the melting of the polar ice caps a result of our need for more and more energy?

(a) (b)

◀ Figure 6.3
(a) No work needed here.
(b) Work must be done in lifting an object.

51

What is work being done against in the following examples?

(a) 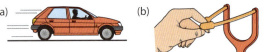 (b) (c)

▶ **Figure 6.4**
(a) A car travelling along a straight, level track.
(b) A catapult rubber being stretched.
(c) A positively charged rod brought towards another positively charged rod.

Calculation of work

The amount of work done is calculated from the formula:

work = force × distance moved along the line of the force

To use this formula, the force must be measured in newtons and the distance in metres, giving work in **newton metres** (**Nm**).

This is such an important unit that it is given a special name:

1 newton metre is 1 joule (J)

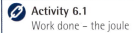 **Activity 6.1**
Work done – the joule

WORKED EXAMPLE

A car travels along a straight level road at a constant speed for 200 m against a frictional force of 300 N. Calculate the work done by the car.

Work = force × distance
= 300 N × 200 m
= 60 000 J

DID YOU KNOW?

Δ is the Greek letter delta, equivalent to D.

QUESTIONS

6.1. Calculate the work done against the pull of gravity when a sack of rice of mass 50 kg (weight 500 N) is lifted from the ground, onto the back of a lorry 1.2 m above the ground.

The work done is the equivalent of the energy transferred or transformed. We use the symbol Δ (delta) to represent a change in a quantity, so we can write

$$\Delta W = F\Delta d = \Delta E$$

In Question 6.1, the work done in lifting the sack is equivalent to the energy gained by the sack, assuming no other energy transfers took place.

6.2 Energy

So what is energy?

Energy is the capacity or ability to do work.

Quite simply, if an object has 500 J of energy, it has the ability to do 500 J of work.

A cricket ball of mass 0.15 kg travelling at a speed of 40 m/s has an energy of 120 J owing to its motion. This means that if it were brought to rest it would do 120 J of work.

▼ **Figure 6.5**
A fast bowler can give a cricket ball 120 J of kinetic energy.

Different types of energy

There are various reasons why an object may be said to have extra energy. Here are some examples.

Kinetic energy – the ability to do work because of an object's movement.

Gravitational potential energy – the ability to do work because of an object's position in a gravitational field.

◀ **Figure 6.6**
The climber has gravitational potential energy.

Activity 6.2
Which type of energy?

Electrical potential energy – the ability to do work because of an electrically charged object's position in an electric field.

◀ **Figure 6.7**
Electrical potential energy is released into other forms of energy in a lightning strike.

▼ **Figure 6.8**
Nuclear potential energy is released into other forms of energy in an atomic explosion.

Chemical potential energy – the ability to do work because of the potential energy of the atoms making up chemicals.

Nuclear potential energy – the ability to do work because of the potential energy of the particles within the nucleus of an atom.

Strain energy – the ability to do work because the molecules making up an object are either crushed together or pulled apart.

Internal energy – the ability to do work because of the temperature of an object.

Sound energy – the ability to do work because of the vibrations of particles in a sound wave.

What types of energy are shown in Figure 6.9?

▼ Figure 6.9
Different types of energy.

Activity 6.3
Energy changes

Energy transfer

Energy can be changed from one form to another. There are two ways of doing this: either by doing work or by radiating energy.

Work

Whenever work is done, energy is transferred from one form to another.

When a car accelerates, a force must be applied to the car. The car (and therefore the point of application of the force) is moving and so work is done. The work done against the accelerating force is equal to the **kinetic energy** gained by the car.

But why was the car able to do work? The energy to do the work comes from the chemical potential energy in the fuel.

The **chemical potential energy** of the fuel is converted into **kinetic energy** of the car.

When a car is moving along a straight, level road at constant speed, there needs to be a driving force. The car is moving, therefore the driving force is also moving. The car does not gain any more kinetic energy; work is

Work, energy and power

now being done solely against friction. Fuel is being burnt, so where does the chemical potential energy go? Feel the tyres of a car after a journey and you will find they are warm – the chemical potential energy has been converted to internal energy. Whenever work is done against friction, the input energy is converted to internal energy.

Radiation

Hold your hands in front of a fire and you can feel the warmth of the fire. Stand in sunshine and the light will dazzle your eyes. A leaf on a tree will absorb light from the Sun to change water and carbon dioxide into glucose.

In all these examples energy is **radiated** from one object and absorbed by another. The fire radiates thermal or **infrared** radiation. The sun radiates, not only infrared radiation, but also **visible** and **ultraviolet radiation.**

Describe the energy changes in Figure 6.10.

(a)

(b)

(c)

(d)

▲ Figure 6.10
(a) A fast moving car braking.
(b) A cyclist going up a hill at a constant speed.
(c) A rocket accelerating upwards.
(d) A catapult firing a rock.

▲ **Figure 6.11**
In all these examples, energy has been changed from one form to another but in no example has it either been created or destroyed.

Conservation of energy

One of the most fundamental laws of physics is The Law of Conservation of Energy.

Energy can be neither created nor destroyed.

For example, at a power station when fuel is burnt, electric potential energy and internal energy are produced, but the sum of these is equal to the original chemical potential energy of the fuel.

Calculation of energy

Gravitational potential energy

A woman lifts a mass m through a height of h onto her head.

The force needed to lift the mass is equal to its weight $= m \times g$ (where g = gravitational field strength).

Work done by the force against gravity = force × distance moved
$$= m \times g \times h$$

The mass now has the ability to do an extra $m \times g \times h$ of work due to its new height. Its potential energy is $m \times g \times h$.

Gravitational potential energy = $m \times g \times h$

WORKED EXAMPLE

A pile driver has a hammer of mass of 200 kg, which is raised through a height of 80 m. Calculate the gravitational potential energy given to the hammer.

Gravitational potential energy = $m \times g \times h$
$= 200 \times 10 \times 8$ J
$= \mathbf{16\,000\,J}$

QUESTIONS

Hint

Remember to convert to base SI units.

6.2 Calculate the gravitational potential energy of the following.
   a) A boy of mass 45 kg, sitting in a tree 12 m above the ground.
   b) A box of mass 1.5 kg on a shelf 75 cm above the ground.

Kinetic energy

A force of F acts on a stationary spacecraft of mass m for time t.

The acceleration of the craft $= \dfrac{\text{force}}{\text{mass}} = \dfrac{F}{m}$

Work, energy and power

The velocity (v) of the craft = acceleration × time

$$v = \frac{F}{m} \times t$$

or

$$F = \frac{mv}{t}$$

The distance moved by the craft = average velocity × time

$$= \tfrac{1}{2} v \times t$$

Work done on the craft = force × distance

$$= \left(\frac{mv}{t}\right) \times \tfrac{1}{2} v \times t$$

The craft can now do an extra ($\tfrac{1}{2}mv^2$) of work due to its speed. Its kinetic energy is $\tfrac{1}{2}mv^2$.

Kinetic energy = $\tfrac{1}{2}mv^2$

▲ Figure 6.12
Work is done, giving these masses gravitational potential energy.

WORKED EXAMPLE

A golf ball of mass 75 g is moving with a speed of 40 m/s. Calculate the kinetic energy of the golf ball.

$$\text{Kinetic energy} = \tfrac{1}{2} mv^2$$
$$= \tfrac{1}{2} \times 0.075 \times 40^2 \text{ J}$$
$$= 60 \text{ J}$$

Hint

75 g = 0.075 kg

QUESTIONS

6.3 Calculate the kinetic energy of the following.
   a) A car of mass 800 kg travelling at 15 m/s.
   b) A cricket ball of mass 300 g travelling at 25 m/s

Activity 6.4
Kinetic energy

6.3 Energy resources

For many years the world has relied on **fossil fuels** to provide the raw energy to run industry and provide energy for transport. Fossil fuels, such as coal, oil and natural gas are made from rotting animal and vegetable matter, taking millions of years to form. When they are burnt, the chemical potential energy of the fuels can be converted to internal energy to drive turbines, or to run engines. However there are problems with fossil fuels. They are finite, so once we have used the Earth's supply it will take millions of years for them to be replaced. On combustion, they release **pollutants** into the air – even with modern methods of cleaning the waste gases, some pollutants are released. One of the most important pullutants is carbon dioxide, which rises into the upper atmosphere where it acts like a blanket, not allowing energy to radiate away from the Earth. This is known as the **greenhouse effect** and it is slowly causing the Earth to get warmer, with potentially catastrophic effects.

Mankind needs to develop different sources of energy if we are to avoid major problems in the future. Some examples are

Hydroelectricity – the gravitational potential energy of water stored in reservoirs can be used to generate electricity.

Tidal energy – there are two tides each day. The gravitational potential energy and the kinetic energy of the sea water can be used to turn turbines to generate electricity.

Wave energy – the kinetic energy of waves out at sea can be used to generate electricity.

Wind energy – the kinetic energy of moving air particles can be used to drive turbines.

Geothermal energy – the energy from the hot rocks underneath the Earth's surface can be used to generate electricity.

Solar energy – the radiated energy from the Sun can be used to either heat water for domestic use or to directly generate electricity using solar cells.

Biofuels – crops can be fermented to form ethanol, which can then be distilled to fuel vehicles.

Nuclear fission – the energy of the nuclei of unstable atoms can be used to heat water to drive turbines and generate electricity.

6.4 Power

What makes a racing car more powerful than a family car? So far we have looked at work and energy, but now we need to consider power. The designers of a racing car need to make it not only go faster than an ordinary car but also accelerate at a greater rate. This means that it must give the car more kinetic energy in a shorter time interval; we say the engine has more power.

Power is defined as the rate of doing work or transferring energy. It is measured in joule/second or **watts** (**W**)

▼ Figure 6.13
The racing car is much more powerful than the family car.

▲ Figure 6.14
The wind turbine produces 7500 joule of energy each second – its power output is 7500 W or 7.5 kW.

Work, energy and power

▲ Figure 6.15
This power station produces 1500 MW.

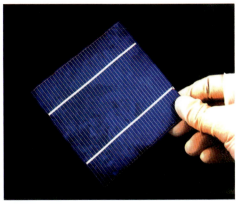

▲ Figure 6.16
This solar cell produces 1.5 mW of energy.

QUESTIONS

6.4 List the three energy generators shown in Figures 6.14, 6.15 and 6.16 in order of increasing power output. Where do you think the racing car engine would fit?

Activity 6.5
Measuring power

Calculating power

$$\text{power} = \frac{\text{work done}}{\text{time taken}}$$

To use this formula the work should be measured in joules and the time in seconds, giving the unit of power as the joule/second.

This is such an important unit that it is given a special name.

1 joule/second is 1 watt (W)

Efficiency

No machine converts all the input energy into useful output work or energy. There are always other forms of energy produced, usually waste thermal (internal) energy.

QUESTIONS

6.5 Calculate the power of the following.
   a) A torch bulb which uses 90 J in 60 s.
   b) A heater in a fish tank which uses 3600 J in 4 hours.
   c) A motor which does 4.5 MJ of work in 2 minutes.

▶ Figure 6.17
In a motorboat engine, less than 25% of the input energy is converted into energy to drive the boat through the water. The remainder goes to internal energy (the engine gets hot!) and sound energy.

59

QUESTIONS

6.6 What types of energy do the following have?
   a) A rollercoaster train at the top of the ride.
   b) A sprinter as she crosses the finish line.
   c) An elastic band which is stretched.

6.7 What energy changes occur when
   a) an athlete throws a javelin?
   b) a steam train leaves a station?
   c) a radio is switched on?

6.8 Calculate the gravitational potential energy of an aeroplane of mass 200 tonne at a height of 4000 m above the Earth.

6.9 Calculate the kinetic energy of a sprinter of mass 60 kg running at 36 km/h.

6.10 Calculate the power produced by the following.
   a) A car moving at 15 m/s against a frictional force of 200 N.
   b) A hoist which lifts a bag of cement of mass 50 kg through 8 m in 20 s.
   c) A skater of mass 45 kg who accelerates from rest to 12 m/s in 4 s.

Hint

The engine of a car travelling at v m/s against a force of F produces an output power of $F \times v$.

Summary

Now that you have completed this chapter, you should be able to:

- define work and energy
- recognise that work is measured in joules
- recognise that energy is measured in joules
- understand and recognise different types of energy
- describe energy conversions
- understand conservation of energy
- describe different energy sources
- understand that power is how fast work is done
- recall and use the equation for the work done when a force moves
- recall and use the equations for gravitational potential energy, and the kinetic energy of an object
- recall and use the equation for power.

Chapter 7
Kinetic molecular model of matter

▲ **Figure 7.1**
Diamonds – the most sought after crystals of all. The photograph shows an uncut diamond, but even in its natural state we can see the geometric shapes which nature makes.

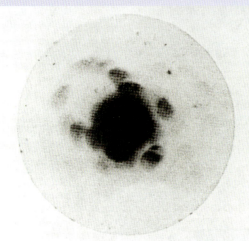

▲ **Figure 7.2**
Visible light has too great a wavelength to be able to look deeper into crystals. Lawrence Bragg, at the age of 22 and having just graduated, was the first person to realise that X-rays could be used to study the structure of crystals. Reflections from successive sheets of atoms reinforce each other to produce these spots.

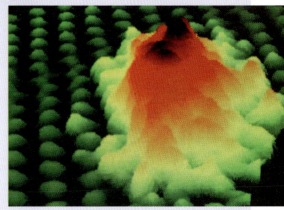

▲ **Figure 7.3**
The latest electron microscopes can resolve images to less than the diameter of an atom – so that we can actually see individual atoms. The photograph shows where two gold crystals meet. They are joined by a complex arrangement of atoms. The purity of the signal makes it possible to distinguish individual atoms and deduce their positions in three dimensions.

What is matter made from? Why do gases behave differently from liquids and why do liquids behave differently from solids? In this chapter we shall describe one model of matter, a model that explains the difference between the states of matter. We shall look at some of the evidence supporting this model and some of the phenomena that the model will explain.

7.1 What is matter made from?

If you look around you will see many different things. These things will probably come into one of two categories: **solids** (such as wood, iron and brick) and **liquids** (such as water, milk, and ethanol). The third category of materials – gases (such as air, hydrogen sulphide, chlorine) are generally harder to see.

(a)

(b)

(c)

▲ Figure 7.4
(a) Solids are rigid and have a definite shape and size. A relatively large force is needed to change the shape or the size of a solid.
(b) Liquids do not have definite shape, they will tend to take the shape of their container or if spilt, spread across the bench. However they do have a fixed volume, unless large forces are applied to change it.
(c) Gases have no fixed shape and no fixed volume. Many are colourless and that is why they are hard to see – we can only detect them by other properties such as their smell. Here, the brown gas nitrogen dioxide is clearly visible.

Matter is made up from tiny particles, called **molecules**. What evidence do we have for the existence of these particles?

Look at some salt crystals under a microscope. Each tiny salt grain is a marvel of geometric shapes. Now stack some oranges, or polystyrene balls to make a pyramid. Is it possible that the salt crystals are made up in the same way, with the tiny particles stacked up like the oranges?

This is evidence, not proof, that matter could be made up of particles.

DID YOU KNOW?

The particles which make up a crystal are called atoms. The atoms are made up of still smaller particles called electrons, protons and neutrons.

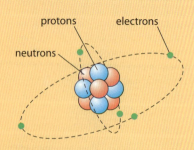

▲ Figure 7.5
The basic structure of an atom.

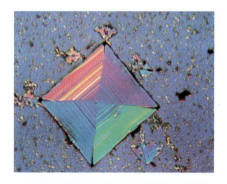

▲ Figure 7.6
Atoms in the salt crystal on the left are stacked in a similar way to the oranges.

Brownian motion

If you look through a microscope at a drop of milk diluted with water, you will see bright specks of light moving randomly in all directions.

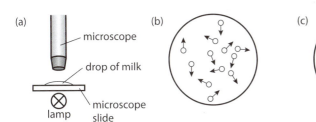

▶ **Activity 7.1**
Growing crystals

◀ **Figure 7.7**
(a) Investigating Brownian motion.
(b) Specks of light moving in random directions.
(c) Path of a single speck of light.

The specks of light are tiny fat globules. They are moving because they are continually bombarded by the very much smaller water molecules, which themselves are far too small to see. We now have very strong evidence for our theory.

S The bombardment of the fat globules is rather like having a large steel ball bearing being bombarded by very much smaller ball bearings. Each hit causes the large ball bearing to change its speed and its direction of motion.

 DID YOU KNOW?

Robert Brown 1773–1855

Robert Brown was a Scottish botanist. What is a botanist doing in a physics book?

He initially worked on the fertilisation of ova in plants. He then studied the structure of pollen, and it was when doing these experiments that he first observed the movement of pollen grains in water. It was not the first time that this had been observed but prior to Brown it had been assumed that the motion was due to the 'living nature' of pollen, and scientists thought they were seeing the 'very rudiments of life'. Brown, being a good scientist, questioned this. He repeated the experiment with pollen from different species and found similar movement in all. He then tried pollen that had been preserved in alcohol for twelve months (clearly dead). The movement still occurred. Finally he tried non-living material (ground rock) and found the same effect. It was now clear to Brown that the movement was not due to the particles having 'life', but was due to the bombardment of the particles by water molecules. The effect is now known as Brownian motion in his honour.

This botanist thoroughly deserves to be in a physics book!

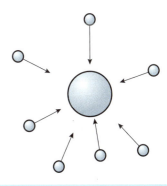

▲ **Figure 7.8**
Large particle bombarded by smaller particles.

Activity 7.2
A model of a liquid and a gas

Activity 7.3
Brownian motion

 **QUESTIONS**

7.1 Brownian motion can be seen using smoke particles in air. What causes the smoke particles to move in this case?

How big are the molecules?

A simple experiment can be done to estimate the maximum diameter of the molecules.

A trough or bowl of water is dusted with a light powder, which floats on its surface. The diameter of a drop of oil is measured before it is placed onto the surface of the water. When it is placed on the water, it clears dust from a circle, showing a clear patch. The diameter of this circle is also measured.

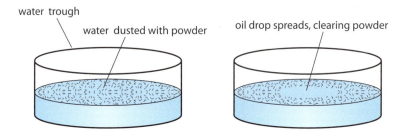

▶ **Figure 7.9**
Experiment to estimate the maximum size of an oil molecule.

By comparing the original volume of the drop with the area of the circle, the thickness of the circle can be found. The thinnest this circle can be is one molecule thick, so we have an upper estimate of the molecule's diameter.

Experiments like this give the diameter of the oil molecule to be in the region of about 10^{-8} to 10^{-9} m.

Activity 7.4
Estimating molecular size

7.2 The kinetic model of matter

Solids

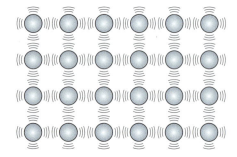

▶ **Figure 7.10**
Molecules in a solid vibrate about fixed positions. The molecules are closely packed, so it is difficult to compress a solid. The rigid structure and the difficulty of changing the shape of a solid are due to the forces between the molecules.

Liquids

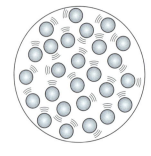

◀ **Figure 7.12**
A drop of water forms below a tap.

▶ **Figure 7.11**
The forces in a liquid are big enough to form drops of liquid and hold them together. The particles are still fairly closely packed, but now they do not have fixed positions and are free to move around the liquid in random directions.

64

Gases

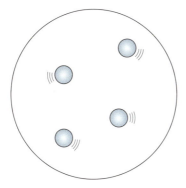

◀ **Figure 7.13**
The molecules in a gas are a long way apart and the forces between them are negligible. The particles are totally independent and move with complete freedom. Just as in a liquid, the direction of the movement of the molecules is random.

 DID YOU KNOW?

We often use the term *model* in science. We can never say that something is definitely 'this' or definitely 'that', we can only say that it *behaves* as though it is this, but it does not behave as though it is that. In the model we use here, we consider the molecules to be like tiny hard balls, but are they really like this? Probably not. However, this model is useful in that it helps us to explain properties of matter and to make predictions.

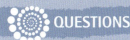 **QUESTIONS**

7.2 Explain why a solid is very much harder to compress than a gas.

7.3 Explain why it is much harder to break a solid apart than to shatter a drop of liquid.

Heating matter

When matter is heated, energy is given to the molecules. Generally, the molecules gain kinetic energy. In a solid they vibrate faster and in a liquid or a gas they move faster. Not all the molecules move at the same speed or in the same direction. The average kinetic energy of the molecules is a measure of the temperature of the material – the higher the average kinetic energy of the molecules, the higher the temperature.

◀ **Figure 7.14**
The liquid is heated, giving energy to the molecules and making them move faster.

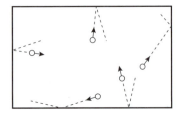

▲ Figure 7.15
Gas molecules collide with each other and with the container walls.

Pressure exerted by a gas

A gas is stored in a container. The gas molecules move at random and collide with the container walls and bounce off. Each time the wall is hit there is a small force on the wall. There are billions of collisions with the wall each second, and the overall effect of these forces is to produce a pressure on the wall.

If the gas is heated, the molecules move faster. Therefore they collide with the walls more frequently and each collision is harder. The result is that the pressure increases when the temperature increases.

Change in pressure with changing volume, at constant temperature

We can investigate the change of pressure with the changing volume using the apparatus shown in Figure 7.16. Air is trapped in the glass tube by the oil. The pressure is altered by pumping air into the reservoir, and this pushes the oil up the glass tube, compressing the air trapped in the tube. The pressure of the trapped air is equal to the pressure of the air in the reservoir. This pressure is measured by the pressure gauge.

▶ Figure 7.16
Investigating pressure and volume.

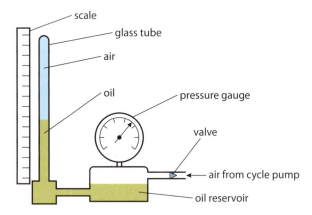

Activity 7.5
Pressure and volume of a gas

The results obtained are shown on the graph in Figure 7.17. We can see from the graph that as the pressure is increased so the volume decreases. This type of relationship is known as an **inverse** relationship and it follows the rules

halve the volume – double the pressure

double the volume – halve the pressure

triple the volume – divide the pressure by three.

▶ Figure 7.17
The relationship between pressure and volume.

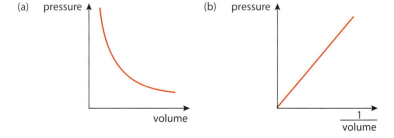

Kinetic molecular model of matter

The results are explained in Figure 7.18. In the first diagram, the particles are well spaced and the distances travelled between collisions with the walls are quite large. If the piston is pushed in, the particles are much closer and the distance between collisions with the walls is much smaller, so the collisions are more frequent, causing a higher pressure.

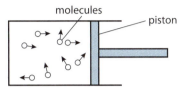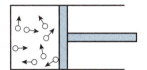

Figure 7.18
The effect of reducing volume of a gas.

Boyle's law

If we look at the results from the experiment and calculate the value of 1/volume for each pressure, then plot pressure against 1/volume, we get a graph, as shown in Figure 7.17(b). This is a straight-line graph through the origin. We have already seen that this tells us that one variable is proportional to the other. In this case

$$\text{pressure} \propto \frac{1}{\text{volume}}$$

or

$$\text{pressure} = \frac{\text{constant}}{\text{volume}}$$

Rearrange the equation:

$$\text{pressure} \times \text{volume} = \text{constant}$$

A useful way of rewriting this is

$$p_i v_i = p_f v_f$$ (where p_i = initial pressure, v_i = initial volume
p_f = final pressure, v_f = final volume)

Hint
The Boyle's law formula assumes that the temperature remains constant.

DID YOU KNOW?

Robert Boyle was born in 1627, the fourteenth child of the Earl of Cork. He is referred to as the father of modern chemistry.

One of his earliest successes was the invention of an effective vacuum pump. He published his findings of the pressure–volume relationship in the second edition of his treatise 'The Spring and Weight of Air' in 1662.

He was a founding member of the Royal Society (1662) which still exists today and is the oldest continuous scientific society in the world.

WORKED EXAMPLE

A cylinder of hydrogen contains 0.32 m³ of hydrogen at a pressure of 250 kPa.

Calculate the volume of the hydrogen at atmospheric pressure, assuming that there is no change of temperature.
(Atmospheric pressure = 100 kPa)

$$p_i v_i = p_f v_f$$

$$f = \frac{p_i v_i}{p_f}$$

$$v_f = \frac{250 \text{ kPa} \times 0.32 \text{ m}^3}{100 \text{ kPa}}$$

$$v_f = 0.80 \text{ m}^3$$

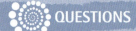

QUESTIONS

7.4 Explain why a gas exerts a pressure on a container.

7.5 A gas has volume 4.5 m³ at atmospheric pressure. The pressure is then increased to 1.5 × atmospheric pressure, with no change in temperature. What is the volume of the gas at this new pressure?

7.6 An air bubble has an initial volume of 2.4 cm³ when it is released from the mask of a diver at a depth of 25 m. The volume increases to 9.0 cm³ when it reaches the surface.
Given that the pressure at the surface of the water is 100 kPa, calculate the pressure 25 m below the water surface.

7.7 A boy pushes the piston of a cycle pump while holding his thumb over the end of the piston.
State what happens to the pressure of the air in the pump and explain this in terms of the kinetic model of matter.

7.8 Explain why a cylinder of carbon dioxide might explode in a laboratory fire.

7.9 A gas is contained in a rigid metal cylinder. The temperature of the cylinder is raised from 20 °C to 60 °C.
a) State what will happen to the pressure of the gas.
b) Explain your answer to a) in terms of the movement of the molecules.

7.10 A boy fires a marble at a cricket ball.
a) State what will happen to the two balls after the collision.
b) Use your answer to a) to explain why Brown's observations of pollen grains on water give evidence that the water molecules are moving.

7.11 A gas, at a pressure of 2.0×10^5 Pa, is contained in a cylinder. The piston of the cylinder is moved outwards so that the volume of the gas is increased from 250 cm² to 400 cm².
a) Calculate the new pressure of the gas.
b) Explain, in terms of the movement of its molecules, why there is a change in pressure of the gas.

7.12 The volume of a diver's air tank is 16 000 cm³. It contains air at pressure of 4.59×10^5 Pa.
Calculate the volume the air would occupy if it were released directly into the atmosphere.
You may assume there is no change of temperature of the air.
(Atmospheric pressure = 1.02×10^5 Pa.)

Summary

Now that you have completed this chapter, you should be able to:

- distinguish between gases, liquids and solids
- recognise the evidence for the existence of molecules
- describe, in terms of molecules, the structures of solids, liquids and gases
- recognise and describe Brownian motion
- describe, in terms of forces and distances between particles, the difference between solids, liquids and gases
- understand that when a gas is heated, the kinetic energy of the individual molecules increases
- recall that when the volume of a gas is decreased, its pressure increases
- recognise and use the equation, pressure × volume = constant.

Chapter 8

Expansion and temperature

▶ Figure 8.1
It might be cold in Antarctica — temperatures as low as −40 °C are not uncommon — but what is the lowest temperature that can be reached? At really, really low temperatures (−270 °C), gases freeze and other materials exhibit startling new properties. Metals become superconductors; they conduct electricity with no resistance. Helium becomes a superfluid, it flows without any frictional forces.

▶ Figure 8.2
The temperatures in a supernova (an exploding star) can reach 15 000 000 000 °C.

Temperature is a measure of how hot or cold an object is. In this chapter we look at measuring temperatures. We look at different types of thermometer and how scales are marked on them. We also look at the expansion of solids, liquids and gases, as a result of temperature rise, and how expansion is used in the design of different devices in industry and the home.

8.1 Expansion of solids, liquids, and gases

We can observe the expansion of a solid by setting up the experiment shown in Figure 8.3. A large mass holds one end of the stand steady. The rod rests on a sewing needle, which has been pushed through a drinking straw. This amplifies the expansion of the rod as it is heated, enabling it to be seen easily.

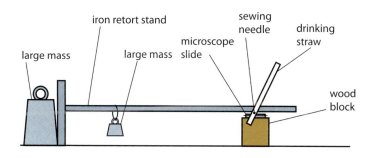

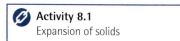

Figure 8.3
When the rod is heated with a Bunsen burner, it rolls the needle along, causing the straw to rotate.

Activity 8.1
Expansion of solids

When any material is heated it tends to expand. The molecules themselves do not change size. The expansion is due to the molecules moving further apart. In a solid they vibrate more and their average separation increases.

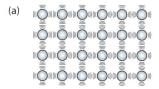
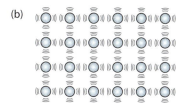

Figure 8.4
(a) The body is cool so the molecules vibrate with small amplitude.
(b) The body is heated causing the molecules to vibrate with a larger amplitude. Their average separation increases, so the body expands.

Different materials expand by different amounts. Metals expand more, for a given temperature rise, than non-metals. The table shows the expansion for different materials.

Material	Expansion (mm/100 °C)
Glass	0.09
Concrete	1.20
Iron	1.24
Copper	1.76
Aluminium	2.34
Lead	2.90

Table 8.1
Comparative expansion of some solids.

The expansion is given in the number of millimetres a one-metre bar would expand if heated through 100 °C.

71

▲ Figure 8.5
Expansion of railway lines.

▶ Figure 8.6
Expansion of bridges.

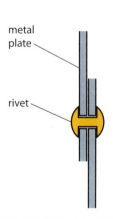

▲ Figure 8.8
Hot riveting.

Effects of expansion

Railway lines

In hot weather, railway lines expand. This can cause the lines to buckle, as in Figure 8.5. To avoid this problem, gaps are left between sections of line to allow for expansion. The two rails are joined by a piece of iron called a fishplate. The holes in the fishplates are oval to allow the bolts to slide as the rail expands or contracts. You can hear and feel the joints as the train runs over them.

Bridges

Bridges expand in hot weather. Just as with railway lines, this can cause buckling and damage to road surfaces. To avoid this problem, there is a gap between the bridge and the road. The bridge is built on rollers so it can move when it expands. The gap is usually filled with flexible filler, but you can often feel the gap as you drive over it.

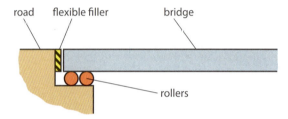

Telegraph wires

Telegraph wires expand in summer, causing them to hang loosely between the telegraph poles. In the winter when they contract, they become tighter.

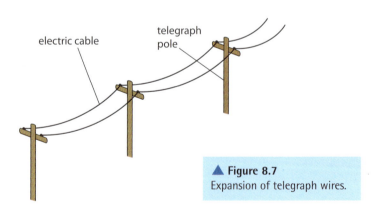

▲ Figure 8.7
Expansion of telegraph wires.

Hot riveting

When steel plates are riveted together to build a ship, the rivets are heated to red heat as they are inserted. When they cool, they contract and pull the plates tightly together, to make a watertight joint.

Bimetal strip

A bimetal strip is made from two different metals bonded together. The metals expand at different rates. Copper expands more than iron for the same temperature rise, so the strip bends with the copper on the outside of the curve.

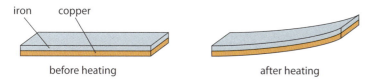

◀ Figure 8.9
Expansion of a bimetal strip.

QUESTIONS

8.1 Figure 8.10 shows a bimetal strip being used as a thermostat for an oven. Study the diagram. The two metals are copper and iron.
   a) Use the information in Table 8.1 to explain which side of the strip should be made out of copper.
   b) Explain how the temperature control knob adjusts the temperature at which the thermostat switches off.

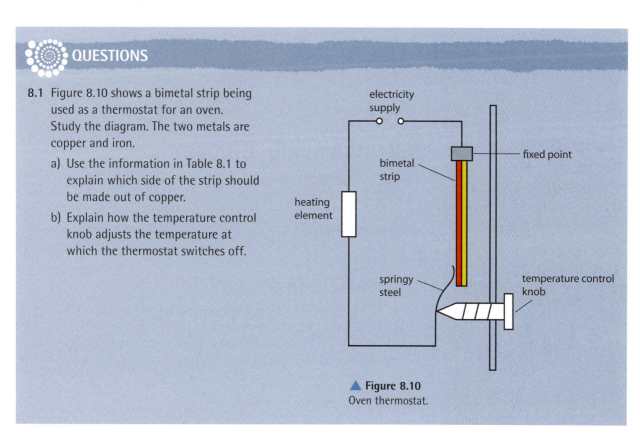

▲ Figure 8.10
Oven thermostat.

Expansion of liquids

The expansion of liquids can be shown by filling a flask with a coloured liquid. Plunge the flask into a bowl of hot water and watch the level in the tube rise. Liquids usually expand more than solids. The flask containing the liquid also expands in this experiment: if you observe very carefully you will see the liquid level drop slightly before rising. This is caused by the flask heating up before the liquid, and thus expanding first.

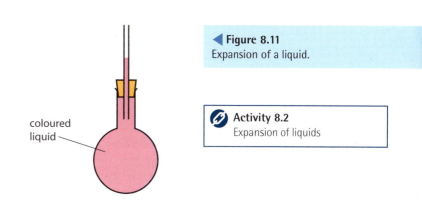

◀ Figure 8.11
Expansion of a liquid.

Activity 8.2
Expansion of liquids

Expansion of gases

The expansion of gases can be shown using the apparatus in Figure 8.12. Air is trapped in a flask by a liquid piston. The flask is heated by putting it in hot water. The liquid piston will move up the tube as the trapped air expands. It will be observed that the expansion is much larger than the expansion of a liquid.

▶ **Figure 8.12**
Expanding gases.

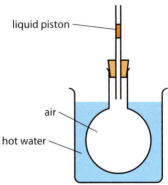

> **Activity 8.3**
> Expansion of gases

8.2 Measuring temperature

To measure temperature we need a property that changes with temperature. The most commonly recognised thermometer uses the expansion of a liquid, but many other things can be used: the expansion of a gas at constant pressure, the flexing of a bimetal strip, the change of resistance of a metal wire, even the change in colour of crystals.

The liquid-in-glass thermometer

Figure 8.14 shows a simple liquid-in-glass thermometer. The liquid usually used is ethanol or mercury. When the bulb is heated, the liquid expands and moves along the capillary tube. The greater the temperature change, the further the liquid moves. The liquid expands the same amount for each degree rise in temperature so the divisions on the scale are equal distances apart. We say the scale is **linear**.

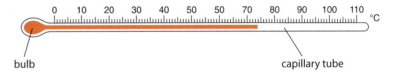

▲ **Figure 8.14**
Liquid-in-glass thermometer.

The **sensitivity** and the **range** of the thermometer (Figure 8.15) can be determined by altering the size of the bulb and the diameter of the capillary tube. If a large bulb or a narrow capillary tube is used, this will mean the liquid will move a relatively long way for a given temperature change, thus increasing the sensitivity of the thermometer. However, it will also mean that the range of the thermometer is decreased, as the difference between the highest and the lowest temperatures that the thermometer can measure is smaller.

> **DID YOU KNOW?**
>
> A thermochromic strip has crystals which change colour when the temperature changes.
>
>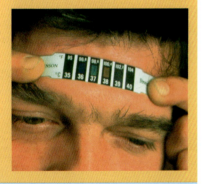

▲ **Figure 8.13**
A thermochromic strip is often used to measure body temperature.

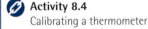

> **Activity 8.4**
> Calibrating a thermometer

Expansion and temperature

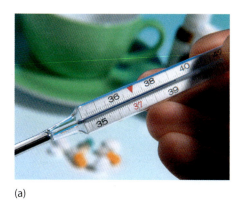

(a) (b)

▲ **Figure 8.15**
(a) The clinical thermometer is very sensitive. It can measure to the nearest 0.1 °C, but has a limited range; it can only measure temperatures from 32 °C to 42 °C. (b) The laboratory thermometer has a large range; it can measure temperatures from −10 °C to 110 °C, but it is not very sensitive. It can only measure to the nearest 1 °C.

Calibration of a thermometer

To mark a scale on a thermometer, we must have two temperatures which are easily repeatable to act as references. These are called fixed points. On the Celsius scale the **lower fixed point** is the melting point of pure ice, this is given the value 0 °C. The **upper fixed point** on this scale is the boiling point of pure water at standard atmospheric pressure, which is given the value 100 °C.

Once marks have been made on the thermometer stem at the lower and upper fixed points, the scale can be divided into 100 equal divisions.

The thermocouple thermometer

Any property that changes with temperature can be used to make a thermometer. One example is the thermocouple. A thermocouple is made from two different types of wire joined as shown in Figure 8.18. When the two junctions are at different temperatures, a small emf (see Chapter 16) is generated. This can be measured on a sensitive voltmeter. The greater the temperature difference, the larger the emf produced. When using the thermocouple, junction 2 is kept at a constant temperature (perhaps by attaching it to a block of ice), while junction 1 is used as the probe.

To use a thermocouple to measure temperature a calibration graph is used. The emfs when the probe junction is in melting ice (V_0) and boiling water (V_{100}) are plotted onto a graph. These two points are joined by a straight line and we can get a good approximation for the temperature by taking a reading from the graph.

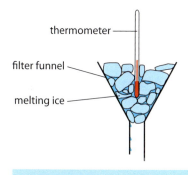

▲ **Figure 8.16**
To find the lower fixed point the thermometer is put in melting ice.

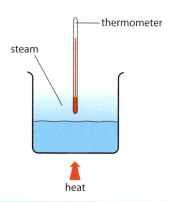

▲ **Figure 8.17**
To find the upper fixed point the thermometer is put above boiling water in the wet water vapour.

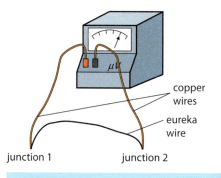

▲ **Figure 8.18**
Thermocouple.

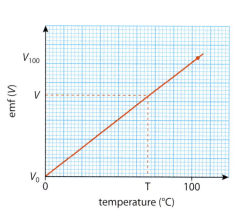

◀ **Figure 8.19**
Calibration graph for a thermocouple.

75

▶ **Table 8.2**
Advantages of a thermocouple thermometer over the liquid-in-glass thermometer.

Advantage	Reason
Quick acting, so can measure changing temperatures.	The only part of the thermocouple that needs to change temperature is junction 1 which is very small.
It has a large range.	Mercury and alcohol freeze so they cannot measure very low temperatures. Also, metals with high melting points can be used to make the thermocouple so temperatures can be measured where liquids would evaporate.
The meter can be remote from the area where the temperature is being measured. This means the operator can be in a central control room.	The wires can be as long as required.

Activity 8.5
Calibrating a thermocouple

▶ **Figure 8.20**

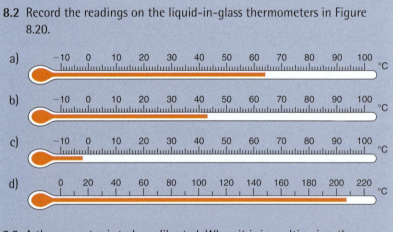

QUESTIONS

8.2 Record the readings on the liquid-in-glass thermometers in Figure 8.20.

8.3 A thermometer is to be calibrated. When it is in melting ice, the length of the mercury thread is 20 mm, and when in wet water vapour it is 140 mm long.
   a) Calculate the temperature when the thread is 50 mm long.
   b) Calculate the length of the thread when the temperature is 60 °C.

8.4 One way of removing a nut which has got stuck on a bolt is to heat the nut. It is often more effective to heat the nut rapidly rather than to raise its temperature slowly. Suggest reasons for this.

8.5 A train wheel has an iron tyre. The iron tyre has a slightly smaller diameter than the diameter of the wheel. In order to put the tyre onto the wheel it is heated to a high temperature.
   a) Explain why the tyre can now be put on the wheel.
   b) Explain the advantage of this system rather than having a tyre with an internal radius equal to the wheel.

8.6 A student puts a corked bottle of water in a microwave oven and heats it until the temperature of the water reaches 80 °C. He does the same with a corked bottle of air of the same size. The cork in the bottle of air pops out of the bottle but the cork in the bottle of water remains in place. Use your knowledge of expansion to explain these observations.

8.7 A clinical thermometer is designed to measure the temperature of the human body, which ranges from about 34 °C to 42 °C. For convenience, the thermometer needs to be less than 150 mm in length.
   a) State what range of temperatures the thermometer should be designed to read.
   b) State two features that could be used to make the thermometer more sensitive than a laboratory thermometer.

8.8 Figure 8.21 shows a thermocouple thermometer.

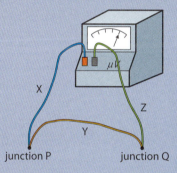

◀ Figure 8.21

   a) Suggest suitable materials for wires X, Y and Z.
   The voltmeter reads 25 μV when junction P is placed in boiling water and junction Q is placed in melting ice.
   b) (i) Calculate the reading on the voltmeter when junction P is placed in boiling ethanol at 80 °C.
      (ii) Calculate the temperature of a cup of tea if the voltmeter reading is 12 μV when junction P is placed in it.
   (In both cases junction Q is kept in melting ice.)

8.9 Figure 8.22 shows a laboratory thermometer.

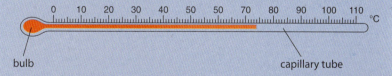

◀ Figure 8.22

   a) Use the information in the diagram to explain the terms (i) range and (ii) sensitivity.
   b) Describe two situations in which a thermocouple would be more suitable for measuring a temperature than the laboratory thermometer in the diagram.

Summary

Now that you have completed this chapter, you should be able to:

- recognise that solids, liquids and gases expand when heated
- describe some effects and uses of thermal expansion
- appreciate that for thermometers to operate, they require a physical property that changes
- describe the structure of a liquid-in-glass thermometer
- understand the need for fixed points
- describe how to calibrate a thermometer
- recognise the different expansion of solids, liquids and gases
- recognise and understand the term *range*
- recognise and understand the term *sensitivity*
- recognise and understand the term *linearity*
- describe the structure of a thermocouple
- understand the properties of a thermocouple which make it particularly suitable for use in different circumstances.

Chapter 9

Internal energy and changes of state

Clouds, the bringer of rain, the giver of life. There are many different types of cloud.

▲ Figure 9.1
These large fluffy clouds are called cumulus. They are fairly low level and form due to warm air rising and cooling. As the air cools, the water vapour it holds condenses to form droplets.

◀ Figure 9.2
Nimbocumulus are more developed cumulus clouds. If the conditions are right, the clouds can grow to a height of 10 000 m. At the top of the cloud ice particles form, and lower down the water droplets grow larger and the cloud looks much darker. This will lead to rain, often heavy, and sometimes with thunder and lightning.

▲ Figure 9.3
Stratus cloud is a heavy grey cloud that covers the sky. It can form at either a relatively high level (when it is known as altostratus) or very low levels. Sometimes the base will stretch right down to the ground, causing fog.

▲ Figure 9.4
Cirrus clouds are very high wispy clouds, which are made up of ice crystals.

How much energy is needed to make a body hot? How much energy is needed to melt a solid or turn a liquid into a vapour? Why do solids turn to liquids, and liquids to gases when heated?

In this chapter we look at the quantity of energy needed to raise the temperature of a body and go on to look at the energy required to change matter from one phase to another. We shall also explain, using the kinetic theory of matter, what happens when materials change phase.

9.1 Thermal capacity

Activity 9.1
Heating liquids

We have already seen that when a body is heated, its molecules gain kinetic energy. We call the energy gained by the molecules **internal energy**. When there is a rise in temperature, the overall internal energy of the body increases.

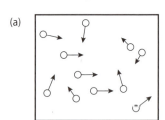 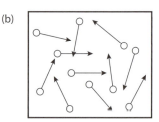

▶ Figure 9.5
Internal energy in the particles increases from (a) to (b).

Set up the apparatus in Figure 9.6. Make sure the water and the paraffin are at the same temperature. Record the time it takes each liquid to raise its temperature by 5 °C. It takes less time for the paraffin to heat up than the water. This shows that less energy is needed to raise the temperature of the paraffin.

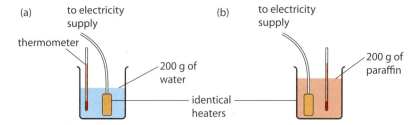

▶ Figure 9.6
Investigating thermal capacity.

The energy required to increase the temperature of a body by 1 °C is called the **thermal capacity** of the body.

Different materials of the same mass have different thermal capacities. For the same temperature rise, it requires about 5 times as much energy to heat 1 kg of water, as it does to heat 1 kg of sand. This explains why, on a hot day when you walk on a sandy beach, the sand burns your feet – but the sea remains cool.

▶ Figure 9.7
The sand gets very hot whilst the water remains cool.

Specific heat capacity

The **specific heat capacity** of a material is the thermal capacity of 1 kg of the material.

$$\text{Specific heat capacity} = \frac{\text{energy transfer}}{\text{mass} \times \text{temperature change}}$$

or

$$c = \frac{\Delta E}{m \times \Delta \theta}$$

Internal energy and changes of state

In this formula, energy is measured in joules, mass in kilograms and temperature in degrees Celsius.

So the unit of specific heat capacity is joule/(kilogram × degree Celsius) or in symbols **J/(kg °C)**. Sometimes the mass is measured in grams so the unit becomes J/(g °C).

It is easier to use the specific heat capacity formula if you remember it in the form:

Energy transfer = mass × specific heat capacity × temperature change

$$\Delta E = m \times c \times \Delta \theta$$

Specific heat capacities compare the energies required to raise the temperatures of different materials, rather than particular bodies. The specific heat capacities of some common materials are given in Table 9.1.

> **Activity 9.2**
> Measuring specific heat capacity

> **Hint**
> Remember from Chapter 6 that we use the symbol Δ to signify 'change in'.

▼ **Table 9.1**
Specific heat capacities for some common materials.

Material	Specific heat capacity (J/kg °C)
Aluminium	900
Copper	390
Iron/steel	450
Water	4200
Sea water	3900
Paraffin	2100

DID YOU KNOW?

When the word *specific* is used in science it means 'per unit mass'. So *specific volume* of a material would be the volume of a material that has a mass of 1 kg.

WORKED EXAMPLE

A domestic hot water tank holds 150 kg of water. The water is at a temperature of 12 °C. Calculate the energy required to raise the temperature of the water to 48 °C.

Temperature change = (48 − 12) °C
= 36 °C

Energy transfer = mass × specific heat capacity × temperature change

ΔE = 150 × 4200 × 36 J
= 22 680 000 J
= **23 000 000 J** to 2 sig. figs.

> **Hint**
> It is correct to give the answer to 2 significant figures because the given quantities (mass, specific heat capacity, temperatures) are themselves given to only two significant figures.

Measurement of specific heat capacity of aluminium

Apparatus to measure specific heat capacity is set up as in Figure 9.8. The temperature of the aluminium block is recorded and the heater switched on for a few minutes. The heater is switched off and the maximum temperature of the block is recorded.

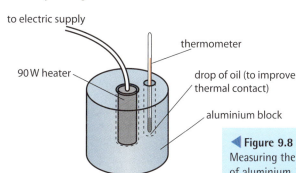

◀ **Figure 9.8**
Measuring the specific heat capacity of aluminium.

Hint

You will observe that this figure is significantly higher than the value given in Table 9.1. Not all the energy goes to heating the aluminium – a considerable quantity will be lost to the surroundings. How could we improve the experiment to reduce energy losses?

> ### WORKED EXAMPLE
>
> Sample results:
> Mass of block = 1.0 kg
> Initial temperature = 12 °C
> Final temperature = 21 °C
> Time = 2 minutes = 120 s
> Temperature change = (25 − 12) °C
> = 9 °C
> Energy = power × time
> = 90 W × 120 s
> = 10 800 J
>
> $\Delta E = m \times c \times \Delta\theta$
>
> $c = \dfrac{\Delta E}{m \times \Delta\theta}$
>
> $= \dfrac{10\,800}{1.0 \times 9}$ J/(kg °C)
>
> = 1200 J/(kg °C)

> ### QUESTIONS
>
> 9.1 A glass of orange juice is put in a refrigerator to cool. Explain the effect on the molecules of the orange juice.
>
> 9.2 Calculate the energy required to raise the temperature of an iron block of mass 25 kg through a temperature rise of 40 °C.
>
> 9.3 A domestic immersion heater has an output power of 12 kW. Calculate the time it would take to raise the temperature of a cylinder containing 120 kg of water from 5 °C to 45 °C.

9.2 Change of state

Gently heat a beaker of crushed ice, which has only just been taken out of the freezer.

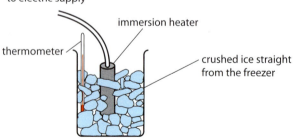

▶ Figure 9.9
Investigating temperature and change of state.

You find that the temperature of the ice gradually increases from about −4 °C until it reaches 0 °C. It will then remain at this temperature until *all* the ice has melted. Only then will the temperature start to rise again.

Internal energy and changes of state

It is clear that energy is still being given to the ice whilst it is melting. This energy is being used, not to raise the temperature of the ice, but to change it from solid to liquid. This energy is called the **latent heat of fusion.**

When a liquid solidifies, the latent heat of fusion energy is given out by the substance to the surroundings.

> **Activity 9.3**
> Cooling curves

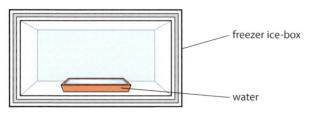

◀ Figure 9.10
A freezer removes energy from water so that it turns into ice.

The temperature at which a liquid changes to liquid, without a change in temperature, is called the **melting point** of the substance.

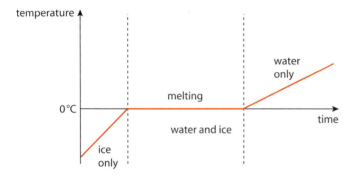

◀ Figure 9.11
The flat portion of the graph shows the period when the ice is melting.

The kinetic model again!

When a solid is melting, the energy given to the molecules is not used to give them more kinetic energy. This is why the temperature remains constant. It is used to do work against the forces holding the molecules together as the molecules are moved slightly further apart. As a result the molecules gain potential energy.

Once the water in a kettle starts boiling, the temperature remains constant at 100 °C, just as the temperature stays at 0 °C when ice is melted. The energy that converts the liquid to vapour is called the **latent heat of vaporisation**.

The temperature at which a liquid changes to vapour, without change in temperature, is called the **boiling point** of the substance.

▼ Figure 9.12
Water in a boiling kettle stays at 100 °C.

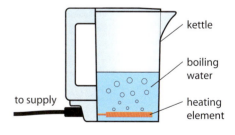

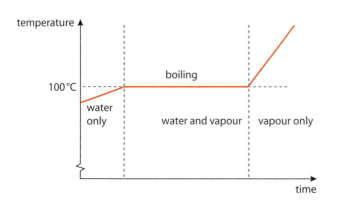

◀ Figure 9.13
The flat portion of the graph shows the period when the water is boiling.

83

The kinetic model yet again!

When a liquid turns to a vapour, just as in melting, the energy given to the molecules is not used to give them more kinetic energy. Again it is used to do work against the remaining forces holding the molecules together as they are moved much further apart. Once again the molecules gain potential energy.

Condensation

When vapour cools, it will turn back into liquid. This process is called **condensation.**

(a)

(b)

(c)

▶ **Figure 9.14**
(a) When a kettle of water boils, a cloud of steam is formed above the kettle. The steam is not really water vapour, it is small droplets of water which have cooled and condensed in the air. If you look very carefully at the spout of a boiling kettle there is a small gap between the visible steam and the spout. This space will contain genuine water vapour.
(b) Clouds are made up of droplets of water. As the warm, damp air rises, it cannot hold as much water vapour. The vapour condenses to form clouds.
(c) When the air cools at night, vapour condenses onto cobwebs and other objects forming drops of dew.

In Chapter 21, we will see how we can trace the paths of radioactive emissions by allowing ethanol vapour to condense onto the ions left by the emissions.

Internal energy and changes of state

Specific latent heat of fusion

The specific latent heat of fusion of a material is the energy required to convert a unit mass of solid into liquid without change in temperature.

Energy transferred = mass of solid changed to liquid
× specific latent heat of fusion

$$\Delta E = \Delta m \times \ell_f$$

In this formula, energy is measured in joules and mass in kilograms (or grams), so the specific latent heat is measured in **joules/kilogram (J/kg)**, or **J/g**.

To measure the latent heat of fusion, the melting ice is placed in a filter funnel. A heater is switched on and a beaker is placed under the funnel to collect the water from the melted ice. After several minutes, the heater is switched off and the beaker is removed. The mass of melted ice can now be measured.

Activity 9.4
Measuring latent heat

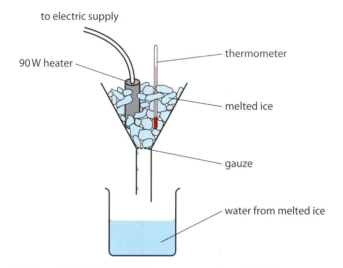

◀ Figure 9.15
Measuring latent heat of fusion.

WORKED EXAMPLE

Sample results:

$$\begin{aligned}
\text{Power of heater} &= 90\,\text{W} \\
\text{Mass of empty beaker} &= 48\,\text{g} \\
\text{Mass of beaker + melted ice} &= 84\,\text{g} \\
\text{Time} &= 2\,\text{minutes} = 120\,\text{s} \\
\text{Mass of ice melted} &= (84 - 48)\,\text{g} \\
&= 36\,\text{g} \\
\text{Energy input} &= 90 \times 120\,\text{J} \\
&= 10\,800\,\text{J} \\
&= m \times \ell_f \\
\ell_f &= \frac{\Delta E}{m} \\
&= \frac{10\,800}{36}\,\text{J/g} \\
&= 300\,\text{J/g}
\end{aligned}$$

Hint

The answer is a little lower than the accepted value of 330 J/g. Energy is also absorbed from the surroundings, which melts some of the ice. You can allow for this by also collecting water from the ice for 2 minutes without the heater switched on. This mass of water is equal to the mass of water melted by the surroundings. This mass is then subtracted from the mass collected to give a better result.

Specific latent heat of vaporisation

The specific latent heat of vaporisation of a material is the energy required to convert unit mass of liquid into vapour without change in temperature.

Energy transferred = mass of liquid changed to vapour
× specific latent heat of vaporisation

$$\Delta E = \Delta m \times \ell_v$$

This formula is almost identical to the formula for the latent heat of fusion. Again energy is measured in joules, mass in kilograms (or grams), so the specific latent heat is measured in joules/kilogram (J/kg), or J/g.

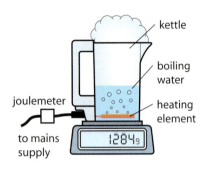

▲ **Figure 9.16**
Measuring latent heat of vaporisation

> ### WORKED EXAMPLE
>
> Sample results:
>
> Power of kettle = 2.0 kW
> Time for which kettle switched on = 4.0 minutes
> Mass of kettle and water before heating = 1434 g
> Mass of kettle and water after heating = 1284 g
> Mass of water converted to vapour = 1434 g − 1284 g
> = 150 g
> Energy supplied = power × time
> = 2.0 × 1000 × 4.0 × 60 J
> = 480 000 J
>
> $\Delta E = m \times \ell_v$
>
> $\ell_v = \dfrac{\Delta E}{m}$
>
> $= \dfrac{480\,000}{150}$ J/g
>
> = 3200 J/g

Hint

The answer must be in J/g since the mass was given in grams (g).

This is significantly higher than the actual value (2300 J/g). Can you suggest why?

> ### QUESTIONS
>
> 9.4 Calculate the energy needed to convert 200 g of copper from solid to liquid at its melting point.
> (Specific latent heat of fusion of copper = 176 J/g)
>
> 9.5 Liquid nitrogen is used to cool materials rapidly.
> Calculate the energy 20 g of nitrogen takes from the surroundings when it vapourises at its boiling point.
> (Specific latent heat of vaporisation of nitrogen = 200 J/g)

Internal energy and changes of state

Evaporation and boiling

On a sunny day, a puddle of water will slowly disappear. The liquid water has turned into vapour. Clearly the water has not boiled – it has **evaporated**.

Evaporation and boiling are quite different.

• Evaporation is a surface effect.	• Boiling occurs throughout the liquid with bubbles of vapour forming in the liquid.
• Evaporation occurs at all temperatures.	• Boiling occurs at a single temperature known as the boiling point.
• Evaporation is a quiet process.	• Boiling is a vigorous process.

> Activity 9.5
> Cooling on evaporation

Evaporation occurs when molecules leave the surface of a liquid. Any molecules near the surface can escape but the most energetic molecules are the most likely to escape. This results in the average kinetic energy of the remaining molecules being reduced. Consequently, the temperature of the remaining liquid falls.

This can be experienced when you come out of the sea on a sunny day. The evaporating molecules escape, leaving the lower energy (cooler) ones behind.

In evaporation not all the molecules that leave the surface actually remain as vapour. There are a few molecules above the surface forming a vapour. Figure 9.17 shows the surface of a liquid. Molecules 1 and 3 escape entirely from the liquid.

Molecules 2 and 4 have plenty of energy to escape but hit another molecule and bounce back into the liquid.

Evaporation increases when
- the temperature increases
- the surface area of the liquid is increased
- there is a breeze across the surface of the liquid.

Clothes left crumpled up take a long time to dry because the surface area exposed to air is reduced. A sunny, windy day is best for drying clothes. The raised temperature means that more molecules have sufficient energy to escape, and the wind blows away those molecules which have already escaped, so they cannot themselves go back into the liquid or bounce other molecules back into it.

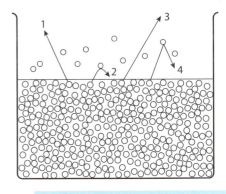

▲ Figure 9.17
Molecules escaping the surface of a liquid.

▶ Figure 9.18
Good conditions for evaporation!

87

> ### QUESTIONS
>
> 9.6 Suggest why sweating helps cool the body.
>
> 9.7 When a cup of tea is too hot to drink, people blow across the surface.
> Explain why this increases the rate of cooling of the tea.

9.3 Thermal energy transfer

Conduction

When a glass rod is heated, the molecules near the source of energy vibrate faster. This vibration is passed on to neighbouring molecules, which also vibrate, and the energy spreads along the rod. We call this process **thermal conduction**.

Figure 9.20 shows a demonstration that different materials conduct at different rates. Each rod is the same size and is coated in candle wax with a small ball bearing stuck on the end. The boiling water melts the wax and the ball bearings fall to the ground. The ball bearing on the copper rod falls to the ground first, followed by the one on the aluminium rod and finally the one on the iron rod. This shows that copper is the best **conductor** of the three metals, followed by aluminium and iron.

▲ **Figure 9.19**
Thermal conduction in a solid.

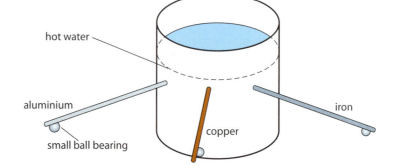

▶ **Figure 9.20**
Investigating conduction in metals.

> **Activity 9.6**
> Conduction

Using conductors

Saucepans are often made with copper bases. Copper is an excellent conductor so the energy from the stove passes quickly through the base.

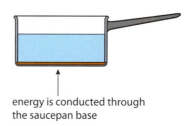

▶ **Figure 9.21**
The copper found in the base of many saucepans is a good thermal conductor.

Internal energy and changes of state

This simple experiment shows that copper is an excellent conductor. When a Bunsen burner flame is lit beneath the copper gauze, the heat is conducted away by the copper, so the gas above does not get hot enough to ignite. It can be shown that there is gas above the gauze by lighting the flame above the gauze as in the second diagram. Finally, it is possible to light the flame above the gauze, leaving the gas under it unburnt. This principle is used inside a Davy Safety Lamp.

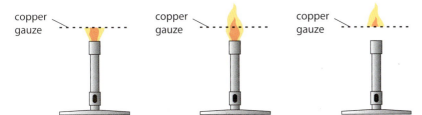

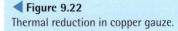

Figure 9.22
Thermal reduction in copper gauze.

> ### DID YOU KNOW?
>
> Sir Humphrey Davy was one of the leading scientists of the early eighteenth century. Among other things, he discovered the anaesthetic effect of nitrous oxide, one of the earliest anaesthetics.
>
> He is best known for his invention of the Davy Safety Lamp. He produced his first safety lamp in 1815 in response to miners in the north-east of England. Candles were the only form of light the miners had, and there was a major problem with the naked flames igniting methane, which was found in the mines.

Figure 9.23
The Davy Safety Lamp.

The Davy Safety Lamp burns inside a copper cage (Figure 9.23). If there is a build up of inflammable gases, the flame inside the cage flares up without igniting the gas outside, giving miners the ability to safely detect the gases.

The cooling fins on a motorcycle engine are made from brass. Like copper, brass is a good conductor. The fins are used so that the surface area of hot metal in contact with the air is increased. This increases the rate of cooling.

Figure 9.24
Cooling fins.

Conductors and insulators

Materials that are very poor conductors are called **insulators**. Generally, metals are good conductors whilst non-metals are good insulators.

When we wish to avoid transfer of thermal energy we use insulators.

▲ Figure 9.25
Animals and birds trap air in their fur or feathers. The air acts as an insulator which keeps them warm in cold weather.

▲ Figure 9.26
Cloth is a good insulator, so we do not burn our hands when picking up hot utensils with oven mitts.

A more detailed model of conduction

Metals have many free electrons in their structure. A simple model is to imagine these free electrons to be rather like a gas, which transfers the energy from a hot to a cooler part of the metal. The energy transferred by the electrons is significantly greater than the energy transferred from molecule to molecule, thus making metals much better conductors than non-metals.

Activity 9.7
Convection

Convection

Place a crystal of copper sulfate at the bottom of a beaker. Heat the water gently near the crystal. You will see the blue colour of the copper sulfate rise up and across the beaker.

When the water around the crystal is heated it expands, becomes less dense and floats to the surface. Cold water takes its place, and this in turn is heated and rises. This method of energy transfer is called **convection**.

▶ Figure 9.27
Demonstrating convection 1.

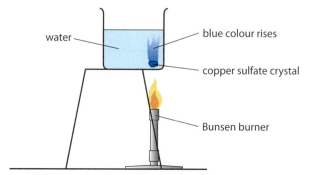

Internal energy and changes of state

In Figure 9.28 the candle heats the air in the left hand chimney. This rises up the chimney and cold air replaces it, dragging the smoke through the apparatus. In this way, a **convection current** is set up. Mines used to be ventilated in this way, by lighting a large fire at the bottom of one of the shafts. Nowadays large fans instead of fires are used to extract the stale air.

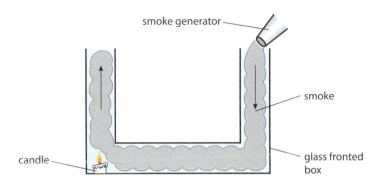

Figure 9.28
Demonstrating convection 2.

Winds are formed by convection. The simplest example is a sea breeze. During the day, the land is much hotter than the sea, so the air above the land rises up and cool air from above the sea takes its place. A convection current is set up. At night the land cools much more quickly than the sea. This causes a breeze in the opposite direction, as now the air above the sea is warmer than the air above the land.

On a larger scale, hot air above the continents in equatorial regions rises upwards, causing some of the major global weather systems.

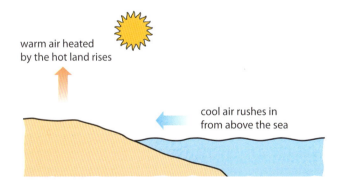

Figure 9.29
Convection causes sea breezes.

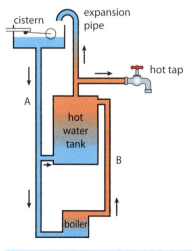

▲ **Figure 9.30**
Domestic hot water system.

QUESTIONS

9.8 Figure 9.30 shows a domestic hot water system.
   a) Explain why hot water goes up pipe B, from the boiler to the hot tank.
   b) Explain why the pipe to the hot tap is connected to the pipe coming from the top of the hot tank.
   c) Explain why there is a pipe from the bottom of the hot water tank to A.

Activity 9.8
Radiation

Radiation

Thermal energy reaches Earth from the Sun through 150 million kilometres of vacuum. There is no matter in a vacuum, therefore the energy cannot be transmitted by either conduction or convection. It is transmitted by thermal **radiation**, or more accurately, **infrared radiation**.

Infrared radiation is part of the same family of radiation as visible light. This family of radiation is called the **electromagnetic spectrum**. We will look at it in detail in Chapter 12.

▶ Figure 9.31
Mirrors reflecting both visible light and infrared radiation at a solar power station near Seville in Spain.

The greenhouse effect

Figure 9.32 shows how a greenhouse works. Energetic infrared radiation and visible radiation from the Sun pass through the glass of the greenhouse and are absorbed by the plants and the ground. The plants and the ground re-emit this as low-energy infrared radiation. The low-energy infrared radiation cannot get through the glass and is reflected inside the greenhouse. The temperature inside the greenhouse rises.

A similar thing is happening to the Earth. When we burn fossil fuels, we produce more and more carbon dioxide. The carbon dioxide is released into the atmosphere, where it allows visible light and high-energy infrared radiation from the Sun to pass through, but reflects the low-energy infrared radiation from the Earth.

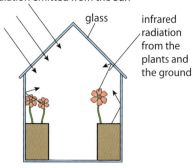

▲ Figure 9.32
Warming in a glasshouse.

▶ Figure 9.33
(a) During the day, infrared radiation is absorbed by the Earth. As the Earth warms up, an increasing quantity is radiated away.
(b) On a clear night, infrared radiation is emitted from the Earth and the temperature rapidly drops.
(c) On a cloudy night, the clouds reflect much of the infrared radiation so the temperature does not drop as rapidly.

(a)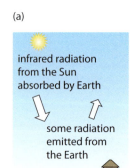

(b)

(c)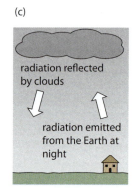

Internal energy and changes of state

It is believed that the greenhouse effect is causing the temperature of the Earth to gradually increase, with potentially catastrophic effects.

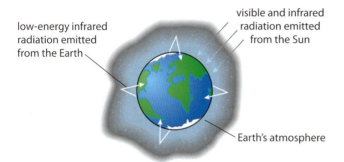

◀ Figure 9.34
Global warming in action! (Note: atmosphere thickness is exaggerated in this diagram.)

Emission of infrared radiation

A metal cube is filled with hot water. An infrared detector is placed equal distances from the different coloured faces. It reads slightly higher when placed near the matt black face than when placed near the silver face. Each face is at the same temperature. This shows that a black surface is a much better emitter than a shiny silver surface.

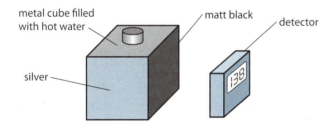

▲ Figure 9.35
Dull surfaces are good emitters.

Absorption of infrared radiation

Two small beakers, containing equal masses of water, are placed equal distances from a radiant heater. One beaker is painted matt black; the other has a shiny silver surface. The temperature of the water in the matt black beaker rises much faster than the temperature of the silver beaker. This shows that matt black is a better absorber than silver.

Activity 9.9
Absorption of radiation

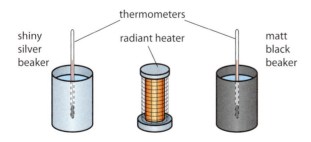

◀ Figure 9.36
Dull surfaces are good absorbers.

These experiments show that not only is black a better emitter than silver, it is also a better absorber. Experiments can be done with different materials and the rule is that the better a surface is at absorbing radiation, the better it is at emitting radiation.

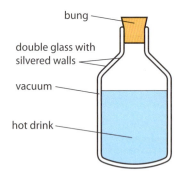

▲ Figure 9.37

▶ Figure 9.38

▶ Figure 9.39

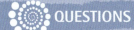 QUESTIONS

9.9 Figure 9.37 shows the structure of a vacuum flask.
  a) Name and describe the ways in which the bung reduces energy loss from the drink.
  b) Name and describe the ways in which the vacuum stops energy loss.
  c) Explain whether the flask could be used to keep an iced drink cool.
  d) Explain why the walls of the flask are silvered.

9.10 Insulators are used in the home to reduce energy loss to the outside.
Study Figure 9.38 and list the ways in which energy is conserved.

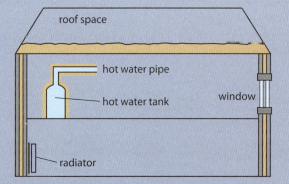

9.11 500 g of water at 22 °C is placed in a freezer.
Calculate the energy that needs to be removed from the water to convert it all into ice.
(Specific heat capacity of water = 4.2 J/g,
specific latent heat of fusion of water = 330 J/g)

9.12 Figure 9.39 shows the apparatus used to measure the specific heat capacity of brine.
  a) State the measurements that must be made.
  b) State two sources of error that are likely to occur in this experiment and describe their effect on the final result.

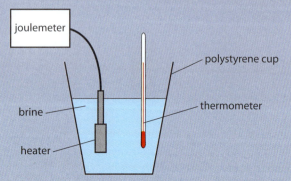

94

Internal energy and changes of state

9.13 In an experiment to measure the specific heat capacity of steel, a mass of 320 g of steel rivets is placed in a beaker and heated using a 30 W electrical heater. After a period of two minutes the temperature of the rivets rises from 7 °C to 32 °C.

Calculate the specific heat capacity of the steel.

9.14 A block of ice of mass 2.4 kg and initial temperature 0 °C is left outside. It absorbs energy from the surroundings at a steady rate of 480 W.

Calculate the time it will take to completely melt.
(Specific latent heat of fusion of water = 330 J/g)

9.15 A student is doing an experiment investigating cooling.

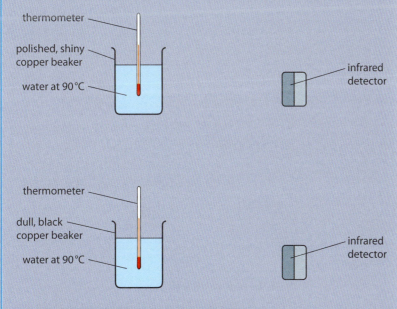

◀ Figure 9.40

Figure 9.40 shows the apparatus he used.
He makes the following observations.

1. The reading on the infrared detector is higher in the second experiment.
2. The beaker in experiment 2 cools faster than in experiment 1.

a) Explain what conclusions the student can obtain from the experiments.

b) After completing these experiments he puts the same mass of cold water in each beaker and places the two beakers the same distance from a radiant heater.
Explain what results you would expect the student to observe.

95

Summary

Now that you have completed this chapter, you should be able to:

- understand the term *thermal capacity*
- understand that a rise in temperature of a body is caused by an increase in the kinetic energy of the molecules
- understand that during melting, a body's temperature remains constant
- understand that during boiling, a body's temperature remains constant
- describe solidification
- describe condensation
- describe evaporation in molecular terms
- describe thermal conduction
- describe experiments to demonstrate thermal conduction
- understand the term *insulator*
- recognise some uses of insulators
- describe convection
- describe experiments to demonstrate convection
- describe thermal radiation as infrared radiation
- recognise that infrared radiation is a part of the electromagnetic spectrum
- describe experiments to detect infrared radiation
- Identify and explain some of the effects of conduction, convection and radiation
- describe experiments to measure the specific heat capacity of a material
- recall and use the equation $\Delta E = m \times c \times \Delta\theta$
- use and recall the equation $\Delta E = m \times \ell$
- distinguish between boiling and evaporation
- understand the factors which affect the rate of evaporation from a body
- describe experiments to show the properties of good/bad emitters and absorbers.

Chapter 10

Waves, light and sound

In this chapter we will look at waves and their properties. We will see that it is important to have an understanding of waves in order to study light and sound.

▲ Figure 10.1
The ultimate thrill – surfing a big one!

10.1 Waves

Throw a stone in a pond and watch the ripples spread out.

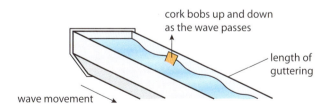

◀ Figure 10.2
Movement of water to make waves.

If there is a leaf or other small object floating on the pond you will see it bob up and down, or move round in circles, but it will not move along with the wave. The same effect can be seen if a small cork is floated on water in a length of guttering.

97

If you shake a spring from side to side you can produce waves. The more rapidly you move your hand then the closer together the waves — but they still travel down the spring at the same speed.

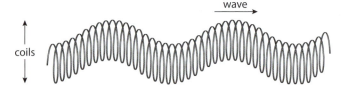

Figure 10.3
A transverse wave in a slinky spring.

Activity 10.1
Waves on springs

The individual particles in water waves, and the wave produced on the spring do not move along with the wave but simply vibrate at right angles to the direction of travel.

Terminology

The **speed** of a wave is the distance the wave travels per unit time.

The **wavelength** of a wave is the distance between identical points on successive waves.

The **frequency** is the number of complete waves passing a point per unit time.

The **amplitude** of a wave is the maximum displacement of a point from its rest position.

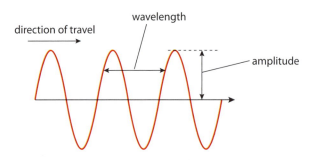

Figure 10.4
Wave terminology.

Table 10.1
Units for waves.

Hint

λ is the Greek letter lambda, it is equivalent to ℓ.
1 hertz (Hz) is the name given to a frequency of 1 wave per second.

Property	Unit
Speed (v)	metre per second (m/s)
Wavelength (λ)	metre (m)
Frequency (f)	hertz (Hz)
Amplitude (A)	metre (m)

The wave equation

In Figure 10.5, imagine that in one second, a wave travels from point X to point Y. If the distance between each wave is 12 cm, wave X will have travelled four lots of 12 cm, which is 48 cm. So in one second, the wave has travelled 48 cm, giving a speed of 48 cm/s. We can see that the speed is found from the frequency (4 Hz or 4 waves per second) multiplied by the wavelength, in this case 12 cm.

◀ Figure 10.5
Wave speed.

More generally, if a wave has a frequency of f, it will make f complete waves in 1 second. If each wave has a wavelength λ then the disturbance will travel a distance of $f \times \lambda$ in one second.

This gives us the equation:

speed = frequency × wavelength
v = f × λ

WORKED EXAMPLE

A coin is dropped into a pool. Waves spread out from the centre with a frequency of 6 Hz and a wavelength of 15 cm.

Calculate the speed of the waves.

Speed = frequency × wavelength
Speed = 6 Hz × 15 cm
= **90 cm/s**

Hint

Remember: 1 Hz means 1 wave per second.

Two types of wave

So far we have looked at waves in which the particles vibrate at right angles to the direction of travel of the wave. Such waves are called **transverse waves** (transverse means across).

Instead of moving our hand across when we make a wave on a slinky type spring, we can move it back and forth in the direction the wave travels. This type of wave is a **longitudinal wave**.

Activity 10.2
Transverse and longitudinal waves

◀ Figure 10.6
A **longitudinal wave** in a slinky spring.

The particles now vibrate back and forth parallel to the direction in which the wave travels. This forms regions where the coils are closer together than the average and regions where they are further apart are formed.

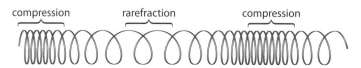

◀ Figure 10.7
Structure of a longitudinal wave.

The regions where the coils are close together are called **compressions**, and the regions where they are further apart than average are called **rarefactions**.

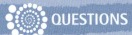

QUESTIONS

10.1 Figure 10.8 shows a locomotive hitting some trucks. When it hits the first truck a pulse is sent down the line of trucks.

movement of the locomotive

Is the wave formed longitudinal or transverse? Explain your answer.

10.2 Figure 10.9 shows how a rod vibrates when it is struck at point P. Which distance on the diagram is equal to one wavelength? What is the amplitude?

10.3 a) A boy produces a series of waves on a spring of length 2.4 m. It takes 0.8 seconds for the waves to travel the length of the spring. Calculate the speed at which the wave travels.
b) Describe how the waves would change if the boy moved his hand the same distance but at a faster rate.
c) Describe how the wave would change if the boy moved his hand further for each wave produced.
d) The boy makes one complete cycle of his hand (from one side to the other and back) in 0.40 s. Calculate the frequency of the waves.
e) From your answers to a) and d) calculate the wavelength of the waves.

10.4 The waves in a water tank have a wavelength of 25 mm and they move across the tank at a speed of 350 mm/s.
Calculate the frequency of the waves.

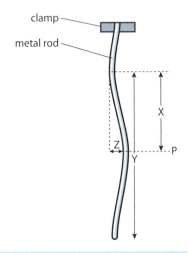

▶ Figure 10.8

▲ Figure 10.9

Properties of waves – the ripple tank

We can use water waves to study the behaviour of waves.

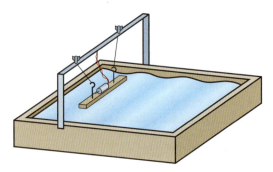

▶ Figure 10.10
The ripple tank.

Activity 10.3
The ripple tank

The motor produces waves, which move across the tank. We often represent the wave by a single line drawn across the crest of a wave; this line is called a **wavefront**. The ripple tank can be used to study either straight or circular wavefronts.

100

Waves, light and sound

Reflection

When a barrier is put in the tank the waves reflect from it (Figure 10.11). We can see that straight wavefronts are reflected at the same angle as they come in.

Circular wavefronts reflect back to form another set of circles, which are centred at a point an equal distance from, and on the other side of, the barrier as the centre of disturbance of the original waves.

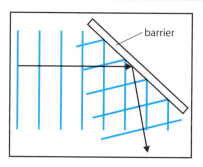

▼ Figure 10.11
Straight wave fronts reflecting off a straight barrier.

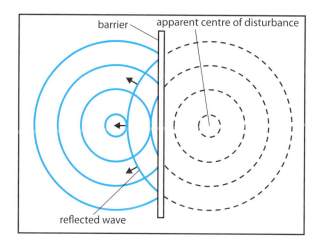

◀ Figure 10.12
Circular wavefronts reflecting off a straight barrier.

Refraction

We can investigate the effect of changing the depth of the water by putting a sheet of glass or perspex in the tank.

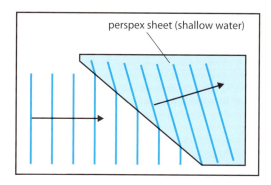

◀ Figure 10.13
Change in wavefronts due to change in water depth.

The waves slow down when they enter the shallow water. As a result the wavelength is shortened. The waves get left behind and change direction.

◀ Figure 10.14
Refraction of waves in the sea. As the water gets shallower near the shore the waves change direction.

Diffraction

One of the most amazing properties of waves is their ability to spread around corners. If we have a narrow gap, or a small object, the waves spread around it, so that there are waves where one might expect there would be none. This is called **diffraction**.

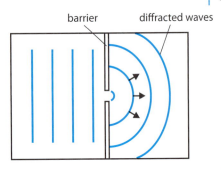

▲ Figure 10.15
When the gap in a barrier is small, the waves spread out, almost in semicircles.

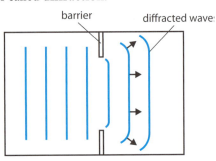

▲ Figure 10.16
When the gap is larger, the spreading is not as clear. There is a large straight part to the wavefront, with just a bit of spreading around the edges.

▶ Figure 10.17
Diffraction round an object. If the object is smaller than the wavelength of the waves, the waves pass by without it affecting them. If slightly larger, there is still enough spreading for there to be only a little bit of calm water.

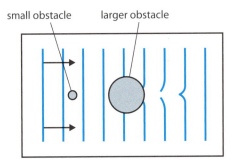

The amount of diffraction is dependent on the size of the gap or obstacle. For a significant effect, the gap or obstacle needs to be of similar size to, or smaller than, the wavelength of the wave.

Diffraction is important because it is a property that particles do not exhibit, so it enables us to identify whether radiation from a source is transmitted by particles or waves.

Diffraction of radio waves

Radio waves have wavelengths ranging from over a kilometre, for long wave radio transmissions, to less than a millimetre, for television transmissions. The long wave broadcasts can be received by the farm in Figure 10.18 as the wave diffracts round the mountain. Television broadcasts (with much shorter wavelengths) would not be received, unless they were sent via a satellite.

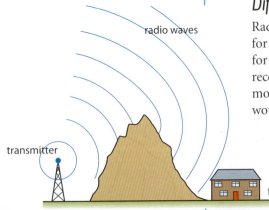

◀ Figure 10.18
The radio wave diffracts round the mountain.

Waves, light and sound

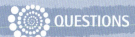

QUESTIONS

10.5 A girl allows a drop of water to fall into a ripple tank. Circular waves are set up.

Draw a diagram to show how the waves spread out. Draw 4 wavefronts and suitable arrows to show how the wavefronts move.

10.2 Sound

Production of sound

Figure 10.19 shows some sources of sound. In each there is a vibrating object. Identify what is vibrating in each case.

Sounds are made by vibrating sources. When a drum is struck, the drum skin vibrates back and forth. As it does so, it pushes the air molecules, producing a longitudinal wave.

Activity 10.4
Production of sound

▲ Figure 10.19
Different ways of producing sounds.

103

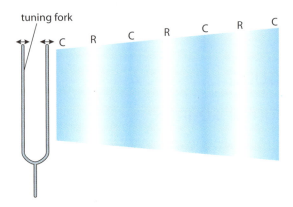

A tuning fork produces sound as its prongs vibrate. The regions on Figure 10.20, which are marked C, represent compressions, where the air molecules are pushed together, producing a pressure slightly greater than atmospheric pressure. The regions marked R represent rarefactions, where the air molecules are pulled apart and the air pressure is slightly less than atmospheric pressure.

▶ Figure 10.20
A tuning fork vibrates.

A sound wave is a longitudinal wave. It may also be described as a pressure wave. It is these small variations in pressure which our ears detect, and which we hear as sound.

The transmission of sound

Sound will not travel through a vacuum

Set up a battery driven bell in a bell jar as in Figure 10.21. Turn the bell on and then slowly pump out the air from the bell jar. As the air is removed from the bell jar, the sound level gradually fades until it can not be heard. This demonstrates that sound needs a medium to be transmitted through.

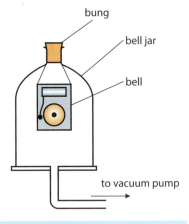

▲ Figure 10.21
A ringing bell makes no sound inside a vacuum.

Sound travels through liquid

If you swim underwater you can hear noises as water slaps against the sides of the pool.

Activity 10.5
Transmission of sound

▶ Figure 10.22
Dolphins communicate by a series of clicks, which travel through the sea.

104

Waves, light and sound

Sound travels through solids

Hit an iron railing. An observer at the other end will hear two distinct sounds. First the sound which is passed through the iron and a little while later the sound which travels through the air.

Activity 10.6
Tin can phone

◀ Figure 10.23

Table 10.2 shows the speed of sound in different materials.

You will observe that sound travels faster through solids than liquids, and slowest of all through gases

Material	Speed (m/s)
Steel	5000
Aluminium	5100
Water	1500
Air at 0 °C	320
Air at 20 °C	340
Carbon dioxide	280

▲ Table 10.2
The speed of sound through various materials.

Measurement of the speed of sound in air

When you watch a game of cricket and see the batsman hit the ball, there is a clear delay before you hear the sound. The delay is caused because sound travels much more slowly than light, and the distance from the spectator to the middle of the pitch is large enough for the effect to be noticed.

We can use this effect to measure the speed of sound.

 Activity 10.7
Measuring the speed of sound

◀ Figure 10.24

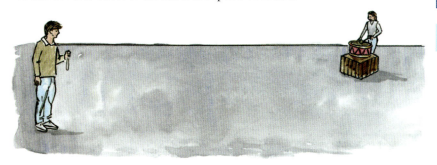

One student is given a drum and another is given a stopwatch. The student with the stopwatch walks to the far side of a sports field. He starts the stopwatch when he sees the first student strike the drum. He stops it again when he hears the sound. Finally, the distance between the drummer and the timer is measured.

This type of experiment can only give a rough estimate of the speed of sound, because the uncertainty in measuring the time interval is so great.

 WORKED EXAMPLE

Sample results:

$$\text{Time} = 0.8\,\text{s}$$
$$\text{Distance between the students} = 250\,\text{m}$$
$$\text{Speed} = \frac{\text{distance}}{\text{time}}$$
$$= \frac{250}{0.8}\,\text{m/s}$$
$$= 320\,\text{m/s}$$
$$\text{Speed of sound in air} = 320\,\text{m/s (to 2 sig. fig.)}$$

Echoes

Sound reflects from hard surfaces, which is why we hear echoes. We can use echoes to measure the speed of sound.

▶ **Figure 10.25**
Using echoes to measure the speed of sound.

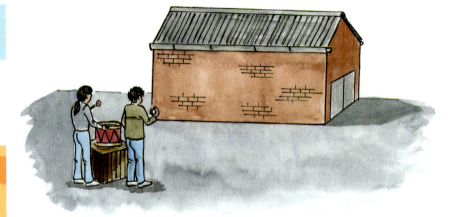

DID YOU KNOW?

In Greek mythology, the unhappy nymph Echo was condemned to repeat the last words spoken to her. She fell in love with the beautiful youth Narcissus. He rejected her and was punished by falling in love with his own reflection. He was trapped by the sight of his own beauty and died. Yellow narcissus flowers grew where he died.

The boy starts the stopwatch when the girl strikes the drum. She then hits the drum each time she hears an echo. After a total of, say, eleven strikes, he stops the stopwatch. This method has the advantage over the previous method of increasing the time interval between starting and stopping the watch, thereby increasing the accuracy of the experiment.

WORKED EXAMPLE

Sample results:

Distance from drummer to wall, $d = 22$ m

Number of drum strikes $= 21$

Time, $t = 2.6$

$$\text{Speed} = \frac{\text{distance}}{\text{time}}$$
$$= 2 \times n \times \frac{d}{t}$$
$$= \frac{2 \times 20 \times 22}{2.6} \text{ m/s}$$
$$= \mathbf{340 \text{ m/s}} \text{ (to 2 sig. fig.)}$$

Hint

$n = 20$ because the first drum strike simply gives the starting time. The sound travels to and from the wall between each strike, so we multiply the distance from the wall by two.

Echo sounding

Ships sometimes use echo sounding (or sonar) to find the depth of the sea or to locate wrecks or shoals of fish. Pulses of high frequency sound are sent downwards and the time taken for the echo to return is measured.

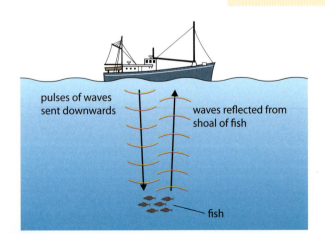

◀ **Figure 10.26**
Echo sounding.

Waves, light and sound

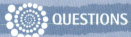

QUESTIONS

10.6 Give evidence that sound travels faster in solids than in gases.

10.7 A survey ship is measuring the depth of the ocean. A pulse of sound is emitted and the echo is heard 0.24 s later.
Calculate the depth of the ocean.
(Speed of sound in water = 1500 m/s)

Listening to sounds

We can study sound waves using a loudspeaker and a cathode ray oscilloscope.

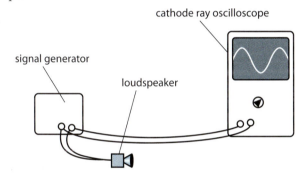

◀ **Figure 10.27**
Displaying sound waves using a cathode ray oscilloscope.

The sound produced by a signal generator produces a simple waveform.

⚡ **Activity 10.8**
The cathode ray oscilloscope

▲ **Figure 10.28**
(a) The oscilloscope shows a displacement-time graph of the waves.
(b) When the loudness of the sound is increased the maximum displacement of the wave, or amplitude, increases.
(c) When the pitch is increased, the number of waves produced in a given time, or frequency, is increased.

If you display a single note from a musical instrument then the wave shape is different from the wave shape from a signal generator. Each instrument will have its own characteristic wave shape. It is this that makes the same note sound different when played on different instruments.

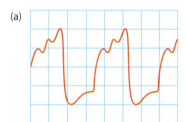
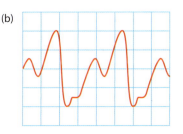

◀ **Figure 10.29**
(a) Waveform from a saxophone.
(b) Waveform from a trombone.

107

DID YOU KNOW?

Dogs can hear much higher frequency sounds than humans. Dog whistles are designed so dogs can hear them but they do not disturb people.

Range of hearing

The human ear is a very sensitive detector. However, it can only detect sounds within the range of about 20 Hz to 20 kHz. As you grow older, your range of hearing decreases, particularly at higher frequencies. Some young children can hear the high-pitched squeaks (about 30 kHz) that bats use to navigate.

QUESTIONS

Unless otherwise stated, take the speed of sound in air to be 320 m/s.

10.8 A pianist plays a note of 256 Hz followed by a note of 330 Hz. Explain how the pitches of the two notes compare.

10.9 Which of the following frequencies of sound could an average person detect?
a) 100 Hz, b) 200 mHz, c) 10 kHz, d) 2 MHz, e) 10 Hz.

10.10 Figure 10.30 shows a ripple tank being used to demonstrate the reflection of water waves.
Copy and complete the diagrams to show the wavefronts after reflection.

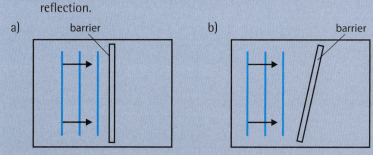

▶ Figure 10.30

10.11 Figure 10.31 shows a ripple tank being used to demonstrate refraction.
Copy and complete the diagrams to show the wavefronts after refraction.

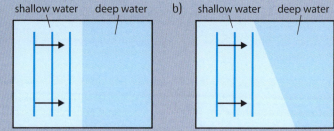

▶ Figure 10.31

10.12 A golfer is waiting to take his shot. He observes another golfer on a different hole hit the ball. He estimates that he hears the sound of the club striking the ball 1.5 s after he sees it.
Calculate the distance the other golfer is from him.

10.13 A boy stands 75 m from a cliff. When he shouts he hears an echo. Calculate the time interval between the boy shouting and his hearing the echo.

10.14 Figure 10.32 shows the traces on a cathode ray oscilloscope of two sound waves produced by different musical instruments.

(a)  (b)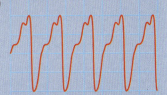

◀ Figure 10.32

The controls on the oscilloscope are the same for both sounds.
a) State and explain how the pitch of the two sounds compare.
b) State and explain how the loudness of the two sounds compare.

10.15 Figure 10.33 shows wavefronts in a ripple tank approaching a gap in a barrier.
a) Carefully copy the diagram and draw in three more wavefronts after they have passed through the barrier.
b) The experiment is repeated with a gap of twice the wavelength of the waves.
Draw a second diagram to show the results you would expect this time.
c) Name the property of waves that these experiments demonstrate.

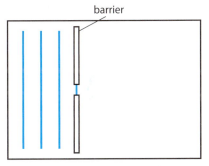

▲ Figure 10.33

10.16 Fig. 10.34 is a graph showing how the pressure changes as a sound wave passes a point.

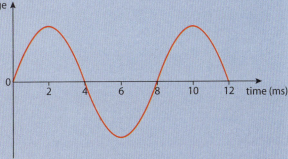

◀ Figure 10.34

a) Copy the graph and label on it a point where there is (i) a compression and (ii) a rarefaction.
b) Use the graph to find the frequency of the sound.
c) Calculate the wavelength of this sound wave.

Summary

Now that you have completed this chapter, you should be able to:

- understand that waves transfer energy from one place to another

- recognise and use the terms *wave speed, frequency, wavelength* and *amplitude*

- recognise that the particles in a transverse wave vibrate at right angles to the direction of the movement of the waves

- recognise that the particles in a longitudial wave vibrate parallel to the direction of the movement of the waves

- use a ripple tank to demonstrate the properties (reflection, refraction and diffraction) of water waves

- describe the production of sound by vibrating sources

- recognise that a sound wave is a longitudinal wave

- relate the loudness of a sound to its amplitude

- describe how an echo is a reflection of a sound wave

- relate the pitch of a sound to its frequency

- recognise and use the equation $v = f \times \lambda$

- recognise that sound is a pressure wave made up of a series of compressions and rarefactions

- recognise that sound travels at different speeds in different media.

Chapter 11

Light and lenses

Spectacles, telescopes, microscopes, and cameras all use lenses, and there is even a lens in your eye. An understanding of light is essential for an understanding of these instruments. This chapter concentrates on light waves and on simple converging lenses and explains some of their properties and uses.

▲ **Figures 11.1 and 11.2**
How can the same camera take both these photographs?

11.1 Reflection of light

Light travels in straight lines

Light travels in straight lines. This is why shadows are formed.

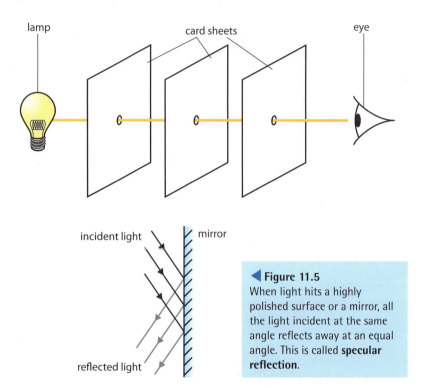

▶ **Figure 11.3**
A simple experiment shows that light travels in straight lines.

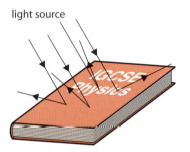

▲ **Figure 11.4**
When light strikes a rough surface, like the cover of a book, the light is **scattered** in all directions. We call this **diffuse reflection**.

◀ **Figure 11.5**
When light hits a highly polished surface or a mirror, all the light incident at the same angle reflects away at an equal angle. This is called **specular reflection**.

Terminology

Remember the angles of incidence and reflection are the angles between the rays and the normal, **not** between the rays and the surface.

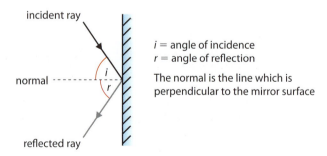

Activity 11.1
Light travels in straight lines

▶ **Figure 11.6**
The diagram shows reflection of a single ray of light.

i = angle of incidence
r = angle of reflection

The normal is the line which is perpendicular to the mirror surface

Laws of reflection

Activity 11.2
The pinhole camera

Activity 11.3
Reflection

There are two laws of reflection.

1. The angle of incidence is equal to the angle of reflection.
2. The incident ray, the normal and the reflected ray all lie in the same plane.

Law 2 means that the two rays and the normal can all be drawn on a sheet of paper.

112

Light and lenses

> **DID YOU KNOW?**
>
> Figure 11.7 shows a small source of light. Light is emitted from the source in all directions and a small cone of light is refracted by the cornea and the lens to form an image on the back of the eye (the retina). The light sensitive cells in the retina send the image to the brain.

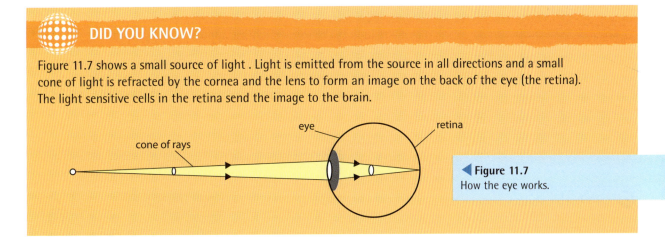

◀ Figure 11.7
How the eye works.

Image in a plane mirror

Figure 11.8 shows a cone of rays leaving an object and striking a mirror. The beam reflects from the mirror and enters the eye. The image formed on the retina is exactly the same as though the light had come from point **I**. The brain traces the beam back as though it had come from point **I** and the person sees the image at **I**. This happens for every point on the object, so the person sees a complete image of the object.

You will observe that the beam of light does not actually pass through **I**, it only appears to come from that point. This type of image cannot be projected onto a screen; it is a **virtual image**.

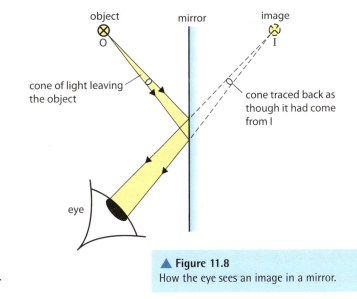

▲ Figure 11.8
How the eye sees an image in a mirror.

Locating the image in a plane mirror

Push a pin (the object pin) into a drawing board and place a mirror near it (Figure 11.9). When you look into the mirror you can see an image of the pin. Take a second pin (the search pin) and place it so that it appears to be at the same point as the image. Move your head from side to side and adjust the position of the search pin until it is in exactly the same place as the image, no matter where you look from.

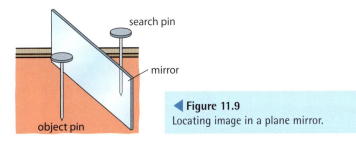

◀ Figure 11.9
Locating image in a plane mirror.

Measure the distance of the object pin and the distance of the search pin from the mirror. You should find them to be equal (Figure 11.10). The image produced by a plane mirror is exactly as far behind the mirror as the object is in front.

▶ Figure 11.10
Location of object and image in a plane mirror.

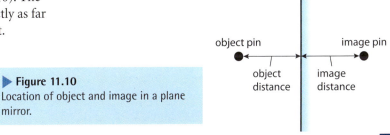

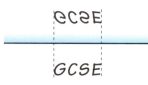

▲ Figure 11.11
Letters appear the wrong way round when viewed in a mirror.

Mirror writing

When you look in the mirror, writing appears back to front.

It is not only writing that is reversed in this way, any image is reversed. When you look at yourself, your left hand side appears to be your right and vice versa. The double reflection means this image ends up the right way round.

Activity 11.4
Image in a plane mirror

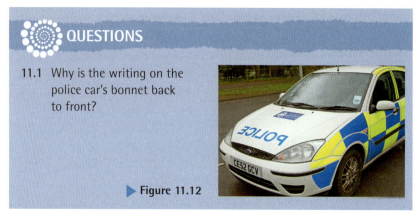

QUESTIONS

11.1 Why is the writing on the police car's bonnet back to front?

▶ Figure 11.12

Fun with mirrors

Two mirrors at right angles produce three images. One image is formed in each mirror, as you would expect. The third image is produced by light reflecting from both mirrors before entering the eye. This third image is laterally inverted.

The periscope can be used to see over obstructions without showing yourself. They can be used for viewing sporting events where you are not tall enough to see over other people (Figure 11.14). Submarines use them to look for ships, without having to surface (Figure 11.15).

▼ Figure 11.13
Three images.

▶ Figure 11.14
Periscope.

▼ Figure 11.15
Submarine periscope.

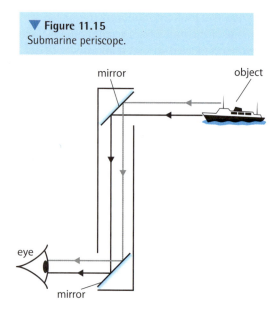

Light and lenses

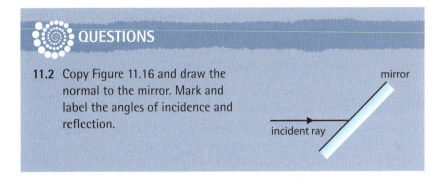

QUESTIONS

11.2 Copy Figure 11.16 and draw the normal to the mirror. Mark and label the angles of incidence and reflection.

◀ Figure 11.16

11.2 Refraction of light

Refraction

Shine a torch into a tank of water. When the light hits the water, some of the light is reflected, but some enters the water. The beam of light that enters the water changes direction as it enters the new medium.

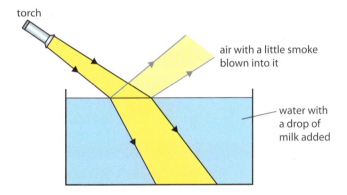

◀ Figure 11.17
Investigating refraction.

Activity 11.5
Refraction of light

If we compare this with refraction of water waves in Chapter 10, we see that the process is very similar. When light goes from one medium to another, it changes speed and, unless incident at right angles to the boundary, changes direction.

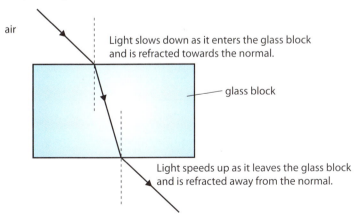

◀ Figure 11.18
Refraction of light through a glass block.

The general rule is that when light goes from a dense medium (such as water) to a less dense medium (such as air) it speeds up, and is refracted *away* from the normal. If it goes from a less dense to a more dense medium its speed decreases and it is refracted *towards* the normal.

Different media cause different degrees of refraction. Light travelling from air into glass will refract more than light going from air to water. It follows that if light travels from water to glass then it will refract towards the normal, because glass is more dense than water.

Terminology

Remember just as in reflection, the angles of incidence and refraction are the angles between the rays and the normal, **not** between the rays and the surface.

If we look at Figure 11.19, we see that with a parallel-sided block, the emergent ray is refracted so that it is parallel with the incident ray.

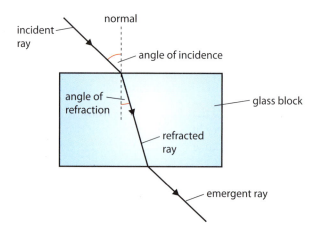

▶ **Figure 11.19**
Refraction in a parallel sided block.

DID YOU KNOW?

Why does a swimming pool look shallower than it really is?

Light coming from the toy at the bottom of the pool is refracted away from the normal as it leaves the pool. The child sees a virtual image of the toy at X.

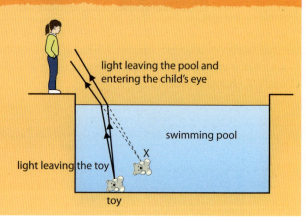

▶ **Figure 11.20**
The pool appears shallower due to refraction.

Refractive index

The refractive index of a material measures how much refraction takes place when light enters that material. It is defined by the equation:

refractive index = $\dfrac{\text{speed of light in a vacuum}}{\text{speed of light in the medium}}$

or in symbols: $n = \dfrac{c_0}{c_m}$

Units

Both speeds are measured in the same units and therefore cancel. This means that refractive index has no units; it is a pure ratio.

WORKED EXAMPLE

Glass has a refractive index of 1.5. Given that the speed of light in a vacuum is 3×10^8 m/s, calculate the speed of light in glass.

$$\text{refractive index} = \frac{\text{speed of light in a vacuum}}{\text{speed of light in the medium}}$$

$$1.5 = \frac{3 \times 10^8}{v_g} \text{ m/s} \quad \text{where } v_g = \text{speed of light in glass}$$

$$v_g = \frac{3 \times 10^8 \text{ m/s}}{1.5}$$

$$= 2 \times 10^8 \text{ m/s}$$

You will see from Table 11.1 that the refractive index of air is very close to 1. This means there is very little refraction when light travels between vacuum and air. For this course we will assume refraction due to air is negligible.

Another equation for refractive index

It is not easy to measure the speed of light — either in a vacuum or in glass or water! If we wish to measure the refractive index of a material in the laboratory, we measure the angles of incidence and refraction and use the equation:

$$\text{refractive index} = \frac{\text{sine of the angle of incidence}}{\text{sine of the angle of refraction}}$$

$$n = \frac{\sin i}{\sin r}$$

▼ Table 11.1 Refractive indices.

Material	Refractive Index
Diamond	2.42
Glass (lead crystal)	1.58–1.84
Glass (crown)	1.49–1.52
Perspex	1.49
Water	1.33
Air	1.0003

WORKED EXAMPLE

A ray of light enters a pond at an angle of incidence of 34°. Given that the refractive index of glass is 1.33, calculate the angle of refraction of the ray.

$$n = \frac{\sin i}{\sin r}$$

$$\sin r = \frac{\sin i}{n}$$

$$\sin r = \frac{\sin 34}{1.33}$$

$$= \frac{0.559}{1.33}$$

$$= 0.420$$

$$r = 25° \quad \text{(to 2 sig. fig.)}$$

Hint

Don't forget the last step. Until then we have only found the value of sin r.

QUESTIONS

(Use values of refractive index from Table 11.1 where necessary. Speed of light in a vacuum = 3×10^8 m/s)

11.3 When light is shone at a glass block at angle of incidence of 48° the angle of refraction is 28°. Calculate the refractive index of the glass.

11.4 Calculate the speed of light in water.

Critical angle and total internal reflection

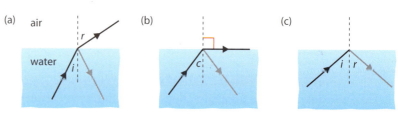

▶ Figure 11.21 Critical angle and total internal reflection.

Figure 11.21(a) shows a ray of light leaving water and entering air. Most of the light is refracted but a small amount is reflected back into the water. Air is less dense than water and so the emerging ray is refracted away from the normal. The angle of refraction is bigger than the angle of incidence.

If the angle of incidence is increased, two things happen. More of the incident light is reflected and the angle of refraction increases. Figure 11.21(b) shows the situation when the angle of incidence is such that the refracted ray travels along the water surface. The angle of refraction is now 90°. This is the largest angle of incidence at which any light can escape from the water and is called the **critical angle**.

If the angle of incidence is increased further (Figure 11.21(c)) all the light is reflected back into the water. This is called **total internal reflection**.

You will see how, as the refractive index of the material increases, the critical angle decreases.

Activity 11.6 Critical angle

▼ Table 11.2 Critical angles.

Material	Critical angle
Water	49°
Glass (crown)	42°
Glass (lead crystal)	33°
Diamond	24°

DID YOU KNOW?

It is the small critical angle that makes diamonds sparkle. They are cut so that light entering the front of the diamond is totally internally reflected back into the diamond, before escaping from the front once more.

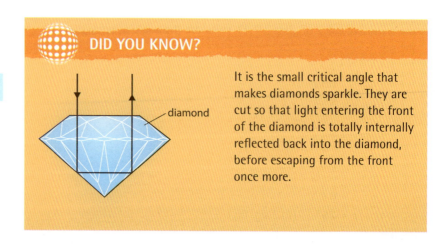

▶ Figure 11.22

Look at Figure 11.21(b). If we consider light going from air into water, the angle of incidence is equal to 90° and the angle of refraction is equal to the critical angle c.

$$n = \frac{\sin i}{\sin r} \quad \text{but } i = 90° \text{ and } \sin 90° = 1$$
$$\text{and } r = c$$

$$n = \frac{1}{\sin c}$$

This enables us to determine the refractive index of a material by measuring the critical angle.

WORKED EXAMPLE

The refractive index of a sapphire is 1.76. Calculate its critical angle.

$$n = \frac{1}{\sin c}$$
$$\sin c = \frac{1}{n}$$
$$= \frac{1}{1.76}$$
$$= 0.568$$
$$c = \mathbf{34.6°}$$

Hint

Don't forget the last stage.

Use of total internal reflection

Right-angled prisms can be used in optical instruments instead of mirrors. One example is the periscope. The critical angle for a fairly high density glass can be as small as 39°. Light entering the prism at (nearly) right angles to one face will hit the back face with an angle of incidence of about 45°. This is well in excess of the critical angle and so the light will be totally internally reflected.

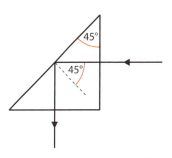

▲ Figure 11.23
Total internal reflection in a right-angled prism.

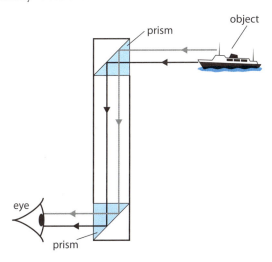

◀ Figure 11.24
Ray diagram for a prism periscope.

Light can travel down a glass fibre, undergoing internal reflection each time it hits a wall. These fibres are known as **optical fibres**.

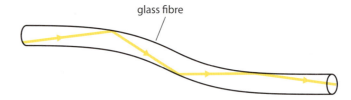

▶ **Figure 11.25**
Optical fibres of various types are used in medicine (the endoscope) and in telecommunications.

An endoscope consists of a pair of optical fibres attached to a camera. Light is sent down one fibre, is scattered from the internal organs of the patient and goes up the other fibre to a camera. The image of the internal organs of the patient can be viewed without major surgery.

▶ **Figure 11.26**
Endoscopes are used to look at the internal organs of patients.

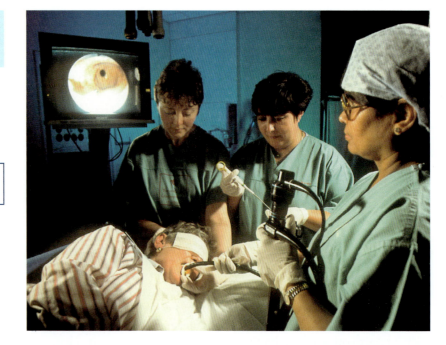

Activity 11.7
Making an optic fibre

In telecommunications, copper cables are increasingly being replaced by optical fibres. Pulses of light replace the electrical signals that were traditionally used. There are many advantages in using optical fibres in this way; there is decreased loss of signal strength, there is less distortion of the signal and the rate of transmission of information is greatly increased.

▼ **Figure 11.27**
A lens can bend light to form an image of an object.

11.3 Lenses

The image formed by a lens is quite different from the image formed by a plane mirror. Most obviously it may be upside down (**inverted**). The rays of light actually pass through the image and can be projected on to a screen. This type of image is called a **real image**. We also notice that, in this particular example, the image is smaller than the original object; we say that it is **diminished**.

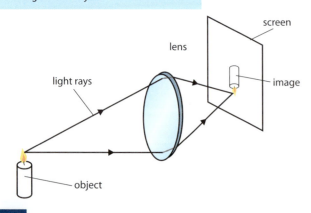

Light and lenses

Parallel light passing through a lens

We can see that light initially parallel to the principal axis is brought to a point before diverging out again. The point where the light converges is called a **principal focus**. The distance between the optical centre of the lens and a principal focus is the **focal length** of the lens. The focal length tells us how 'strong' the lens is – the shorter the focal length, the stronger the lens.

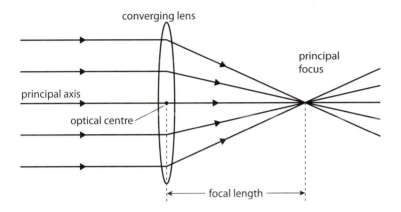

Figure 11.28
A converging lens focuses parallel rays to a point.

The optical centre of the lens is the point where light passes through the lens without being deviated.

A lens has two principal **foci** because light can pass either way through the lens, so there is a principal focus either side of it.

Activity 11.8
More on the pinhole camera

Activity 11.9
Tracing rays through a converging lens

Activity 11.10
Locating images

Locating images in a converging lens

We have already seen how a converging lens can produce an image. If we know the position of an object relative to the lens, and know the focal length of the lens, then we can predict where the image will be formed, by drawing a scale diagram. We need a minimum of two rays, from the tip of the object, whose paths we can predict. In practice there are three such rays:

1. The ray that is initially parallel to the principal axis – this will pass through the principal focus after refraction.
2. The ray through the optical centre of the lens – this passes through the lens without being deviated.
3. A third ray is not strictly necessary but is a useful check. This passes through the second principal focus and after passing through the lens, travels parallel to the principal axis.

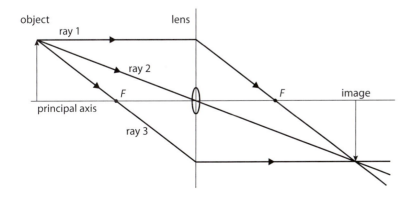

Figure 11.29
Drawing a ray diagram.

121

To improve the accuracy of your drawing it is best to draw the lens as a straight line with a small representation at the centre to indicate that it is a converging lens.

WORKED EXAMPLE

An object of height 1 cm is placed 15 cm from a converging lens of focal length of 10 cm.
By drawing a diagram to a stated scale find the size and position of the image. Give a full description of the image.

Hint
You do not need equal horizontal and vertical scales.

Scales, vertical 2 : 1   horizontal 1 : 4

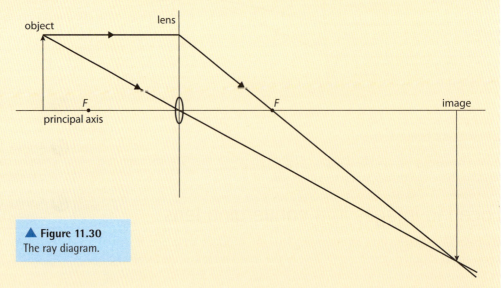

▲ **Figure 11.30**
The ray diagram.

On the diagram the image is 7.5 cm from the lens, so with scaling the actual image will be 7.5 cm × 4 = 30 cm from the lens.
On the diagram the height of the image is 4 cm so the actual height is
4 cm ÷ 2 = 2 cm.
The image is real, inverted and enlarged.

QUESTIONS

11.5 a) A candle is placed 16 cm from a converging lens of focal length 8 cm.
   Draw a diagram to a stated scale to find where the image is formed.
   Give a full description of the image.
   b) Draw a second diagram to show where the image is formed when the object is moved 2 cm further away from the lens. Describe how the image changes.

Light and lenses

Up to this stage we have only looked at the images formed when the object is placed at a distance greater than the focal length from the lens.

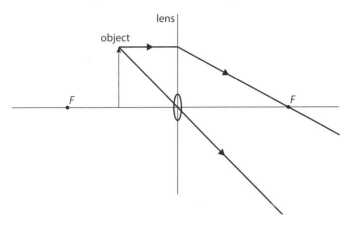

◀ **Figure 11.31**
A ray diagram for an object placed nearer to the lens than the focal length.

The object is now so close to the lens that the rays are still spreading after passing through the lens. This is similar to the formation of an image in a plane mirror. The eye in Figure 11.32 sees an image, as the brain thinks the rays of light come from point P. The image formed is **virtual**, **upright**, and **enlarged**. A magnifying glass is simply a converging lens used in this way.

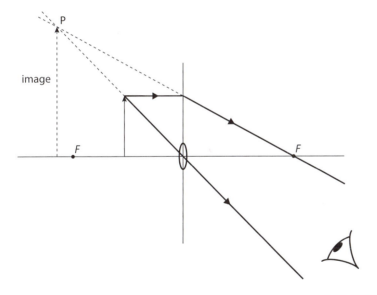

◀ **Figure 11.32**
The converging lens as a magnifying glass.

QUESTIONS

11.6 A converging lens is used as a magnifying glass to look at a flower's stamen. Draw a simple diagram to show where the observer should look from, where the stamen should be placed relative to the lens, and the position of the principle foci of the lens. What happens to the size of the image formed when the lens is moved further away from the stamen?

11.7 The image formed when using a magnifying glass is a virtual image. Explain why the image cannot be cast on a screen.

(Use values of refractive index from Table 11.1 where necessary. Speed of light in a vacuum = 3×10^8 m/s)

11.8   a) Draw a diagram to show the path of a ray of light as it travels from a lamp underneath a swimming pool into the air. Label the ray A.
b) Draw a second ray, on the same diagram, to show the path of a ray that has an angle of incidence at the surface equal to the critical angle. Label this ray B.
c) Draw a third ray, on the same diagram, to show the path of a ray that has an angle of incidence at the surface greater than the critical angle. Label this ray C.

11.9   An object of height 1.5 cm is placed 25 cm from the optical centre of a converging lens of focal length 12 cm.
a) Draw a ray diagram to a stated scale to find the position of the image that is formed.
b) Give a full description of the image.

11.10   Copy Figure 11.33 and show where the image of the arrow is formed.

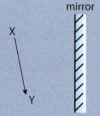

▶ Figure 11.33

Draw rays from the points X and Y to show how the image is formed.

11.11   A ray of light enters a swimming pool at an angle of incidence of 18°.
Calculate the angle of refraction of the light.

11.12   A converging lens has a focal length of 12 cm. It is used to view an object that is 8 cm from the optical centre of the lens.
Draw a ray diagram to a stated scale to show where the image is formed.

11.13   The speed of light in ruby is 1.70×10^8 m/s.
a) Calculate the refractive index of ruby.
b) Calculate the critical angle of ruby.

Light and lenses

Summary

Now that you have completed this chapter, you should be able to:

- recognise that light travels in straight lines
- understand and use the laws of reflection
- understand the formation of images in a plane mirror
- understand the nature of an image in a plane mirror
- understand that light is refracted when it moves from one medium to another
- use and understand the terms *angle of incidence* and *angle of refraction*
- trace a ray of light through a parallel-sided block
- identify and use the terms *angle of incidence* and *angle of refraction*
- understand the meaning of the term *critical angle*
- understand the meaning of *total internal reflection* and be aware of how it can be utilised
- understand and use the terms *principal focus* and *focal length*
- describe the formation of images in a converging lens
- understand what is meant by a real image
- construct ray diagrams to locate real images in a converging lens
- understand that refraction is due to the change of speed when light moves from one medium to another
- understand that light can be totally internally reflected when passing from a dense to a less dense medium
- understand the term *critical angle*
- recall and use the equation $n = \dfrac{c_0}{c_m}$
- recall and use the equation $n = \dfrac{\sin i}{\sin r}$
- recall and use the equation $n = \dfrac{1}{\sin c}$
- describe the action and use of optical fibres
- construct ray diagrams to locate virtual images in a converging lens
- describe the use of a converging lens as a magnifying glass.

125

Chapter 12

The electromagnetic spectrum

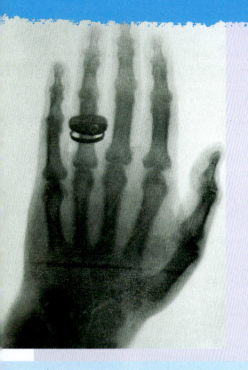

▲ Figure 12.1
The German physicist, Wilhelm Röntgen, discovered X-rays in 1895 whilst experimenting with electron tubes. He called them X-rays because he did not know what they were. Within a week he had taken a photograph of his wife's hand on which her wedding ring is clearly visible. Von Laue later showed that X-rays were part of the electromagnetic spectrum.

▲ Figure 12.2
The Lovell Radio Telescope at Jodrell Bank, Cheshire.
60 years ago we could only look into our universe using visible light. The development of radar during the Second World War led to the development of radio astronomy, the investigation of the radio waves that are emitted by stars and other astronomical bodies. Now there are telescopes which operate in all wavebands of the electromagnetic spectrum.

▶ Figure 12.3
A false colour image of the centre of the Milky Way. The brightest spot at the centre of the photo was produced by a huge X-ray flare near the super-massive black hole at the centre of the galaxy. The X-ray source brightened dramatically and after about three hours it declined rapidly. The flare was caused by material falling into the black hole.

There is a complete family of radiation, some of which you have already met, known as the electromagnetic spectrum. The properties of the different types of radiation in the family are quite different — but they all travel at the same high speed (3×10^8 m/s) in a **vacuum**.

12.1 Light

Refraction of light through a triangular prism

Note that when refracted by a prism, as in Figure 12.5, the light is deviated away from its original direction. This is quite different from refraction through a parallel-sided block where the emergent ray is parallel to the incident ray.

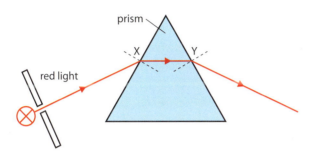

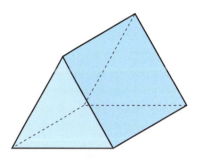

▼ Figure 12.4
A prism is any glass or perspex block – this one is in the shape of an equilateral triangle.

▲ Figure 12.5
If light of a single colour is shone through the prism, it is refracted towards the normal when it enters the prism (at X) and away from the normal when it leaves the prism (at Y).

  Activity 12.1
Tracing a ray through a prism

If white light is shone through the prism the effect is quite spectacular. The white light is split up into the colours of the rainbow; red, orange, yellow, green, blue and violet. This shows that white light is not a single colour; but is made up from the colours of the spectrum. This was first observed by Sir Isaac Newton, when he used a prism to split light from the Sun into its component colours.

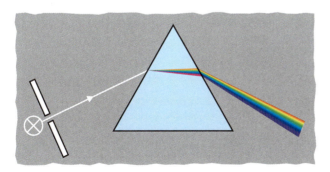

◀ Figure 12.6
Dispersion of white light through a prism.

  Activity 12.2
Dispersion of white light by a prism

The glass of the prism has a slightly different refractive index for different wavelengths of light. Red light is deviated through a slightly smaller angle than orange light, which in turn is deviated through a slightly smaller angle than yellow light and so on. The splitting of white light into its colours in this way is called **dispersion**.

127

> **DID YOU KNOW?**
>
> Light is transmitted by waves, and can be diffracted just as water waves are diffracted! Try looking at a distant light through a small hole in a piece of card – the light source seems to spread out. This is due to diffraction as the light passes through the hole. You may even see different colours as different wavelengths of light are diffracted to different extents.
>
> Each colour of light is really a different frequency of wave (and therefore a different wavelength). Red light has lower frequency (longer wavelength) than violet light, the other colours having frequencies between those of red and violet. A single colour, or frequency, of light is called **monochromatic** light.

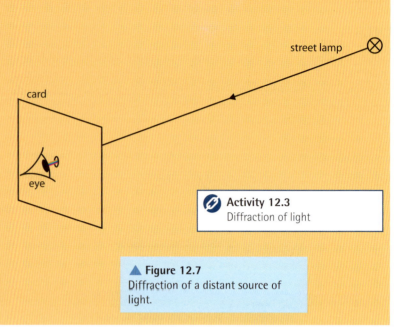

Activity 12.3
Diffraction of light

▲ Figure 12.7
Diffraction of a distant source of light.

▼ Figure 12.8
Testing for infrared radiation.

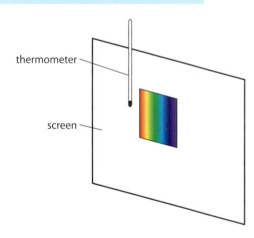

Activity 12.4
Detection of infrared radiation

12.2 Further investigation of the spectrum

If we use a prism to cast a spectrum of the Sun's light onto a screen, we find that there is invisible radiation beyond the red and beyond the violet ends of the visible spectrum.

A thermometer with a blackened bulb placed beyond the red end of the spectrum shows a rise in temperature. This means that radiation is falling on the screen. This is **infrared radiation** – the thermal radiation that we described in Chapter 9.

All warm objects emit infrared light, enabling infrared cameras to be used to take photographs in the dark.

▶ Figure 12.9
A photograph of a capybara taken in the infrared region.

128

If a strip of fluorescent paper is attached to the screen, it can be observed that there is fluorescence beyond the violet end of the spectrum. Energy is incident here; it is being absorbed by the fluorescent paper and re-emitted as visible light. This radiation is known as **ultraviolet radiation**. Overexposure to ultraviolet radiation causes sunburn and skin cancers. However, ultraviolet light is important in the process of photosynthesis in plants.

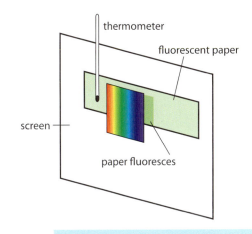

▲ Figure 12.10
Testing for ultraviolet radiation.

12.3 The complete electromagnetic spectrum

There are radiations beyond infrared and ultraviolet. Figure 12.8 shows the different regions of the spectrum and some of their properties and uses.

Activity 12.5
Detecting ultraviolet

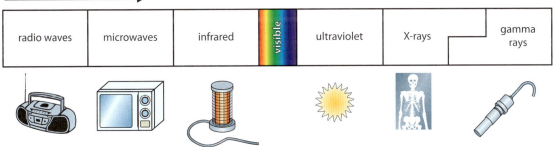

▲ Figure 12.11
The electromagnetic spectrum.

As you go from radio waves to towards X-ray and gamma radiation, the frequency increases and the wavelength decreases. The speed in a vacuum, however, is the same for all types of electromagnetic radiation and is 3×10^8 m/s.

The complete electromagnetic spectrum is split into the regions shown in Figure 12.11. The regions are not sharply divided as the diagram suggests. Just as there are no sharp divides between the colours in the visible spectrum, the regions of the complete electromagnetic spectrum gradually merge one into another.

Radio waves range from wavelengths of 1 km or more down to about 10 cm. Early radio transmissions were made at the longer wavelengths, although as technology improved, the wavelengths used were gradually reduced. The advantage of using shorter wavelength (higher frequency) waves is that the rate of transmission of information is increased. Nowadays, many signals are sent in the microwave or even infrared region.

Microwaves have wavelengths of a few tens of centimetres down to a few millimetres. Microwaves with a wavelength of about 12 cm have the same frequency as one of the frequencies of vibration of the water molecule. This means that they can quickly cause water molecules to vibrate, causing the water itself to heat up rapidly. This makes them useful in cooking: all living material consists of over 90% water (yes, you as well!). The temperature of the water in food is quickly raised and the food is rapidly cooked.

DID YOU KNOW?

Newton identified seven colours in the spectrum: red, orange, yellow, green, blue, indigo and violet. In practice there are many, many different shades as the colours gradually change and merge into one another.

Infrared radiation is the thermal radiation that was described in Chapter 9. Its wavelengths range from a few millimetres to about $0.7\,\mu m$ (7×10^{-7} m).

The human eye can detect radiation of wavelengths between 7×10^{-7} m and 4×10^{-7} m. This is the visible spectrum.

Ultraviolet radiation ranges from 4×10^{-7} m to 1×10^{-8}. Ultraviolet is necessary for life. Plants use ultraviolet light from the Sun to convert water and carbon dioxide into sugars and oxygen in the process called photosynthesis. However, shorter wavelength ultraviolet light can cause damage to living material. Overexposure to it causes sunburn and can even cause melanomas or skin cancers.

X-rays, whose wavelengths range from about 1×10^{-8} m to 1×10^{-11} m, are very penetrating. They are able to travel through human flesh without being absorbed. However, longer wavelength X-rays are stopped by bones, allowing shadow photographs, similar to the one on page 126, to be taken. Like short wave ultraviolet waves, X-rays can damage living material. Because they are so penetrating, they can cause cancerous growths deep in the body.

Gamma rays are formed in radioactive decay. Their wavelengths can be as short as 1×10^{-14} m. Their properties are similar to X-rays but they are even more penetrating.

QUESTIONS

12.1 Using the Internet or otherwise, find a use (not included in the text) for each different type of electromagnetic radiation.

12.2 Give one piece of evidence that light travels much faster than sound.

12.3 Long wave radio waves can have a wavelength of 1500 m. Given the speed of the waves is 3×10^8 m/s, calculate the frequency of these waves.

12.4 The frequency of red light is 4.3×10^{14} Hz. Calculate the wavelength of red light.

Summary

Now you have completed this chapter, you should be able to:

- recognise that white light is made up of the colours of the spectrum
- recognise that infrared radiation is lower frequency than visible radiation
- recognise that ultraviolet radiation is higher frequency than visible radiation
- recognise that all electromagnetic radiation at travels at the same speed in a vacuum.

Chapter 13

Magnetism

Nuclear fusion is the great hope for the clean generation of electricity. Nuclear fusion is the merging of the nuclei of the smallest atoms to form the nucleus of a larger atom, with the release of vast quantities of energy. It is this process that fuels the Sun and other stars and takes place in an H-bomb. For fusion to occur, incredibly high temperatures are needed, so high that matter enters the fourth state, a soup of positive and negative charges called a plasma. The Joint European Torus is an experiment to try to achieve controlled fusion; the plasma is held together by extremely strong electromagnets.

Magnets are used in compasses for navigation. They are used in electric generators and in electric motors. Without the use of magnets, we would be unable to generate large quantities of electrical energy. Our lives would be totally different: there would be no electric light, no television, no Internet, and no washing machines!

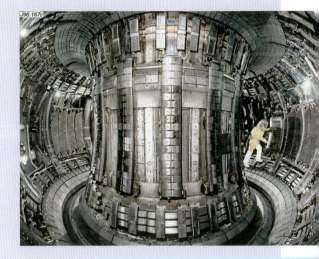

▲ Figure 13.1
The Joint European Torus.

13.1 Magnets

Figure 13.2 shows how a magnet picks up pins. Notice how the pins tend to hold onto the ends of the magnets, as though the magnetism is concentrated at the ends. These ends are the **poles** of the magnet.

Activity 13.1
Which materials are magnetic?

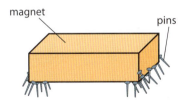

◀ Figure 13.2
Magnets will pick up steel or iron objects.

A magnet freely suspended will rotate and come to rest in a (nearly) north – south direction.

The end that points towards the north is called a **north-seeking pole** (usually shortened to north pole), the other end is called a **south-seeking pole** (or south pole).

▶ Figure 13.3
Freely suspended magnet.

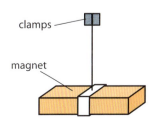

131

Laws of magnetism

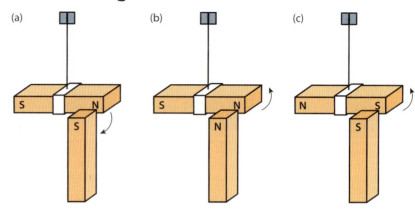

▶ Figure 13.4
(a) A south-seeking pole brought up to a north-seeking pole will attract.
(b) A north-seeking pole brought up to another north-seeking pole will repel.
(c) A south-seeking pole brought up to another south-seeking pole will repel.

Activity 13.2
The compass effect

Activity 13.3
The laws of magnetism

The effects shown in Figure 13.4 can be summed up in the laws of magnetism.

1 Unlike poles attract.

2 Like poles repel.

Induced magnetism

Each pin in Figure 13.5 becomes a temporary magnet, with a north-seeking pole and a south-seeking pole. We call this process **magnetic induction**. When the pins are removed from the magnet, they lose their magnetism once more.

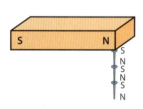

▲ Figure 13.5
A chain of pins can be picked up by a magnet.

Magnetic materials

There are only three elements that are attracted to magnets, or which can be magnetised themselves: iron, cobalt and nickel. Most alloys of iron (steels) are also magnetic, although some stainless steels are not magnetic. Materials that show magnetic properties such as these are described as showing ferrous properties or as **ferromagnetic**.

Activity 13.4
Magnetic induction

▶ Figure 13.6
Iron, nickel, cobalt and steel.

Most types of steel tend to form permanent (or 'hard') magnets, whereas iron will not keep its magnetised state for very long; it forms temporary (or 'soft') magnets. This difference in properties affects the way that iron and steel are used. For example, iron is used for electromagnets (see Section 13.3).

13.2 Magnetic fields

One of the most intriguing aspects of the behaviour of magnets is their 'action at a distance'. They do not need to be touching another magnetic material to attract or repel it, the force acts across empty space or even through other materials. This is not unique: gravity acts in a similar way. A ball is attracted to the Earth even though the ball is not touching the Earth. Similarly, the Earth is attracted to the Sun and they are certainly not touching!

Activity 13.5
Plotting magnetic fields

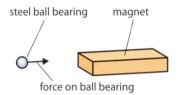
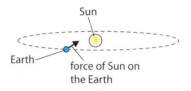

◀ Figure 13.7
Magnetic fields, like gravitational fields, act at a distance.

To help us to explain these effects we say there is a 'force field' around the objects. In the case of gravity, there is a gravitational field, and in the case of the magnets there is a **magnetic field**.

Plotting magnetic fields

The shape of a magnetic field can be represented by **lines of magnetic force**. These represent the direction of the force on a single north-seeking pole at any point in space. There are two methods for finding lines of magnetic force.

Method 1

We place a magnet on a sheet of paper and put a plotting compass close to the north-seeking pole of the magnet.

A dot is placed on the point of the compass needle and the compass is moved so that the tail is on the dot. Another dot is made at the point and the process is repeated until the compass reaches the other pole. The dots are joined to make a line. The compass is now placed at other points near the north-seeking pole of the magnet and more lines are drawn in a similar way.

Method 2

An alternative method of plotting a magnetic field is to use iron filings. The magnet is placed under a piece of paper and iron filings are sprinkled on top. The paper is tapped and the filings line up showing the shape of the field. The lines are not clearly drawn in this method so we do need to use our understanding to draw a meaningful picture.

▲ Figure 13.8
Plotting magnetic fields: method 1.

▶ Figure 13.9
Plotting magnetic fields: method 2.

The magnetic field of a single bar magnet

- The arrows on the lines of force always point away from the north-seeking pole and towards the south-seeking pole (remember they represent the force on a single north-seeking pole).
- Lines of force must always start and finish on a pole and they can never touch nor cross.
- The field is strongest where the lines of force are closest together, which is nearest the poles of the magnet.

Magnetic field of a horseshoe magnet

The field between two opposite poles (or the poles of a horseshoe-shaped magnet) is uniform, except at the edges where there is some fringing.

▲ Figure 13.10
Magnetic field due to a bar magnet.

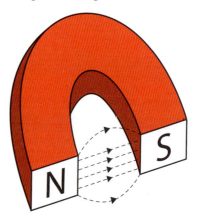

▶ Figure 13.11
Magnetic field between the poles of a horseshoe magnet.

> ### DID YOU KNOW?
>
> The Earth has its own magnetic field. The core of the Earth is made from iron and nickel and it is believed that it is the churning of the liquid iron that produces the Earth's field. This explains why a freely suspended magnet will rotate into a north-south direction.
>
>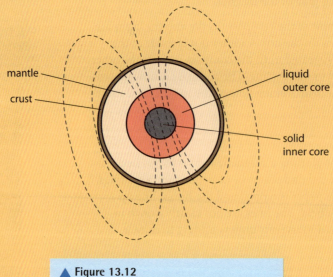
>
> ▲ Figure 13.12
> The Earth's magnetic field.

134

Magnetism

The magnetic field of an electric current

A sheet of paper is placed over a wire and iron filings are sprinkled on it. Switch S is closed and the paper is given a tap. The filings line up across the wire (Figure 13.13). Quite clearly, the filings are affected by the current, which tells us that the current has a magnetic field of its own.

The wire is arranged so that a sheet of card is at right angles to the current. The filings line up, showing circles (Figure 13.14).

A more careful study shows that the field at right angles to a current is a set of circles centred on the current.

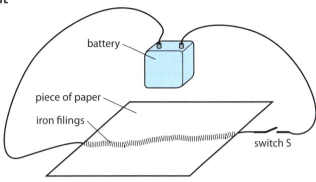

▲ **Figure 13.13**
Magnetic field along a wire with a current flowing through it.

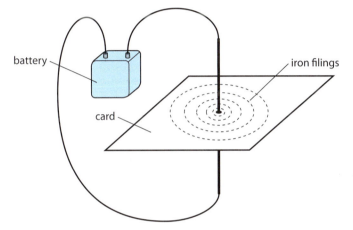

◀ **Figure 13.14**
Magnetic field around a wire with a current passing through it.

Activity 13.6
Magnetic fields of electric currents

The corkscrew rule

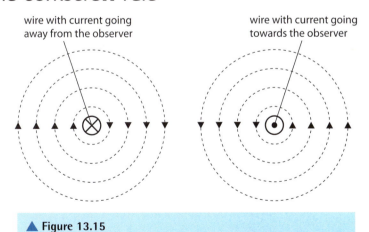

▲ **Figure 13.15**
Corkscrew rule for direction of magnetic field lines around a current.

In order to work out the direction of the magnetic field of a current imagine you are screwing a screw or a corkscrew. The direction the screw moves represents the direction of the current, and the direction you turn the screwdriver represents the field direction. So if you are screwing a screw into the page then you turn the screwdriver clockwise, and out of the page, you would turn it anticlockwise.

▲ **Figure 13.16**
The corkscrew rule.

135

The magnetic field of a current carrying coil

A coil can be imagined as two wires carrying currents in opposite directions (Figure 13.17). The field between the wires add up to make a stronger field (the lines are closer together). The more turns on the coil, the stronger the field will be. Also, if the current is increased, the magnetic field will be stronger.

▶ **Figure 13.17**
Magnetic field lines from a coil.

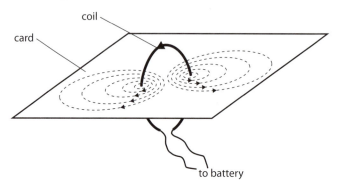

The magnetic field of a solenoid

A solenoid is simply a long coil. The fields of the individual wires add up to produce a very strong field inside the solenoid. Around the outside of the solenoid, the field is very similar to that of a bar magnet (Figure 13.18).

▶ **Figure 13.18**
Magnetic field lines around a solenoid.

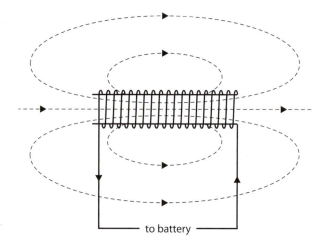

⚡ **Activity 13.7**
Making and destroying magnets

Magnetising magnetic materials

Any ferromagnetic material left in a magnetic field will gradually become very weakly magnetised. Iron-bearing rocks in the Earth's crust are weakly magnetised and show how the Earth's field has changed over geological time. But to make stronger magnets we need to help nature.

▼ **Figure 13.19**
Stroking.

Making a magnet by stroking

A piece of steel is laid on the bench and stroked with a strong magnet using a sweeping motion. The ends of the steel can be tested with a plotting compass, which will show that end A has become a south-seeking pole and end B has become a north-seeking pole.

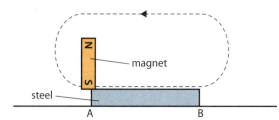

136

Magnetism

Making a magnet by an electrical method

This is the most effective method of making a magnet. A steel bar is placed inside a coil of wire. The wire is attached to a **direct current** supply and the switch is closed, so there is a current in the coil. The current is switched off and the steel is removed from the coil. The steel will now be magnetised.

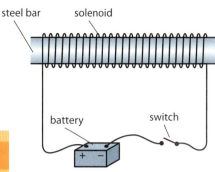

▲ Figure 13.20
Magnetising steel using electrical current.

DID YOU KNOW?

Magnetic materials are made up of mini-magnets. In the unmagnetised material, the mini-magnets are randomly arranged. As the material becomes magnetised, the mini-magnets start to become aligned. When they are fully aligned, the magnet is as strong as it can ever be.

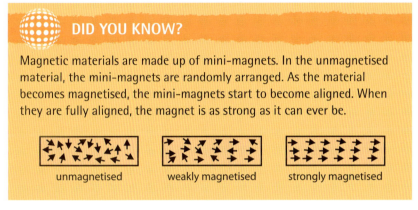

unmagnetised   weakly magnetised   strongly magnetised

Demagnetising magnets

The most effective way of demagnetising a magnet is to put it in a coil and to pass an **alternating current** through the coil. The alternating current changes direction many times a second, and each time the current reverses, the magnet is magnetised in the opposite direction. If the current is gradually reduced to zero each magnetisation will be weaker than the previous one until the magnet is demagnetised. It is most effective to carry this out with the magnet and solenoid lying in an east – west direction.

Alternative methods are to heat the steel up to red heat or to hit it several times with a hammer, with a combination of the two being even more effective. Again, these mechanical methods should be carried out with the magnet lying in an east–west direction.

QUESTIONS

13.1 Why is it more effective to demagnetise a magnet with it lying in an east–west direction?

13.3 Electromagnets

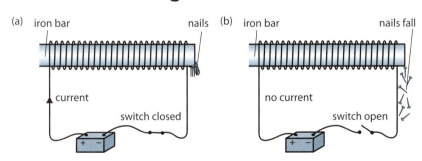

◀ Figure 13.21
An electromagnet.

Activity 13.8
Electromagnets

The apparatus in Figure 13.21 is similar to the apparatus in Figure 13.20, except that the steel bar is replaced with one made of pure or **soft iron**. When the current in the coil is switched on, the iron becomes magnetised and will pick up iron nails (13.21(a)).

When the switch is opened and there is no current, the iron loses its magnetism and the nails fall to the floor (13.21(b)). We now have a temporary magnet, one that only acts as a magnet when there is a current in the coil. We call this type of magnet an **electromagnet**.

Uses of electromagnets

Figure 13.22 shows the structure of an electromagnet that could be used to sort and remove iron-based materials from other waste metals.

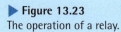
Figure 13.22
Electromagnet for sorting iron scrap.

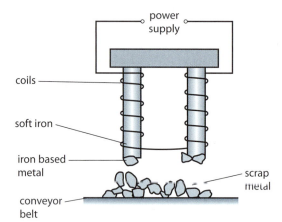

The iron-based metals are attracted to the electromagnet, leaving the other metals on the conveyor belt. The electromagnet can then be swung above a bin, the current switched off and the iron released into the bin.

Relays

A relay is an electromagnetic switch. It is often used when a low-power circuit is used to switch on and off a high-power circuit (see Chapter 19).

▶ Figure 13.23
The operation of a relay.

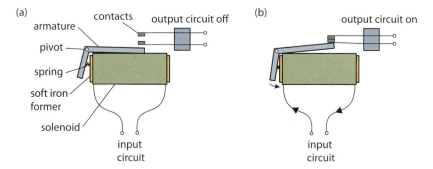

When there is a current in the solenoid, the armature is attracted to the soft iron former and pushes the contacts together, completing the output circuit (Figure 13.23(b)). In this way a small current in the input circuit can control a much larger current in the output circuit.

Magnetism

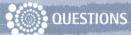

QUESTIONS

13.2 A student is given three boxes, each containing a length of metal.

Both ends of box A attract a magnet.
One end of box B attracts the magnet and the other end repels it.
There is no force when the magnet is brought up to either end of box C.

Suggest, with reasons, what each box contains.

13.3 Figure 13.25 shows a magnet with two pins attached.

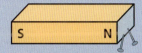

◀ Figure 13.24

a) Copy the diagrams and label the induced poles on the pins.
b) Explain why the pins do not hang vertically downwards.

13.4

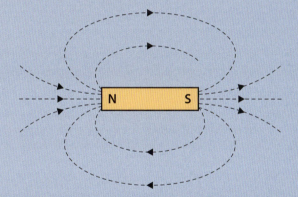

◀ Figure 13.25

A student is asked by her teacher to draw the magnetic field of a bar magnet, above.

State and explain **three** errors in the drawing.

13.5 A student wants to demagnetise a piece of steel. He puts the steel in a coil and connects it to a battery. He then removes the steel from the coil and puts it in the other way round. To his surprise he finds the steel is still magnetised.

a) Explain why this method of demagnetising would not work.
b) Describe the changes you would make to the apparatus and the procedure you would take to successfully demagnetise the steel.

13.6 a) Describe two differences between the structure of a permanent magnet and an electromagnet.
b) Describe the differences between the properties of a permanent magnet and an electromagnet.

▶ Figure 13.26
An electric bell circuit.

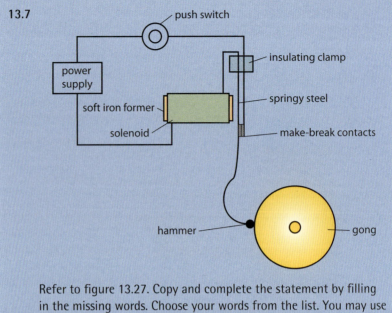

13.7

Refer to figure 13.27. Copy and complete the statement by filling in the missing words. Choose your words from the list. You may use each word once, more than once or not at all.

When the push switch is closed, there is a .... in the coil. This .... the soft iron former which attracts the springy steel towards it. The make-break contacts .... and the circuit is broken. The soft iron core .... its magnetism and the steel springs back with the hammer striking the gong. The circuit is now .... again and the process repeats.

closed   complete   current   demagnetises   gains
incomplete   loses   magnetises   open

Summary

Now that you have completed this chapter, you should be able to:
- state the properties of magnets
- state the laws of magnetism
- recognise the difference between ferromagnetic and non-ferromagnetic materials
- understand the term *magnetic induction*
- understand the meaning of a magnetic field
- understand that a magnetic field may be represented by lines of force
- describe experiments to plot magnetic fields
- describe the magnetic fields around electric currents
- describe how to magnetise and demagnetise magnetic materials
- understand that electromagnets are temporary magnets
- describe some uses of electromagnets.

Chapter 14

Electric current and simple circuits

▲ Figure 14.1
Light from human habitation can be clearly seen from space. This photograph shows the concentration of light in the United States of America and Western Europe.

For centuries the only methods of lighting were the oil lamp or the candle. In the early nineteenth century, gas lighting began to be introduced in the larger towns and cities.

In 1879 Edison developed the first commercially viable electric light bulb and in the following year, some houses were being lit by electricity. But it was only many years later that it became commonplace for ordinary homes to be lit in this way.

Today we take electric lighting for granted and the world is lit up as never before.

Electricity has brought much to civilisation, but at a cost. Can we continue to burn energy to generate electricity to produce light in this way?

14.1 Electric current

A cell is connected to a bulb so that one lead goes from one terminal of the cell to the metal contact on the lamp, and the other goes from the second terminal of the cell to the metal case on the bulb. The lamp is seen to glow.

▶ Figure 14.2
A light bulb.

141

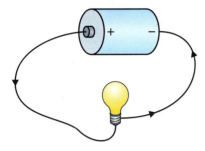

▲ Figure 14.3
Conventional current flow is from positive to negative.

If we use a magnifying glass to look at the lamp we can see a fine metal filament. This filament glows white hot when the bulb is connected to a cell.

When the bulb is connected in a complete circuit, there is a flow of electricity in the circuit. This flow of electricity is an **electric current**. We think of the movement of the electricity as going from the positive terminal of the cell to the negative terminal. This is called the **conventional current**. We can liken the current in a circuit to the flow of water or current in a stream.

Conductors and insulators

Some materials do not allow a current to pass through them. Different materials can be tested using a lamp as an indicator as in Figure 14.4.

Table 14.1 shows some materials that might be tested.

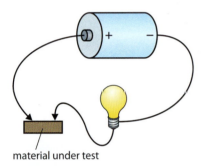

▲ Figure 14.4
Testing current flow.

Material	Lamp lights?
Aluminium	✓
Carbon	✓
Cardboard	☐
Copper	✓
Lead	✓
Perspex	☐
Polythene	☐
Steel	✓
Stone	☐
Wood	☐

◀ Table 14.1
Conducting materials.

Activity 14.1
Conductors and insulators

Materials that allow a current to pass through them are called **electrical conductors**. Materials that do not allow a current through them are called **electrical insulators**.

You can see that non-metals (with the exception of carbon) are insulators and metals are conductors.

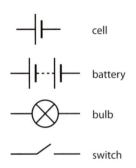

▲ Figure 14.5
Some common circuit diagram symbols.

14.2 Circuit diagrams

Up to now we have drawn the circuits as we might see them but when more complex circuits are used, this becomes impossible. Scientists have developed a system to represent circuits. Connectors are drawn as straight lines and circuit components are represented by symbols that are internationally recognised. A complete list will be found in the Appendix on page 226.

A cell is represented by two vertical lines; the longer, thinner line represents the positive terminal of the cell. A battery consists of several cells, literally 'a battery of cells'. A switch is usually represented in its 'open' position. In this position there is a break in the circuit and there is no current.

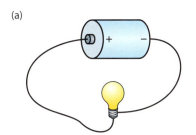 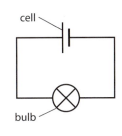

Figure 14.6
A circuit and its circuit diagram.

More circuits

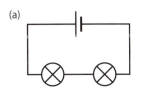 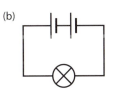 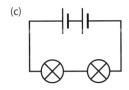

Activity 14.2
Simple circuits

▲ Figure 14.7
(a) If we build the circuit in Figure 14.7(a) we find the lamps light less brightly than in Fig. 14.6. This tells us that there is less current. The extra lamp resists the current. We say there is more **resistance** in the circuit.
(b) In circuit 14.7(b) the lamp lights more brightly than in Figure 14.6. Here the current is larger as the extra cell is able to push through more electricity.
(c) In the circuit in Figure 14.7(c), the two lamps light with the same brightness as the lamp in Figure 14.6. The extra lamp increases resistance and the extra cell increases the voltage, so there is the same current in each circuit.

In these three circuits, the cells and the lamps are put into the circuit so that one comes after the other. This type of circuit is called a **series** circuit.

Measurement of current

 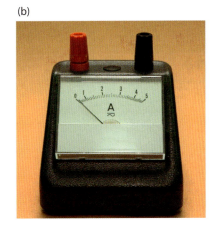

◀ Figure 14.8
(a) A digital ammeter.
(b) An analogue ammeter.

Current is measured in a unit called the **ampere (A)**.

The instrument used to measure current is called an **ammeter**. The ammeter is connected in series in the circuit as shown in Figure 14.9.

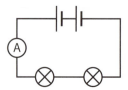

▲ Figure 14.9
Ammeters are connected in series.

The red terminal of the ammeter must be connected to the wire which goes towards the positive terminal of the cell, and the black terminal to the wire which goes towards the negative terminal of the cell. The circuit diagram symbol for an ammeter is a circle with an 'A' in it.

It does not matter where the ammeter is placed in the circuit, so long as it is connected in series. It can be placed before the lamps, between the lamps, after the lamps or between the cells; it will still give the same reading.

▶ Figure 14.10
The ammeter is connected correctly in each of these circuits.

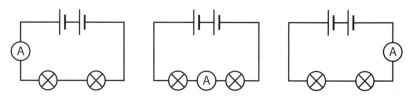

Activity 14.3
Use of the ammeter

We have described current as a flow of electricity – it is the same throughout the circuit. In exactly the same way, the mass of water flowing through a heating system is the same wherever you measure the flow.

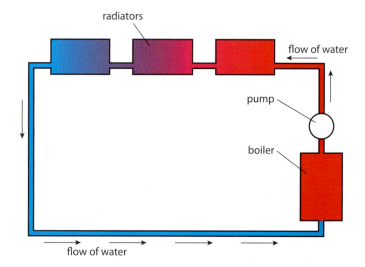

▶ Figure 14.11
The flow of water is the same at all points in the system.

Parallel circuits

In Figure 14.12 the lamps are connected so that there are two branches in the circuit.

Both lamps are lit to the same brightness as the lamp in Figure 14.6. The current has alternative paths to go down, so the resistance in the circuit is less. It is rather like building a second road round a busy town so that more cars can pass each hour.

Activity 14.4
Parallel circuits

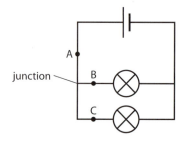

▶ Figure 14.12
These lamps are connected in **parallel**.

144

If an ammeter is placed successively at the points A, B and C in the circuit, then the currents at B and C will add up to the current at A. The current splits at the junction, some going through one lamp, some going through the other lamp. If the two lamps are identical, then half will go through each lamp.

Switches in circuits

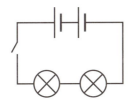

> **Activity 14.5**
> Use of switches

◀ **Figure 14.13**
If the switch is open, the lamp will be off and if the switch is closed the lamp will be lit.

If there is a single break in a circuit there will be no current.

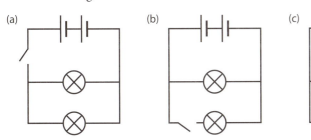

◀ **Figure 14.14**
(a) The switch controls both lamps.
(b) The switch controls the lower lamp only, the upper lamp remains on all the time.
(c) The switch controls the upper lamp only, the lower lamp remains on all the time.

QUESTIONS

14.1 Figure 14.15 shows a circuit that a student has built. Draw the circuit diagram for it using standard circuit diagram symbols.

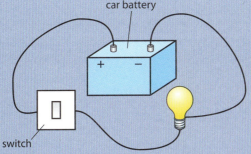

◀ **Figure 14.15**

14.2 Explain what is meant by the following terms.
   a) Conductor
   b) Insulator
   c) Ammeter
   d) Battery

14.3 Consider a lamp powered by a single cell to be lit to normal brightness.

State whether the lamps in Figure 14.16 are lit to more than normal brightness, normal brightness, less than normal brightness, or not at all.

a)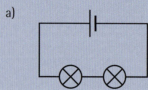

b)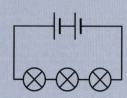

c)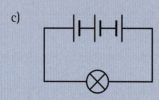

d)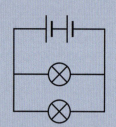

▶ Figure 14.16

14.4 In Figure 14.17, the reading on ammeter A_2 is 0.12 A, and the reading on ammeter A_3 is 0.22 A.

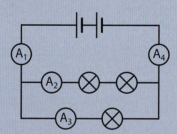

▶ Figure 14.17

a) Calculate the reading on ammeter A_1.
b) Explain why the reading on A_2 is less than the reading on A_3.
c) Write down the reading on ammeter A_4.

14.5 Figure 14.18 shows a circuit with five lamps ($L_1 - L_5$) and four switches ($S_1 - S_4$).

State which lamps the four switches control.

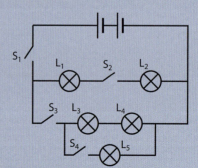

▶ Figure 14.18

Summary

Now that you have completed this chapter, you should be able to:

- recognise electric current as a flow of electricity
- state that the unit of current is the ampere (A)
- state that electric current is measured using an ammeter
- understand and use the terms *electrical conductor* and *insulator*
- interpret and draw simple circuit diagrams
- understand the meaning of a series circuit
- understand the meaning of a parallel circuit
- understand how switches can be used to control components in a circuit.

Chapter 15

Electrostatics

▶ **Figure 15.1**
Thunderstorms occur when charge builds up on the clouds. Eventually the charge becomes so large that the insulating properties of air break down and it becomes conducting. Electrons are torn off the atoms and they and the positive ions conduct the charge. There is so much energy dissipated that the air is superheated and explodes – we hear this as thunder.

Benjamin Franklin (1706–1790) was one of the founding fathers of the United States of America. As well as being a politician and statesman, he was an author, scientist and inventor. He came from a humble background, the tenth son of a candle maker. He was apprenticed as a printer and it was, perhaps, this training that gave him his interest in science.

One of his many inventions was the lightning conductor (which is used to protect buildings from lightning strikes). His most famous experiment, which showed that lightning is an electrical discharge, is surrounded by myth.

◀ **Figure 15.2**
Benjamin Franklin is said to have flown a kite in a thunderstorm and collected the charge produced when the kite was struck by lightning. If he had carried it out as in Figure 15.2, he would certainly not have survived to report the results of the experiment! Nevertheless, it is clear that he carried out some experiments based on this idea, which confirmed the electrical nature of lightning.

Electrostatics

15.1 Electric force

Hold a comb, which has been rubbed on a woollen shirt or jumper, just above some small pieces of paper.

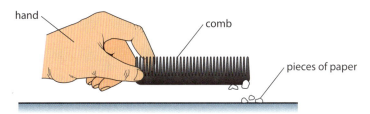

◀ Figure 15.3
A charged comb will pick up pieces of paper.

In addition to gravity and magnetism, this is another example of an 'action at a distance' force. This time it is the **electric force**. We say the comb is **electrically charged**.

We describe the region in which electric charges experience a force, as an **electric field**.

Activity 15.1
Electrostatics effects

More examples of the electric force

Two balloons that have been rubbed with a cloth are suspended close to each other. They will repel each other.

When the balloons are rubbed on the cloth they gain an electric charge. This method of charging objects is called **charging by friction**.

Figure 15.5 shows a series of experiments using different rods. The polythene rods are rubbed on wool or cotton and the acetate rods are rubbed on paper.

This suggests that there are two types of charge; 'polythene type', which we call **negative** charge, and 'acetate type', which we call **positive** charge.

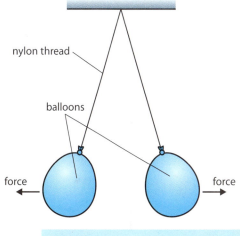

▲ Figure 15.4
Charged balloons.

These observations lead to the laws of electrostatics.
- Like charges repel.
- Unlike charges attract.

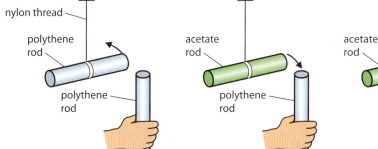

Activity 15.2
Laws of electrostatics

▲ Figure 15.5 Rub polythene rods with wool then acetate rods with paper.
(a) When two polythene rods are brought together they repel.
(b) When an acetate rod is brought near a polythene rod they attract.
(c) When two acetate rods are brought together they repel.

149

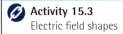
Activity 15.3
Electric field shapes

Electric field

The electric field lines may be drawn in a similar manner to magnetic field lines. The electric field lines show the force on a small positive test charge, so the direction of the field lines is away from positive charges and towards negative charges.

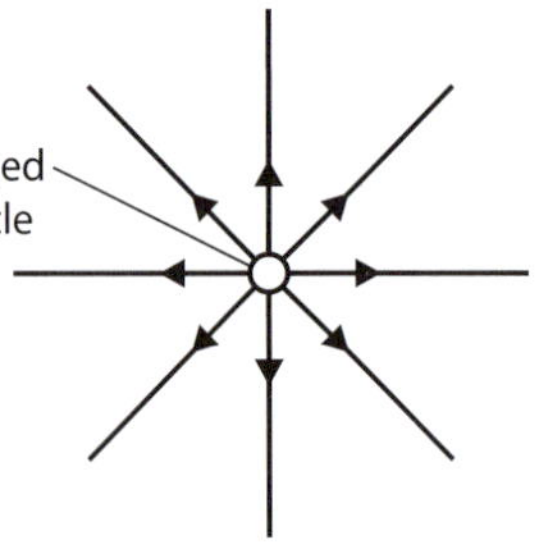

▲ Figure 15.6
The radial field of an isolated point charge.

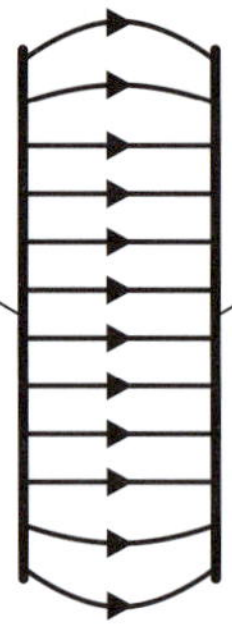

▲ Figure 15.7
The uniform field between two parallel plates.

QUESTIONS

15.1 Is the charge in Figure 15.6 positive or negative?

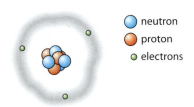

▲ Figure 15.8
The structure of an atom.

Where do the charges come from?

Matter is made up of tiny particles called atoms. The atoms are made up of protons, neutrons, and electrons. The protons carry a positive charge, the neutrons carry no charge, and the electrons carry a negative charge. The protons and neutrons are locked in the central core or **nucleus** of the atom. The electrons surround the nucleus.

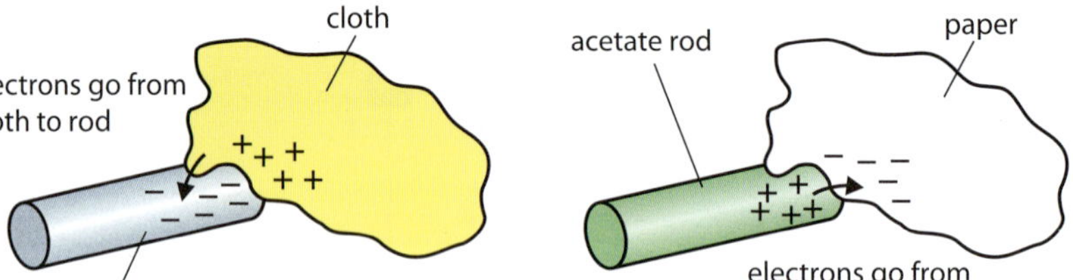

▶ Figure 15.9
Charging polythene and acetate rods.

When a polythene rod is rubbed on a cotton cloth, a few electrons are rubbed off the cloth and stay on the polythene. This leaves the polythene negatively charged and the cloth positively charged. Similarly when an acetate rod is rubbed on paper, some electrons are rubbed off the acetate and stay on the paper. This leaves the acetate positively charged and the paper negatively charged. Note that in both cases it is the electrons that move from one material to the other.

15.2 Current and charge

We can show that charge in electrostatics is closely related to electric current with the demonstration shown in Figure 15.10. A copper sphere is charged from a high-tension supply and is brought near to a positively charged acetate rod. The rod is repelled by the charged sphere.

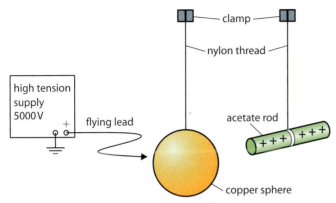

◀ **Figure 15.10**
The rod is clearly repelled by the charged sphere.

Activity 15.4
Electrostatic charge and current

In the previous chapter we described current as a flow of electricity. We now see that it is more precise to say **current is a flow of electric charge**.

Conductors and insulators

Insulators do not conduct charge because all the electrons are tightly bound to the parent atom. In metallic conductors, one or two electrons become unattached from the parent atom and are able to move in the body of the metal. These are called **free electrons**. It is these free electrons that carry the charge in a current. When a cell is connected across the ends of the metal the electrons move towards the positive terminal. Electrons are negatively charged, so the electron flow is in the opposite direction to the conventional current. This sometimes causes confusion, as the conventional current shows the flow of positive charge. The understanding of the two branches of electricity grew separately and we have to live with this small difficulty.

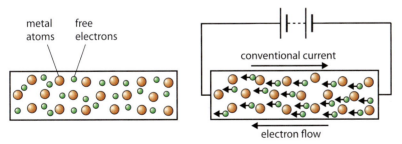

◀ **Figure 15.11**
The flow of free electrons is in the opposite direction to conventional current.

The unit of charge is the **coulomb** (C).

1 coulomb is the charge that passes any point in a circuit when a there is a current of 1 ampere in the circuit for one second.

From the definition we see that

charge = current × time

$Q = It$

151

WORKED EXAMPLE

A light bulb is switched on for 15 minutes. The current in the bulb is 3.0 A.
Calculate the charge passing through the bulb.

$Q = It$

To use this formula, the time must be measured in seconds.
15 minutes = 15 × 60 s = 900 s
Q = 3.0 A × 900 s
   = **2700 C**

QUESTIONS

15.2 Calculate the charge passing through an ammeter when there is a current of 4.0 mA for 28 s.

15.3 In an experiment to electroplate a spoon, a total charge of 18 C passes through the circuit in 2 hours. Calculate the current in the circuit.

Charging by induction

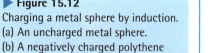
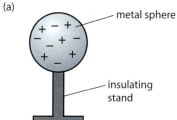
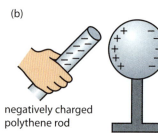
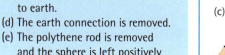
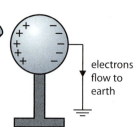
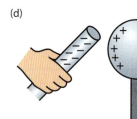
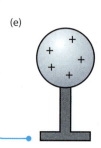

▶ **Figure 15.12**
Charging a metal sphere by induction.
(a) An uncharged metal sphere.
(b) A negatively charged polythene rod is brought near to the sphere. Electrons are repelled to the far side of the sphere.
(c) An earth connection is made to the sphere. Electrons are repelled to earth.
(d) The earth connection is removed.
(e) The polythene rod is removed and the sphere is left positively charged.

 Activity 15.5
Charging by induction

Electrostatics

QUESTIONS

15.4 a) State the laws of electrostatics.
b) A student has four charged rods. Rod A is positively charged. She makes a table to show what happens when each of the rods are brought up to each other.

	Rod A	Rod B	Rod C	Rod D
Rod A	X	Attract	Attract	Attract
Rod B	Attract	X	Repel	Attract
Rod C	Attract	Repel	X	Attract
Rod D	Attract	Attract	Attract	X

What conclusions can you make about the charge on each rod?

15.5 a)

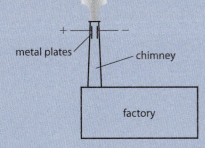

◀ Figure 15.13

Figure 15.13 shows a system used for reducing pollution from a factory chimney.
Suggest why this reduces pollution from the chimney.
b) It is often observed that dust collects much more on a television screen than on the surrounding area. Suggest what this observation tells us about the television screen.

15.6 Fig.15.14 shows two metal plates.
a) Copy and complete the diagram to show the electric field between the plates.
b) Explain what would happen to a small, negatively charged dust particle that is put between the plates.

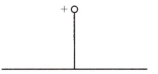
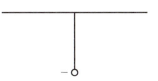

▲ Figure 15.14

15.7 The circuit in Figure 15.15 shows a lamp being lit by a battery.
a) What does the arrow labelled X show?
b) There is a current of 0.50 A in the bulb.
  (i) Calculate the charge passing through the bulb in 5 minutes.
  (ii) Calculate the number of electrons passing through the bulb in that time. (An electron has a charge of 1.6×10^{-19} C)

15.8 An electron has a charge of 1.6×10^{-19} C.
Calculate the current if 10^{15} electrons pass through a conductor each second.

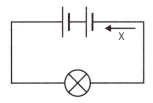

▲ Figure 15.15

15.9 Explain how you could charge a metal sphere negatively, using the method of induction.

Summary

Now that you have completed this chapter, you should be able to:

- recognise that electrical charges can be produced by friction
- recognise that there are two types of charge
- state the laws of electrostatics
- recognise that current is a flow of electric charge
- understand the meaning of the term *electric field*
- understand the difference between conductors and insulators
- understand that the electric field can be represented by lines of force
- recall and use the equation $Q = I \times t$.

Chapter 16

Potential difference and more circuits

Interest in developing electrically driven cars has increased in recent years, owing to the pollution caused by petrol driven cars and the limited availability of oil.

Alessandro Volta invented an early battery (a 'voltaic pile') in about 1800. It was the first device that produced a steady electric current. However, it is only recently that battery technology has developed to the extent that battery-powered cars are viable.

The limited range of purely electrically driven cars is one of their major disadvantages — an alternative is the hybrid car which has both electric and petrol engines. For town driving, the electric motor is used, and for longer journeys the petrol engine is used.

▲ Figure 16.1
The Ze-0 electric car was unveiled at the 2008 British International Motor Show. It has a range of 100 kilometres using metal-hydride batteries. Modern electric cars use the energy converted in braking to help recharge the batteries, which increases their range. For a full recharge, the batteries are plugged into the mains overnight.

16.1 Potential difference

For a current to light a bulb there must be a source of electricity, such as a cell. It is the cell that causes the charge to move. The cell gives the charge electrical potential energy. In Figure 16.2, the charge at point X in the circuit will have very little energy. The cell gives the charge energy so that it has a lot of energy when it is at point Y. Work is done as the charge travels through the bulb and the potential energy is converted into internal energy.

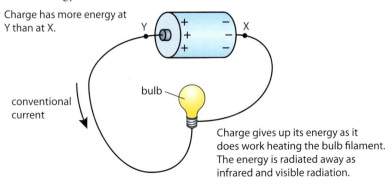

◀ Figure 16.2
Battery powering a light bulb.

155

We say there is a **potential difference** between points X and Y. The potential difference is measured in a unit called the **volt**. The instrument used to measure potential difference is the **voltmeter**.

The volt is defined as the potential difference between two points when 1 coulomb of charge gains (or loses) 1 joule of energy as it passes between the two points.

$$1\ V = 1\ \frac{J}{C}$$

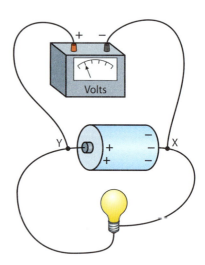

Figure 16.3
The voltmeter acts as a probe testing the energy of the charge at each of the two points.

DID YOU KNOW?

The current is the same all the way round the circuit just as the flow of water is the same all the way round a heating circuit. The water in the system gives up its internal energy as it goes through the radiators. In a similar way, the electric charge gives up potential energy as it goes through a lamp.

One lead from the voltmeter is connected to point Y and the other to point X. Note that the positive terminal of the voltmeter is connected to the positive end of the cell.

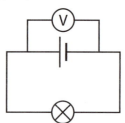

Figure 16.4
Circuit diagram showing the circuit in Figure 16.3. The symbol for the voltmeter is the circle with a 'V' in it.

Measuring the potential difference across cells

Activity 16.1
Measuring potential difference

(a) 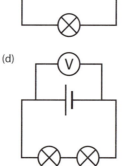 (b) 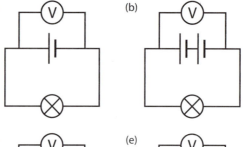 (c)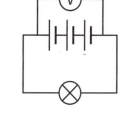

(d) 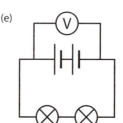 (e) (f)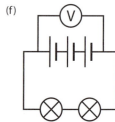

Figure 16.5
The potential difference is measured in the circuit diagrams here and the results recorded in Table 16.1.

156

Potential difference and more circuits

Circuit	Potential difference (V)
a	1.5
b	3.0
c	4.5
d	1.5
e	3.0
f	4.5

◀ Table 16.1
Potential difference measured from the circuits in Figure 16.5.

Hint

The potential difference does *not* depend on the number of bulbs in the circuit. It depends only on the number of *cells* in the circuit. Each cell gives each coulomb of charge 1.5 joules of energy.

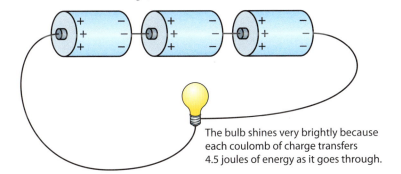

◀ Figure 16.6
More cells in a circuit increases the potential difference.

  Activity 16.2
Measuring potential difference in a circuit

16.2 Cells and e.m.f.

A typical dry cell gives each coulomb of charge about 1.5 V of energy; we say that the **e.m.f.** of the cell is 1.5 V. We use the term e.m.f. when a source of electricity gives energy to the charge. Different types of cell have different values of e.m.f., depending on the chemicals in the cell. Table 16.2 gives some examples.

Use a dry cell to light a bulb for about a minute. If you then feel the cell, you will find it is warm. Some work is done in actually driving the current through the cell. In doing this work, the potential energy of the cell is converted to internal energy in the cell (Figure 16.7).

The formal definition of e.m.f. takes this into account.

The e.m.f. of a cell is the total work done in driving one coulomb of charge round the complete circuit.

▼ Table 16.2
Cell e.m.f.s.

Type of cell	E.m.f. (V)
Dry cell	1.49
Mercury cell	1.35
Nickel-cadmium cell	1.25
Lead acid cell	2.16

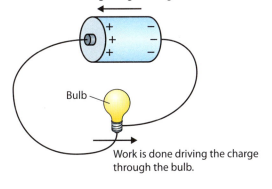

◀ Figure 16.7
Work done in a simple circuit.

157

DID YOU KNOW?

Ω is the Greek capital letter omega, equivalent to O.

16.3 Resistance

We have already seen that the current in a circuit depends on the number of bulbs. The more bulbs, the smaller the current. We say that the bulbs resist the flow of charge.

The **resistance** of an electrical component is defined from the formula:

$$\text{resistance} = \frac{\text{potential difference}}{\text{current}}$$

$$R = \frac{V}{I}$$

Activity 16.3
How does current vary with potential difference?

Units

The base unit of potential difference is the volt (V) and the base unit of current is the ampere (A). The unit of resistance is formed by dividing volts by amperes, giving volts per ampere.

1 volt per ampere is given a special name, the **ohm**.

The symbol given to the ohm is Ω.

Measuring resistance of a constantan wire

To measure the resistance of a component we need to measure both the potential difference across it and the current through it. Figure 16.8 shows the circuit used to measure the resistance of a length of wire.

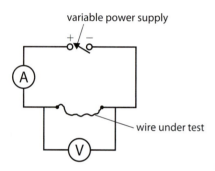

▲ Figure 16.8
Measuring the resistance of a wire.

The values of potential difference and the current are recorded and the resistance calculated.

WORKED EXAMPLE

$V = 6.0$ V
$I = 2.4$ A

$$R = \frac{V}{I}$$
$$= \frac{6.0}{2.4} \, \Omega$$
$$= 2.5 \, \Omega$$

Hint

If potential difference is in volts and current is in amperes, the resistance will work out in ohms.

Resistance and resistors

If a series of readings of current for different supply voltages is taken and a graph of potential difference against current is plotted, a straight-line graph will be obtained, provided the wire does not get hot.

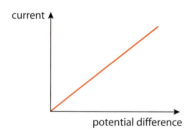

▲ Figure 16.9
V-I graph for a wire.

This shows that the resistance of the wire is constant and does not change with current.

A similar experiment shows that the resistance of the filament of a bulb increases as the current increases. The current heats the filament

158

Potential difference and more circuits

to white heat. The vibration of the atoms increases, making it more difficult for the electrons to pass through it.

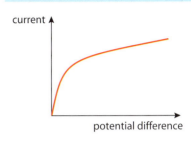

Figure 16.10
V–I graph for a lamp filament.

Figure 16.11
Set value resistances are often required in circuits. These are known as **resistors**.

Figure 16.12
Variable resistors have several uses.

Figure 16.13
Variable resistance in a circuit.

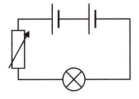

The variable resistance in the circuit in Figure 16.13 is used to control the brightness of the lamp. The smaller the resistance, the larger the current and hence the brighter the lamp.

Figure 16.14
Circuit diagram symbols for (a) a resistor and (b) a variable resistor.

QUESTIONS

16.1 Figure 16.15 shows a circuit in which the resistance of a resistor is being measured. The reading on the voltmeter is 1.5 V and the reading on the ammeter is 0.20 A.
Calculate the value of the resistor.

16.2 A battery of e.m.f. 6.0 V is connected across a 45 Ω resistor.
Calculate the current through the resistor.

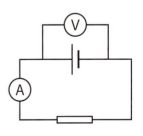

▲ **Figure 16.15**

159

Activity 16.4
How does length affect resistance?

Activity 16.5
How does thickness affect resistance?

Factors affecting resistance

Material

We have already seen that the material an object is made from determines how well it conducts. Non-metals tend to be very poor conductors, whereas metals are good conductors. However some metals conduct better than others. Silver, copper and aluminium are excellent conductors. Iron, lead and the alloy nichrome are much poorer conductors, although still classed as conductors.

Length

For a given material, resistance increases with length.

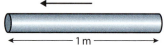

▶ **Figure 16.16**
A two metre length of nichrome wire will have a larger resistance than a one-metre length of the same wire.

The resistance of a wire is proportional to its length.

$R \propto L$

WORKED EXAMPLE

A reel of nichrome wire is marked as having a resistance of 6.6 Ω/m. Calculate the length of wire required to make a resistor of value 50 Ω.

$R \propto L$

or $R = kL$ where k is a constant equal to the resistance per metre.

$50 = 6.6 \times L$

$L = \dfrac{50}{6.6}$ m

$= 7.6$ m   (to 2 sig. figs.)

Diameter

A thicker wire will have less resistance than a thinner one made of the same material and of the same length.

If the cross-sectional area is increased, it is rather like having more wires in parallel. You will recall that connecting resistors in parallel reduces the total resistance.

▶ **Figure 16.17**
Resistance is higher in thinner wires.

The resistance of a wire is inversely proportional to its cross-sectional area

$$R \propto \frac{1}{A} \quad \text{where } A = \text{cross-sectional area}$$

The cross-sectional area $= \pi \left(\frac{d}{2}\right)^2$

Therefore $\quad R \propto \dfrac{1}{d^2}$

WORKED EXAMPLE

A wire of diameter 0.24 mm and resistance 3.6 Ω is replaced by a wire of the same length and made from the same material, but of diameter 0.12 mm.

Calculate the resistance of the replacement wire.

$R \propto \dfrac{1}{A}$ or, more usefully, $R \propto \dfrac{1}{d^2}$

If the diameter is halved (divided by 2) the cross-sectional area is divided by $2^2 = 4$.
Therefore the resistance is increased by a factor of 4.
The new resistance = 3.6 Ω × 4 = **14.4 Ω**

QUESTIONS

16.3 Figure 16.18 shows four wires, all made from the same material. State, giving your reasons, which wire would have the greatest resistance.

◀ Figure 16.18

16.4 Table 16.3 shows the dimensions of different wires made from the same copper-nickel alloy.
The first line shows the resistance of a wire of length 1.0 m and diameter 0.20 mm.
Use this information to calculate the resistance of the remaining wires. Show your working in each case.

	Length (m)	Diameter (mm)	Resistance (Ω)
a)	1.0	0.20	16.7
b)	2.5	0.20	
c)	1.0	0.40	
d)	2.5	0.40	
e)	4.0	0.10	

◀ Table 16.3

16.4 Series and parallel circuits

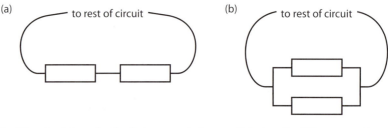

▶ Figure 16.19
(a) Resistors connected in series.
(b) Resistors connected in parallel.

In Chapter 14 we looked at currents in parallel circuits. These questions revise this work.

QUESTIONS

16.5 Ammeter 1 in Figure 16.20 reads 2.4 A.
Write down the readings on ammeters 2 and 3.

▶ Figure 16.20

16.6 The reading on ammeter 2 in Figure 16.21 is 2.0 A, and the reading on ammeter 3 is 5.0 A.
Calculate the reading on ammeter 1.

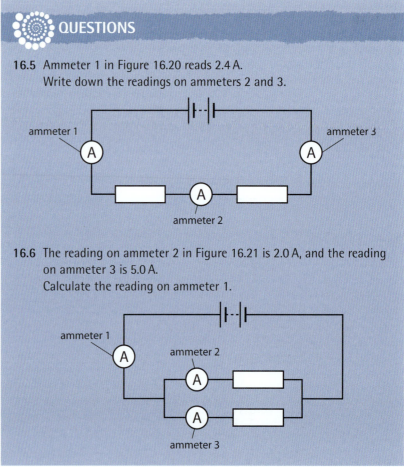

▶ Figure 16.21

Combined resistance of resistors in series

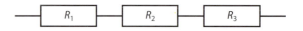

▶ Figure 16.22
Resistors in series.

The combined resistance of resistors in series is the sum of the individual resistors.

$$R_{total} = R_1 + R_2 + R_3$$

162

Potential difference and more circuits

WORKED EXAMPLE

A student connects three resistors of values 6.0 Ω, 4.5 Ω, and 8.0 Ω in series.

Calculate the resistance of the combination.

$$R_{total} = R_1 + R_2 + R_3$$
$$R_{total} = (6.0 + 4.5 + 8.0) \, \Omega$$
$$= 18.5 \, \Omega$$

Activity 16.6
Potential differences in a series circuit

When there is a current, the charge at one side of the battery has more energy than at the other. This energy is converted into internal energy as the charge passes through the resistors. The energy lost by the charge in the resistors must be equal to the excess energy the charge had at the battery. The definition of potential difference is the energy lost or gained by each coulomb of charge as it passes from point A to point B. Therefore it follows that the potential difference across the battery is equal to the sum of the potential differences across the resistors.

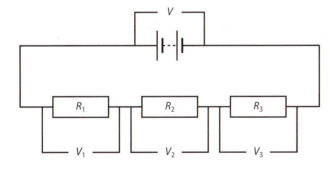

◀ **Figure 16.23**
$V = V_1 + V_2 + V_3$

Activity 16.7
Potential differences and current in a parallel circuit

Combined resistance of resistors in parallel

The potential difference across each of the resistors in Figure 16.24 is the same and this is equal to the resistance across the battery.

The current splits at the junction so the total current from the supply is greater than the current through any of the individual resistors.

We defined resistance from the formula $R = \dfrac{V}{I}$. It follows that the larger the current for the same potential difference, the smaller the resistance. Thus the combined resistance of resistors in parallel is less than that of any of the individual resistors.

▶ **Figure 16.24**
The combined resistance of resistors in parallel is less than that of any of the individual resistors.

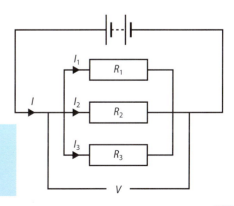

163

No current is lost when it splits at the junction, so it follows that the current from the supply is equal to the sum of the currents in each of the resistors.

$I_{total} = I_1 + I_2 + I_3$

The combined resistance of the resistors is calculated from the formula:

$$\frac{1}{R_{total}} = \frac{1}{R_1} + \frac{1}{R_2} + \frac{1}{R_3}$$

WORKED EXAMPLE

A student connects three resistors of values 6.0 Ω, 4.5 Ω, and 9.0 Ω in parallel.

Calculate the resistance of the combination.

$\frac{1}{R_{total}} = \frac{1}{R_1} + \frac{1}{R_2} + \frac{1}{R_3}$

$\frac{1}{R_{total}} = \frac{1}{6.0} + \frac{1}{4.5} + \frac{1}{9.0}$

Hint
We need to add these fractions.

$= \frac{3 + 4 + 2}{18}$

$= \frac{9}{18} = \frac{1}{2}$

Hint
Don't forget $\frac{1}{2}$ is $\frac{1}{R_{total}}$ and must be inverted.

$R_{total} = 2\,\Omega$

Some practical circuitry

Lighting circuits in the home or other lighting circuits, such as the lighting circuit in a motor vehicle, are always connected in parallel.

There are two reasons for this.

- Lamps are designed to operate at a fixed potential difference – no matter how many lamps are in a parallel circuit, the potential difference across them is always the supply potential difference. In a series circuit, the potential difference is shared out between the lamps, so the more lamps there are, the smaller the potential difference across each one and the dimmer each will be.

▶ **Figure 16.25**
In the first circuit the lamps are in parallel so that there is the same potential drop across each lamp, so each lamp is lit to full brightness. In the second diagram the lamps are in series, the potential difference is shared between them and they will be much dimmer.

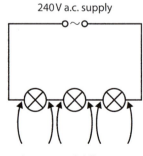

The potential difference is shared between the bulbs.

164

Potential difference and more circuits

- If the lamps are connected in series then they must all be switched on or they must all be switched off, as a single break in the circuit breaks the whole circuit. In the parallel circuit, the lamps can be switched separately as each lamp is in its own separate arm.

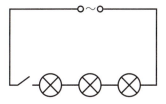
All the lamps must either be switched on or all switched off.

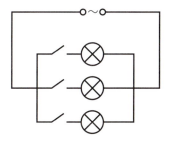
Each lamp can be switched on and off separately.

◀ **Figure 16.26**
Separate switches in parallel circuits.

QUESTIONS

16.7 Three lamps are connected in series. One of the lamps blows. Explain what happens in the rest of the circuit.

16.8 Three bulbs are now connected in parallel. Again, one of the bulbs blows. Explain what would happen in the rest of the circuit.

Electrical safety

Electrical hazards

A potential difference of about 50 V across a person can drive a large enough current through the person to kill them. The potential difference across the mains supply in Britain is about 230 V. It is clear that care must be taken. Figure 16.27 shows some possible hazards.

◀ **Figure 16.27**
(a) Lighting circuits are designed to take a maximum current of 5 A, but the heater takes 12 A. The cables in the wiring circuit will overheat and cause a fire.
b) Water conducts electricity. If a person touches the switch with wet hands, they may well complete a low resistance path to earth. Wall switches are illegal in bathrooms; pull switches must be used.
c) For the same reason, sockets are not allowed in bathrooms. In this case it is even worse – the insulation on both the cable to the socket and the flex to the radio are both damaged. The person could easily touch the bare wires and be electrocuted.

165

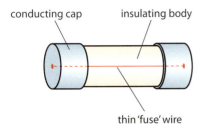

▲ Figure 16.28
A fuse.

▲ Figure 16.29
A circuit breaker.

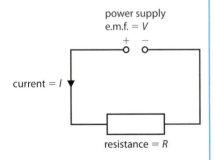

▲ Figure 16.30

▶ Figure 16.31
Light bulbs, power tools, electric irons are all rated in terms of the power needed to run them. For example, the electric iron has a power rating of 800 W. This means that 800 J of electrical energy are converted into internal energy every second.

Fuses

Fuses are designed to protect the user and the wiring. If there is too large a current the fuse wire melts, breaking the circuit. Fuses are always connected in series with the main circuit but different types have different functions.

In a household wiring system there is a fuse box. The fuses in this are designed to protect the wiring. If too large a current flows through the wiring, there is a danger the wires will get hot and start a fire. The fuse is designed to break the circuit before this happens.

You will also find fuses in the plugs of mains appliances such as televisions, washing machines and electric fires. These have a dual function.

- If a loose wire touches the casing of the appliance, it will give anyone touching the appliance a nasty electric shock or even electrocute them. To prevent this, the metal casing of the appliance is connected to Earth. If a live wire does touch the casing there is a large current to Earth which will blow the fuse, isolating the equipment.
- If there is a current larger than that required for the equipment, the fuse will blow in a similar way. This prevents damage to the electronics of the appliance.

You can see that, for safety reasons and to protect your equipment, it is important to fit the correct fuse.

A **circuit breaker** can be used instead of a fuse. Circuit breakers are electromagnetic switches that open automatically if there is too large a current. They have the advantage of being easy to reset and they act more quickly than fuses, so less damage occurs.

16.5 Energy and power

500 W

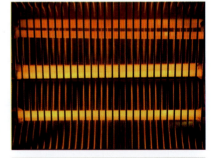

2 kW

800 W

5 W

Potential difference and more circuits

Energy conversion

We have already defined the volt as the potential difference between two points when one coulomb of charge gains (or loses) 1 joule of energy as it moves between the points. This leads to the formula:

$$\text{potential difference} = \frac{\text{energy}}{\text{charge}}$$

Rearranging the formula:

energy = potential difference × charge

and charge = current × time

Therefore, substituting in the previous equation:

energy = potential difference × charge × time

or $E = VIt$

Note that for energy to be calculated in joules, voltage V must be in volts, current I must be in amperes and time t in seconds.

WORKED EXAMPLE

An electric fire takes a current of 12 A when run from a 240 V supply.

Calculate the energy used when the fire is switched on for 1 hour.

$E = VIt$

$E = 240 \times 12 \times 3600$ J

$= 10\,368\,000$ J

$= \mathbf{10\,400\,000\,J}$ or $\mathbf{10\,MJ}$

Hint
Time must be measured in seconds.

Hint
Final answer is rounded to 2 significant figures.

From Chapter 6, you will remember that power is the work done (or energy converted) per unit time.

$$\text{power} = \frac{\text{energy converted}}{\text{time}}$$

If we substitute for the energy from the energy equation we get:

$$\text{power} = \frac{\text{potential difference} \times \text{current} \times \cancel{\text{time}}}{\cancel{\text{time}}}$$

power = potential difference × current or $P = VI$

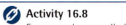
Activity 16.8
Energy and power dissipated

167

WORKED EXAMPLE

A light bulb is labelled 240 V, 60 W.

Calculate the current it will take when operating at its recommended potential difference.

$$P = VI$$
$$I = \frac{P}{V}$$
$$= \frac{60}{240} \text{ A}$$
$$= \textbf{0.25 A}$$

Alternative formulae for energy conversion

We can use the equation *power = potential difference × current* in this circuit.

We also know that potential difference = current × resistance.

Substitute this in the power formula:

power = (current × resistance) × current

or **power = (current)² × resistance** or $P = I^2 R$

In a similar way we can substitute for the current in the original formula to give:

$$\text{energy} = \frac{\textbf{(potential difference)}^2}{\textbf{resistance}} \quad \text{or} \quad P = \frac{V^2}{R}$$

QUESTIONS

16.9 A car headlamp bulb is rated 12 V, 36 W.
Calculate the current it takes when running at its recommended potential difference.

16.10 Calculate the power converted in a 20 Ω resistor when there is a current of 0.50 A.

Potential difference and more circuits

16.11 Calculate the potential difference across a lamp which has a resistance of 4.8 Ω when there is a current of 2.5 A.

16.12

◀ Figure 16.32

Ian uses an extension cable so that he can put the radio on the side of the bath to listen to it. Explain what would happen if he knocked the radio into the bath.

16.13 A 12 V supply is connected across a 6 Ω resistor for 5 minutes. Calculate the energy converted.

16.14 a) Explain what is meant by the term e.m.f.
b) A battery of e.m.f. 6.0 V drives a current of 15 A in a motor. The power converted in the motor is 87 W. Calculate
   (i) the potential drop across the motor
   (ii) the work done per second in driving the charge through the battery.

16.15 Figure 16.33 shows an electron in an electric field. The potential difference between the plates is 5000 V.
a) Calculate the energy the electron gains when it moves from plate A to plate B.
b) Suggest what form of energy the electron gains.

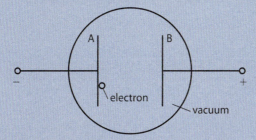

◀ Figure 16.33

(Charge on an electron = 1.6×10^{-19} C)

16.16 A student has three 6 Ω resistors.
She says that she can make seven different values of resistance, using the resistors in different combinations.
Draw a diagram for each combination and calculate the resistance of each.
Draw diagrams to show the different ways the resistors are connected to obtain each value and calculate the value.

169

Summary

Now that you have completed this chapter, you should be able to:

- understand and use the terms e.*m.f.* and *potential difference*

- use a voltmeter to measure potential difference

- understand and use the term *resistance*

- recall and use the equation $R = \dfrac{V}{I}$

- recognise the factors which affect the resistance of a conductor

- understand that the current is the same all the way round a series circuit

- calculate the combined resistance of resistors in series

- understand that the current in each arm of a parallel circuit is less than the current from the source

- understand that the combined resistance of two or more resistors in parallel is less than that of either resistor by itself

- understand why lighting circuits are connected in parallel

- be aware of the hazards of electrical circuits

- understand the use and operation of fuses

- recognise and make calculations using the relationship between resistance and the length and cross-sectional area of conductors

- understand that the sum of potential differences round a circuit is equal to the potential difference across the supply

- understand that the current from the source is equal to the sum of the currents in each branch of a parallel circuit

- calculate the combined resistance of two or more resistors in parallel

- recall and use the equations $E = VIt$

- recall and use the equations $P = VI = I^2R = \dfrac{V^2}{R}$.

Chapter 17

Electromagnetism

▲ Figure 17.1
The maglev train at Shanghai Pudong Airport.

Maglev trains are increasingly common throughout the world, but how do they work?

The train is propelled by a linear induction motor. The track consists of a series of electromagnets, which are magnetised so that north-seeking and south-seeking poles are alternately facing upwards.

The induced magnets in the train are pulled towards the next opposite set of poles. When it reaches that set, the electromagnets in the track change direction so that the train is now pulled towards the next set, and so on.

There is one other effect: the induced poles in the track react with the electromagnets so that the train is pushed upwards. This makes it float about a centimetre above the track so there is no friction between the train and track, unlike in a normal train.

17.1 The motor effect

The force on a current in a magnetic field

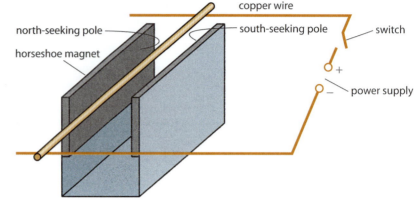

▶ Figure 17.2
Force on a current in a magnetic field.

A thick copper wire is placed between the jaws of a horseshoe magnet, resting on two thick copper wires. (Figure 17.2). These two wires are connected to a power supply unit. When the switch is closed the wire between the jaws of the magnet shoots upwards.

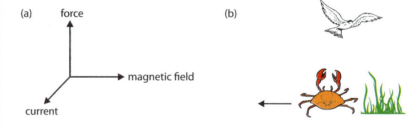

▶ Figure 17.3
(a) The electromagnetic force is quite unlike the gravitational and electrostatic force. The force of gravity and the electrostatic force are in the same direction as the fields. The electromagnetic force is at right angles to both the magnetic field and the current that experiences it.
(b) The electromagnetic force has been likened to the seashore crab: 'On sensing danger from above it looks straight ahead and scuttles away sideways!'

Investigation of the directions of current, field and force

We have already seen that the current, the magnetic field and the force are all at right angles to each other. A current balance can be used to investigate this further.

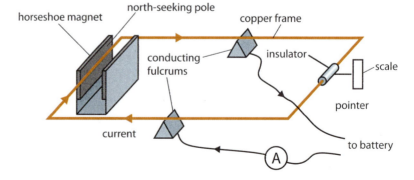

▶ Figure 17.4
A current balance.

Activity 17.2
The motor effect 2

In the experiment shown in Figure 17.4, there is a force upwards on the wire between the poles of the magnet, causing the frame to move so the pointer moves downwards on the scale.

Activity 17.1
The motor effect 1

- If the current is reversed, the direction of the force on the wire is also reversed, so the pointer moves upwards.
- The magnet is now reversed so that the poles are the opposite way round. Again the force is reversed, so once more the pointer moves downwards.
- Increasing the current causes the pointer to move further, showing that the force is greater.

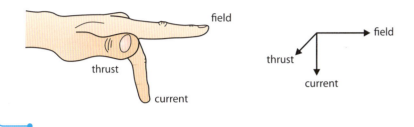

Figure 17.5
We can predict the direction of the force by making a set of axes with the fingers of our **left** hand. The **th**umb represents the force or **th**rust, the **fi**rst finger the **fi**eld and the second finger the **c**urrent. This method for finding the direction of the force is known as Fleming's Left Hand Rule.

The electric motor

A current-carrying coil of wire is placed between the jaws of a magnet. The current in the two sides of the coil are in opposite directions, so the forces on the two sides are also in opposite directions. This produces a turning effect on the coil and the coil rotates about the axle. This is called the **motor effect**.

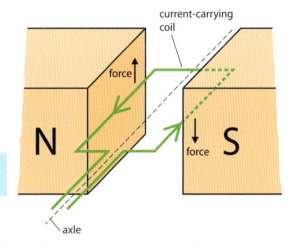

▶ **Figure 17.6**
The motor effect.

The simple electric motor

The current is supplied to the coil using a split **ring commutator** and **carbon brushes**. If the coil were connected directly to the power supply, the wires would twist and break. A further problem is that each half-turn, the direction of the turning effect on the coil would reverse, causing it to vibrate rather than rotate.

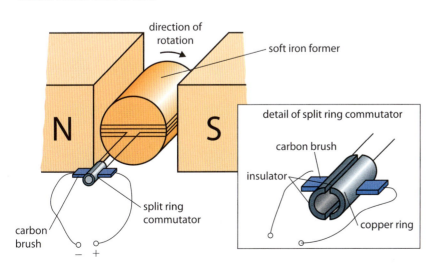

◀ **Figure 17.7**
A simple electric motor.

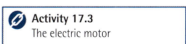
Activity 17.3
The electric motor

173

The coil has many turns and is wound on a soft iron former. The soft iron becomes magnetised, strengthening the magnetic field, so there is a greater turning effect on the coil.

The turning effect can be increased by
- increasing the number of turns on the coil
- increasing the current
- increasing the magnetic field strength.

How the commutator works

▶ Figure 17.8
How a commutator works.

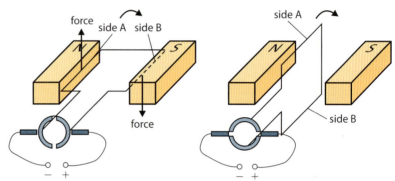

The brushes pass the current to the commutator, which passes the current to the coil, causing it to rotate.

After a quarter of a revolution the brushes are between the split rings, the coil continues to rotate due to its own momentum.

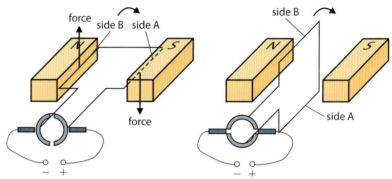

After another quarter revolution the sides of the coil are in contact with the opposite half of the split ring, so the current in the coil reverses and the couple remains in the same direction.

After another quarter revolution the coil is once again vertical, there are no forces on it and it continues to rotate back to the original position.

▼ Figure 17.9

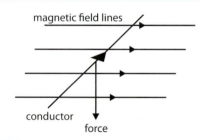

QUESTIONS

17.1 Fig. 17.9 shows a current carrying conductor in a magnetic field.
   a) Suggest two ways in which the force on the conductor could be increased.
   b) State what would happen if the current in the conductor were reversed.

17.2 Give a practical example of the use of an electric motor in
   a) the home, b) industry, c) medicine.

17.2 Electromagnetic induction

An e.m.f. can be generated by moving a wire in a magnetic field. When a wire is moved perpendicularly through a magnetic field, as shown in Figure 17.10, the needle on the **millivoltmeter** gives a kick, showing the induced e.m.f. If the wire is moved parallel to the field from the north-seeking pole to the south, the millivoltmeter does not record a reading. Just as with the motor effect, the field, the movement and the e.m.f. induced are all at right angles. This is the opposite effect to the motor effect. Table 17.1 shows the comparison.

▼ Table 17.1
Comparing the motor effect with electromagnetic induction.

Motor effect	Electromagnetic induction
Current, field and movement are all at right angles to each other.	Induced e.m.f., field and movement are all at right angles to each other.
A current is passed through the conductor causing it to move.	The conductor is moved inducing an e.m.f. in it.

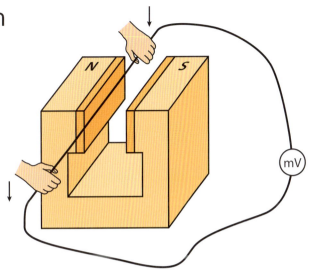

▲ Figure 17.10
Inducing an e.m.f.

Activity 17.4
Electromagnetic induction 1

Factors affecting the magnitude of an induced e.m.f.

When a double loop of wire is used, the kick on the millivoltmeter is twice as large as before. A triple loop induces three times the e.m.f. and so on. This shows that the e.m.f. is proportional to the number of turns in a coil.

The faster the wire is moved, the larger the kick, but the shorter the time it lasts for. This indicates that the speed at which the conductor moves through the magnetic field also determines the magnitude of the induced e.m.f.

It can also be shown that the longer the length of the conductor in the magnetic field then the greater the induced e.m.f.

These rules can be summed up by what is known as Faraday's law of electromagnetism.

The induced e.m.f. is proportional to the rate at which the magnetic field is cut.

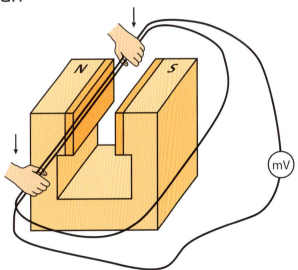

▲ Figure 17.11
Doubling the number of coils doubles the e.m.f.

175

> **DID YOU KNOW?**
>
> The son of a blacksmith, and himself apprenticed to a bookbinder, Michael Faraday became known as the father of electromagnetism. He educated himself by reading and attending evening lectures. He eventually got a job on the staff of Humphrey Davy, the inventor of the miners' safety lamp. In the 1820s, he demonstrated 'electromagnetic rotation', the forerunner of the electric motor. In 1831 he discovered electromagnetic induction. Before this, current could only be produced by batteries. Faraday's discovery opened the door to the possibility of commercial generation of electricity.

▼ Figure 17.12
An a.c. generator.

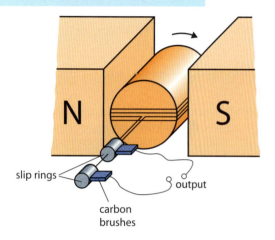

The a.c. generator

We have already seen how electromagnetic induction is the opposite effect to the motor effect. In the same way, the generator is the opposite of the motor. In the motor, the current in the coil causes the coil to rotate. In the generator, the coil is rotated by an external source, and its movement induces an e.m.f.

As the coil rotates, an e.m.f. is induced in the coil. At each half cycle, the direction of the e.m.f. reverses.

Unlike the d.c. motor, the current is taken from the coil using **slip rings** and carbon brushes. This means that the same brush is in contact with the same ring all the time. Consequently the current in the external circuit also changes direction each half cycle.

▶ Figure 17.13
(a) The sides of the coil are cutting the field at right angles, so the rate of cutting is at its greatest. The induced e.m.f. is maximum.
(b) The rate of cutting field decreases, until the coil is vertical and the sides are moving parallel to the field, so the induced e.m.f. is zero.
(c) The coil is again cutting field at the maximum rate, but now each side is moving in the opposite direction to (a), so the induced e.m.f. is in the opposite direction.
(d) Once more the sides of the coil are moving parallel to the field, so the e.m.f. is zero.
(e) The coil is back to the same position as in (a), so the cycle starts again.

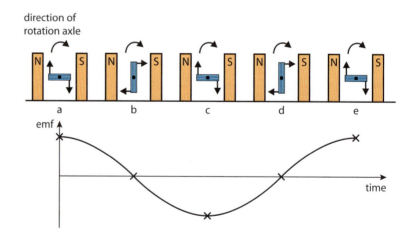

This type of e.m.f., which continuously changes direction, is known as an **alternating e.m.f.** The current it produces is known as an **alternating current (a.c.)**.

This compares with the current from a battery, which is always in the same direction and is known as a **direct current (d.c.)**.

Electromagnetism

QUESTIONS

17.3 Figure 17.14 shows a wire being moved between two magnets.

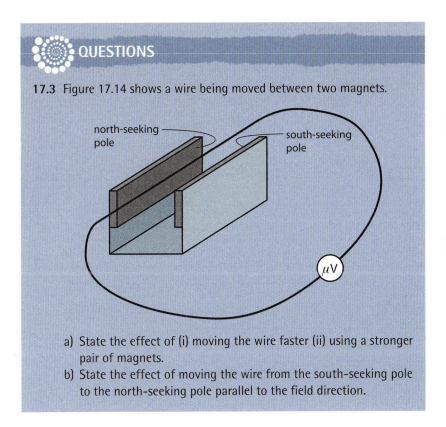

◀ Figure 17.14

◆ Activity 17.5
The electric generator

a) State the effect of (i) moving the wire faster (ii) using a stronger pair of magnets.
b) State the effect of moving the wire from the south-seeking pole to the north-seeking pole parallel to the field direction.

Induction of an e.m.f. in a solenoid

A magnet is moved towards a solenoid, as shown in Figure 17.15(a). As the field from the magnet cuts across the turns of the solenoid, an e.m.f. is induced in the coil, which causes a current in the milliammeter. A similar effect occurs when the magnet is moved away from the coil (Figure 17.15(b), but the current is in the opposite direction. The magnet can be kept still and the solenoid moved; again an e.m.f. will be induced. But if the magnet and the solenoid are moved along together there is no induced e.m.f. — it is the relative movement between the magnet and solenoid that induces the e.m.f.

◆ Activity 17.6
Electromagnetic induction 2

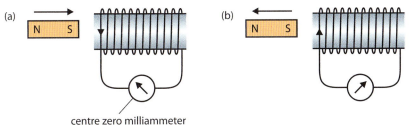

◀ Figure 17.15
Induced e.m.f.

Lenz's Law – are we getting something for nothing?

We studied the magnetic fields of current carrying solenoids in Chapter 13, and the field of a such a solenoid is very similar to that of a bar magnet. When the south-seeking pole approaches the coil in Figure 17.15(a), the current in the coil makes that face of the solenoid into a

177

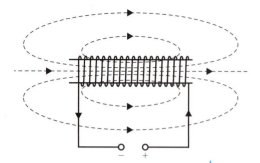

▲ Figure 17.16
The magnetic field of a current carrying solenoid is similar to that of a bar magnet.

south-seeking pole. The two south-seeking poles repel, so work must be done to bring the magnet up to it.

Similarly, when the south-seeking pole is moved away from the solenoid (Figure 17.15(b), a north-seeking pole is induced on that face of the coil. The two poles attract, so again work must be done to move the magnet away.

A German scientist, Heinrich Lenz, summed this up in the law now known as Lenz's law.

The direction of an induced e.m.f. is always in such a direction so as to oppose, or tend to oppose the change that causes it.

Lenz's law is an example of conservation of energy. We use chemical potential energy to do the work to move the magnet against the induced field. This energy is then converted into electrical potential energy.

We clearly do not get something for nothing — to generate electric potential energy we must do mechanical work.

More experiments with solenoids

The experimental set up in Figure 17.17 is similar to that in Figure 17.15, except that the magnet is replaced by a solenoid connected to a battery.

Switch S is closed and the solenoid is brought up to the other solenoid. The millivoltmeter gives a kick, just as though a magnet had been brought up to it. This is not surprising – the first solenoid merely replaces the magnet used in the earlier experiments and its field cuts the turns of the second solenoid.

▶ Figure 17.17
Induced e.m.f. using solenoids.

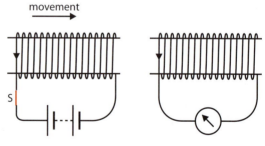

Now for the amazing thing! The switch is now opened, and the needle gives another kick – just as though the solenoids had been moved apart!

The switch is now closed again – again an e.m.f. is induced, this time as if the solenoids had been brought towards each other. The second solenoid 'sees' the magnetic field getting stronger or fading away. The changing magnetic field cuts across the coils of the solenoid and an e.m.f. is induced.

The introduction of a soft iron bar linking the two solenoids, as in Figure 17.18, increases the induced e.m.f.. It magnifies the magnetic field from the first solenoid and channels it through the second solenoid. This is even more effective if a continuous loop of soft iron is used to link the two solenoids.

Electromagnetism

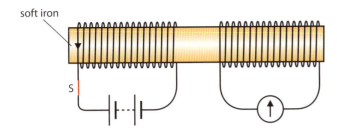

Figure 17.18
The meter kicks when the switch is opened.

The transformer

The transformer consists of two coils, the **primary** and the **secondary**, linked by a soft iron core. In the last section, we saw how a changing magnetic field can induce an e.m.f. In the transformer an alternating current in the primary coil produces a continuously changing or alternating magnetic field. The iron core channels the alternating field through the secondary coil, inducing an alternating e.m.f. across it.

Activity 17.7
The transformer

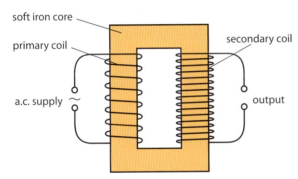

Figure 17.19
The transformer makes use of the interaction of the field between two coils.

The output voltage from the transformer depends on the input voltage and the ratio of the number of turns in the two coils. If there are more turns in the secondary coil than in the primary, the output voltage will be greater than the input voltage. This type of transformer is known as a **step-up transformer**.

If there are fewer turns in the secondary coil than in the primary, the output voltage will be smaller than the voltage. This type of transformer is known as a **step-down transformer**.

Transformers are used in many types of electrical equipment. Television sets have a step-up transformer as high voltages are needed to accelerate the electron beam (see Chapter 18).

A battery charger will have a step-down transformer to reduce the mains voltage to a suitable level to charge a particular battery.

- An alternating current in the primary coil produces a continuously changing magnetic field.
- The soft iron core transmits this field to the secondary.
- The changing magnetic field in the secondary coil induces an e.m.f across the secondary.

The transformer equation

$$\frac{V_{primary}}{V_{secondary}} = \frac{N_{primary}}{N_{secondary}}$$

Where $V_{primary}$ = the voltage across the primary coil
$V_{secondary}$ = the voltage across the secondary coil
$N_{primary}$ = the number of turns in the primary coil
$N_{secondary}$ = the number of turns in the secondary coil

WORKED EXAMPLE

The transformer for an electric train set has 600 turns in its primary coil. It steps the mains voltage of 240 V down to 12 V to operate the train.

Calculate the number of turns required in the secondary coil.

$$\frac{V_{secondary}}{V_{primary}} = \frac{N_{secondary}}{N_{primary}}$$

$$N_{secondary} = \frac{V_{secondary} \times N_{primary}}{V_{primary}}$$

$$= \frac{12 \times 600}{240}$$

$$N_{secondary} = \textbf{30 turns}$$

Are we getting something for nothing?

When a transformer steps a voltage up it might appear that we are getting more energy out of the transformer than we put in. This, however, is not the case; the best we can do is to get the same amount of energy as we put in, and then only if the transformer is 100% efficient. For such a transformer:

$$energy\ input = energy\ output$$

Now electrical energy $= V \times I \times t$

So $V_{primary} \times I_{primary} \times t = V_{secondary} \times I_{secondary} \times t$

$$\boxed{V_{primary} \times I_{primary} = V_{secondary} \times I_{secondary}}$$

Hint

Cancelling t.

WORKED EXAMPLE

A generator uses a step-up transformer to step the output up from 30 V to 240 V to run an emergency lighting system. The maximum current from the generator is 80 A.

Calculate the maximum output current from the transformer, assuming it to be 100% efficient.

$$V_{primary} \times I_{primary} = V_{secondary} \times I_{secondary}$$

$$30 \times 80 = 240 \times I_{secondary}$$

$$I_{secondary} = \frac{30 \times 80}{240}\ A$$

$$= \textbf{10 A}$$

We see from this example with a step-up transformer, that the maximum output current is less than the maximum input current.

Whenever there is a current in a conductor, some energy is converted into internal energy, which heats up the conductor. To reduce heat losses in a step-up transformer, the primary coil (which carries a large current) is made from a few turns of thick wire, whereas the secondary coil (which carries a much smaller current) has many turns of thin wire.

This is reversed for a step-down transformer.

Transmission of electrical energy

Electricity is generated at large power stations and transmitted across the country at around 132 000 V. It is then stepped down for domestic use to around 230 V at local substations.

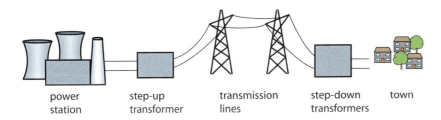

◀ Figure 17.20
Transmission of electricity.

The transmission lines may be several hundred kilometres long, and even if they are thick and made from a low resistance material such as copper, they will still have a significant resistance.

If the energy is transmitted at a relatively low voltage and a high current, there will be a significant amount of heating in the wire. This means energy is wasted in heating the atmosphere.

Power = I^2R, so if the current is halved, the energy loss is cut by a factor of 2^2 or 4. We can begin to see how much energy is saved by transmitting at very high voltages.

Consider a current of 4 A through a resistor of resistance of 6 Ω.

Power = I^2R
= $4^2 \times 6$ W
= 96 W

If the current is halved to 2 A

Power = I^2R
= $2^2 \times 6$ W
= 24 W

The current is halved but the power is quartered.

QUESTIONS

17.4   A transformer has 128 turns on its primary coil and 16 turns on its secondary.
   a) State whether the transformer is a step-up or step-down type.
   b) An alternating supply of 96 V is connected across the primary coil. Calculate the output voltage from the secondary.

17.5   Explain why electrical energy is transmitted across the country at very high voltages.

17.6   A 6 V battery is connected across a transformer. Explain why the output e.m.f. would be zero.

Figure 17.21

Figure 17.22

17.7 Figure 17.21 shows a graph of induced e.m.f. against time, as a coil is rotated in a magnetic field.

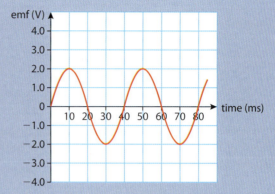

a) Copy the graph and underneath, to the same scale, draw a graph showing the e.m.f. induced when the coil is rotated at twice the speed.
b) Explain the changes you would expect.

17.8 A transformer steps a 12 V supply up to 360 V. Calculate the ratio of the number of turns in the primary coil to the number of turns in the secondary coil.

17.9 Figure 17.22 shows a view, from above, of the design of an ammeter.

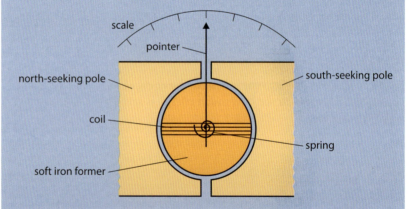

The coil is wound on a soft iron former, which is in a magnetic field. There is also a spring, which limits the rotation of the coil.
a) Explain why the coil is wound on a soft iron former.
b) Suggest why the magnetic poles are circular in shape.
c) Explain in terms of moments why the pointer moves further across the scale when the current increases.

17.10 A transformer has 2000 turns in its primary coil and 125 in its secondary. There is an input potential difference of 240 V across the primary.
a) Calculate the potential difference across the secondary.
b) The current through the primary coil is 0.72 A.
Calculate the current in the secondary coil (you may assume that the coil is 100% efficient).

Electromagnetism

17.11 a) An engineer designs a generator but his customer requires a larger output voltage.
Describe three ways the engineer could modify his design to satisfy his customer.
b) A cyclist is riding along the road, when he decides to switch on his light. The light is driven by a dynamo. He notices that he now has to do more work to keep his bicycle moving at the same speed. Explain, using your knowledge of electromagnetic induction, why he has to do more work.

17.12 Figure 17.23(a) shows a demonstration of energy loss in a transmission line. The two resistance wires have a total resistance of 4 Ω. The bulb is designed to run at 12 V and transfer energy at the rate of 24 W.

a)
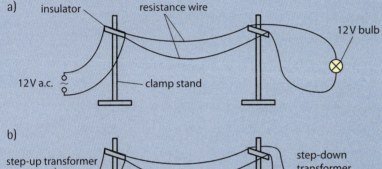

b)

◀ Figure 17.23

a) (i) Calculate the current the lamp is designed to take.
(ii) Calculate the resistance of the lamp.
(iii) Calculate the total resistance in the circuit (assume that the lamp's resistance does not change with temperature).
(iv) Calculate the current in the circuit.
(v) Use the formula $V = I \times R$ to calculate the potential drop across the resistance wires.
(vi) Use the formula $P = I^2 \times R$ to calculate the power loss in the resistance wires.
(vii) Explain why the lamp only lights dimly.
b) Figure 17.23(b) shows the same apparatus but now with a step-up transformer so that the voltage supplied to the resistance wires is 240 V. The second transformer steps the voltage down to supply the 12 V bulb. The power output from the supply remains at 24 W.
(i) Use the formula $P = V \times I$ to calculate the current in the resistance wires.
(ii) Use the formula $V = I \times R$ to calculate the potential drop across the resistance wires.
(iii) Use the formula $P = I^2 \times R$ to calculate the power loss in the resistance wires.
(iv) Explain why the bulb now lights to very nearly full brightness.

Summary

Now that you have completed this chapter, you should be able to:

- describe the effect on a current carrying conductor in a magnetic field

- recognise that the force on a current carrying conductor, the magnetic fields and the current direction are all at right angles to each other

- understand that there is a turning effect on a current carrying coil in a magnetic field

- understand that the magnitude of the turning effect on the coil depends on the number of turns in the coil, the strength of the magnetic field, and the current in the coil

- relate the turning effect to the structure of an electric motor

- understand the use of a split ring commutator and carbon brushes

- describe the induction of an e.m.f. across a conductor due to its movement in a magnetic field

- describe the induction of an e.m.f. across a conductor due to a changing magnetic field

- describe the principles of a moving coil generator

- describe the use of slip rings

- understand and recognise the difference between direct and alternating e.m.f.s and currents

- describe the construction and uses of a transformer

- recall and use the equation $\dfrac{V_{primary}}{V_{secondary}} = \dfrac{N_{primary}}{N_{secondary}}$

- understand how to predict the direction of the force on a current carrying conductor in a magnetic field using Fleming's left hand rule

- recognise the factors which affect the magnitude of an induced e.m.f.

- recognise and explain Lenz's law

- recall and use the equation $V_{primary} \times I_{primary} = V_{secondary} \times I_{secondary}$

- understand why electricity is transmitted at high voltages

- recognise and describe the advantages of transmitting electricity at high voltages.

Chapter 18

Cathode rays

The first moving television images were produced by John Logie Baird in 1924 and as such he is credited as the inventor of television. However, the Marconi-EMI all-electronic method of producing moving images far outstripped Baird's mechanical method. In 1934, the BBC dropped Baird's method and adopted the Marconi-EMI method. The BBC made its first regular television broadcasts in 1936, although they were suspended on the outbreak of the Second World War.

The first colour broadcasts were made in the USA in 1951, although it was not until 1967 that the BBC made their first colour transmissions

Television images are formed by cathode rays hitting a fluorescent screen. The early sets were quite bulky and used a lot of energy. Today, flat-screen televisions using liquid crystal and plasma screens are increasing in popularity.

What of the future? The dream must be of three-dimensional television. Some experts predict that the first demonstration models will be available within the next three years – but others think fifteen to twenty years is a more realistic estimate.

▲ Figure 18.1
Early television.

18.1 Thermionic emission

A white hot metal filament will emit electrons. The internal energy supplied to the hot metal allows electrons to escape from the surface of the metal. This is known as **thermionic emission** (therm = heating; ionic = charge).

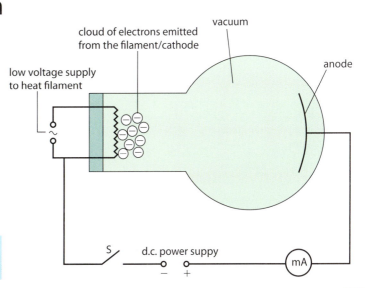

▶ Figure 18.2
A simple thermionic diode.

185

Activity 18.1
Thermionic emission

As the filament of the diode is heated, electrons are emitted from the surface. When switch S is closed the electrons are attracted to the anode, and the **milliammeter** will detect a current in the circuit. If the heater supply is turned off or if the d.c. supply is reversed, there is no current in the circuit. This shows that the particles are emitted from the filament and that they are negative.

18.2 The cathode ray oscilloscope

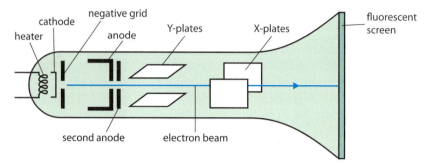

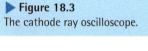
▶ Figure 18.3
The cathode ray oscilloscope.

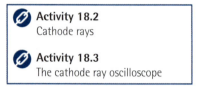
Activity 18.2
Cathode rays

Activity 18.3
The cathode ray oscilloscope

The cathode ray oscilloscope (CRO) is a tool used to measure or monitor voltages. It uses thermionic emission to produce fast-moving beams of electrons. Electrons are emitted from the cathode. The potential difference between the cathode and the anode is a few kilovolts. The electrons are accelerated through this voltage and are shot through the cylindrical anode at high speeds. The electrons cross the tube and strike the screen causing it to fluoresce.

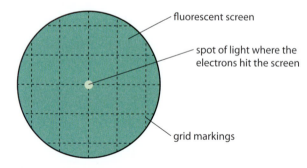

▶ Figure 18.4
The beam can be focused so that a single spot of light is seen on the screen where the electrons hit it.

Deflection of electrons in electric fields
Electrons are negatively charged and are therefore repelled by other negative charges and attracted by positive charges.

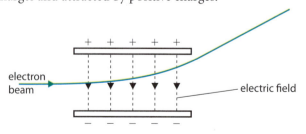

▶ Figure 18.5
The path of an electron through charged plates.

An electron beam is fired between two charged plates. The electrons are attracted by the positive plate and repelled by the negative plate. The beam forms a curve towards the positive plate.

The y-plates

The y-plates deflect the electron beam in a vertical direction.

(a) 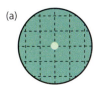 (b) (c) 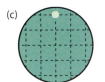 (d)

The cathode ray tube is acting as a voltmeter, measuring the potential difference across the cells. The sensitivity of the plates can be adjusted so that larger or smaller voltages can be measured.

◀ Figure 18.6
(a) No input.
(b) A single cell is connected across the y-plates; the spot of light moves upwards.
(c) Two cells are connected across the y-plates; the spot of light moves twice as far upwards.
(d) A single cell is connected across the y-plates with the opposite polarity; the spot of light moves downwards.

QUESTIONS

18.1 The sensitivity of the y-plates in Figure 18.6 is 2 volts per division. Calculate the e.m.f. of one cell.

The x-plates

The x-plates deflect the electron beam in a horizontal direction. When using the CRO in the usual way they are connected to a time-base voltage.

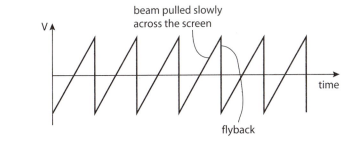

◀ Figure 18.7
Time-base voltage.

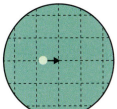
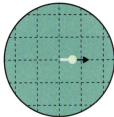
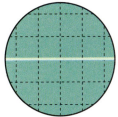

The spot moves slowly across the screen.

The spot moves more quickly, forming a tail.

The spot moves so quickly a continuous line is seen.

◀ Figure 18.8
Increasing the frequency causes a continuous line in the CRO display.

The electron beam moves slowly across the screen, then it flies back to the beginning, and is pulled across again.

Just as the sensitivity of the y-plates can be adjusted, so can the frequency of the time-base. At low frequencies, the spot of light can be seen to move slowly across the screen. As the frequency is increased, the spot moves more quickly and the spot is seen to spread forming a 'tail'. As the spot moves faster, a continuous line is seen.

QUESTIONS

18.2 The frequency of a time-base voltage is 2000 Hz. There are five complete divisions on a CRO screen. Express the time-base speed in terms of milliseconds per division.

Use of the CRO to monitor changing voltages

By connecting the time-base to the *x*-plates and a varying voltage to the *y*-plates, we can produce a visible picture, similar to a graph, on the screen of the CRO.

▶ **Figure 18.9**
Using a CRO to study waveforms.

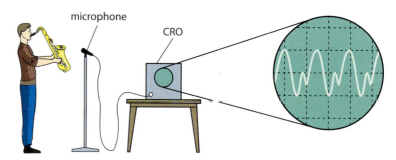

The CRO can be used to study wave shapes and can also be used to calculate the frequency of a wave.

WORKED EXAMPLE

The time-base in the experiment in Figure 18.9 is set at 2.0 ms/division.

Calculate the frequency of the note played by the saxophonist.

There are 2 complete waves in 3 divisions.
1 wave = 1.5 divisions.

time period for one wave = 1.5 divisions × 2.0 ms/division
$$= 3.0 \text{ ms}$$
$$= 0.0030 \text{ s}$$

$$\text{frequency} = \frac{1}{\text{time period}}$$
$$= \frac{1}{0.0030 \text{ s}}$$
$$= 330 \text{ Hz}$$

 Activity 18.4
Use of the CRO to measure time intervals

Deflection of electrons in a magnetic field

We saw in the last chapter how there is a force on current carrying conductors in a magnetic field. In a similar way, a magnetic field will produce a force on a moving charge. This is not surprising, as a current is the movement of electric charge.

Cathode rays

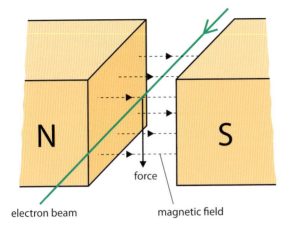

Figure 18.10
Electron beam in a magnetic field.

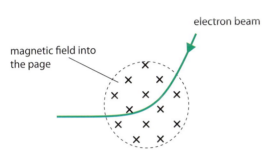

Figure 18.11
Fleming's left hand rule for electron beam in magnetic field.

The rules are exactly the same: the field, the movement of the charge and the force are all at right angles to each other. It is important to remember that when we apply Fleming's left hand rule to electrons, that the conventional current is in the opposite direction to the movement of the electrons.

QUESTIONS

18.3 Figure 18.12(a) shows a cathode ray oscilloscope screen when no voltage is put across the y-plates. The voltage sensitivity is set at 5 V/division.

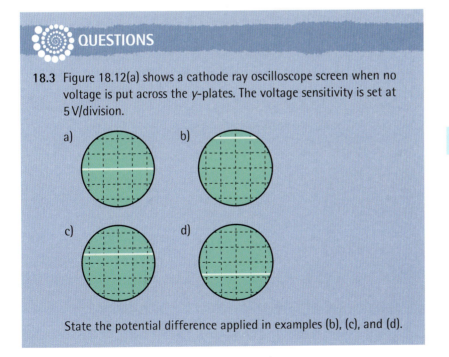

Figure 18.12

State the potential difference applied in examples (b), (c), and (d).

▶ Figure 18.13

18.4 Explain how the frequencies and the amplitudes of the voltages displayed on the CRO screens in Figures 18.13(a) and (b) compare. The controls are set to the same levels in each case.

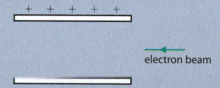
a) b)

18.5 Copy Figure 18.14 and draw the path of the electron beam as it passes between the charged plates.

▶ Figure 18.14

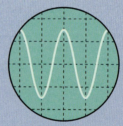

18.6 Figure 18.15 shows the screen of a CRO when an alternating voltage is applied to it.

The controls are set so that the voltage sensitivity is 20 V/division and the time-base is set at 500 ms/division.

▶ Figure 18.15

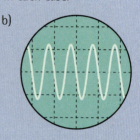

Calculate
a) the amplitude of the voltage and
b) its frequency.

18.7 Figure 18.16 shows an electron beam entering a magnetic field.

▶ Figure 18.16

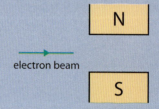

State the direction in which the beam is deflected by the field.

Summary

Now that you have completed this chapter, you should be able to:

- understand the meaning of thermionic emission
- understand that a cathode ray oscilloscope (CRO) can be used to measure voltages
- understand the action of a CRO
- understand that a beam of electrons can be deflected by an electric field
- understand that a beam of electrons can be deflected by a magnetic field
- understand that a cathode ray oscilloscope (CRO) can be used to measure frequencies.

Chapter 19

Electronics

The nineteenth century saw the Industrial Revolution, which turned Western Europe from a rural agricultural society into a city-based industrial society. A second revolution has swept the world in the later part of the twentieth and the early twenty-first centuries.

◀ **Figure 19.1(a)**
The operator console of the 1959 IBM Stretch computer...

A computer of this size would have considerably less computing power than a home computer built only 25 years later. The signals had to travel through kilometres of wiring, which meant that its speed of operation was much slower. The computing power now at our disposal at home was unthinkable only a generation ago. This increase in computing power has been made possible by the development of the integrated circuit.

▼ **Figure 19.1(b)** ... and the rest of the computer!

◀ **Figure 19.2**
A modern integrated circuit (or silicon chip) will contain 40 million or more transistors!

192

Electronics

Where does computing go from here?

Improved software certainly improves the operation of computers and will continue to do so in the future. The miniaturisation of computer chips has just about reached its limit. Totally new technologies will need to be developed to make radical steps forward. The strange quantum behaviour of single protons or electrons has been suggested as one possible avenue to explore.

19.1 Electronic components

◀ **Figure 19.3**
Some more electronic components.

Activity 19.1
Thermistors and LDRs

The thermistor

The **thermistor** is a temperature sensitive resistor. When its temperature increases, its resistance decreases. The thermistor can be used in circuits in which we need to control the temperature. An example is switching on an air conditioner when a room becomes too warm.

▲ **Figure 19.4**
The circuit diagram symbol for a thermistor.

Light dependent resistor

A **light dependent resistor** is often referred to as an **LDR**. As the name suggests, the resistance of a light sensitive resistor depends on the amount of light falling on it. It has a high resistance in the dark, but its resistance decreases when light falls on it.

LDRs can be used in light meters and automatic switches, which turn a light on when it gets dark.

LDRs and thermistors are often referred to as **sensors**. They sense a change in the light level or the temperature and convert it into electric information.

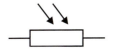

▲ **Figure 19.5**
The circuit diagram symbol for a LDR.

▲ **Figure 19.6**
The circuit diagram symbol for a capacitor.

> **Activity 19.2**
> Capacitors

▶ **Figure 19.7**
Structure of a capacitor

Capacitors

A **capacitor** consists of two conducting plates separated by a thin insulating layer.

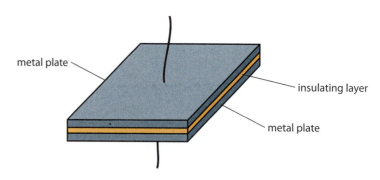

Charging and discharging a capacitor

▶ **Figure 19.8**
Charging a capacitor.

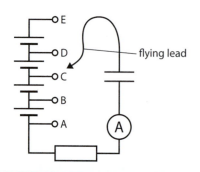

▲ **Figure 19.9**
Charging and discharging a capacitor.

When the capacitor is connected to a battery, charge flows from the battery to the plates, which themselves become charged.

When the flying lead is touched to point B in Figure 19.9, charge flows to the capacitor and a pulse of current is registered on the ammeter. The flying lead is touched on point A. The charge flows off the capacitor and there is an equal-sized current in the opposite direction.

The lead is then touched to point C. Again there is a pulse of current, but this time twice the size of the previous ones. The greater the potential difference put across the capacitor plates, the greater the charge which flows on to the plates.

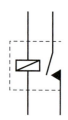

▲ **Figure 19.10**
Circuit diagram symbol for a relay. A relay switch is an electromagnetically operated switch. Its operation is described in Chapter 13.

Changing the resistance in the circuit

The resistor in Figure 19.9 is replaced with a larger value resistance and the experiment is repeated. The maximum current each time the capacitor is charged or discharged is smaller than before, but it lasts for a longer time. The same charge flows onto the capacitor but now it is a slower process.

Electronics

Time delay circuits

Charge flows onto the plates of a capacitor when a potential difference is applied across it:
- The charge increases when the potential difference increases.
- The discharge current decreases when the resistance in the discharge circuit increases.
- The discharge time increases when the resistance in the discharge circuit increases.

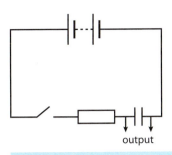

▲ **Figure 19.11**
When the switch is closed, there is a delay before the capacitor is fully charged and therefore a delay before the output reaches the maximum voltage.

Time delay circuits

As it takes a finite time for capacitors to charge or discharge, they can be used in time delay circuits. A circuit such as the one shown in Figure 19.11 might be used as part of a burglar alarm or temperature sensor.

Energy stored in a capacitor

When a capacitor is charged, it can act as a kind of store of electric potential energy. It is used to release large amounts of energy in short bursts.

In Figure 19.12, when the switch is moved from the charging circuit, the capacitor discharges rapidly through the lamp, giving a very bright but short flash of light. This type of system is used in the flash gun on a camera.

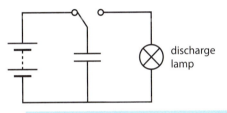

▲ **Figure 19.12**
Circuit for a flash gun.

The potential divider

As the sliding contact in Figure 19.13 is moved along the resistance wire from A to B, the reading on the voltmeter gradually increases.

If the voltmeter is replaced by a lamp, the brightness of the lamp increases as the sliding contact is moved from A to B. This shows how this can be used as a variable voltage supply.

When a variable resistor is used in this way we call it a **variable potential divider** or **potentiometer**.

Figure 19.15 shows two types of potential dividers.

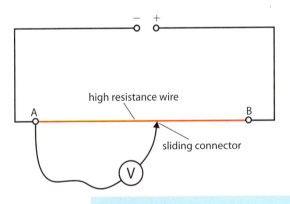

▲ **Figure 19.13**
Potentiometer.

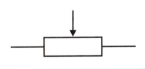

▲ **Figure 19.14**
Circuit diagram symbol for a potentiometer.

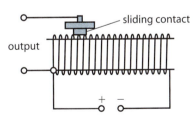

The resistance wire is in the form of a solenoid.

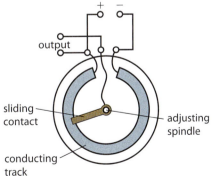

The resistance wire is in the form of a circular strip.

▲ **Figure 19.15**
Two types of potential dividers.

Activity 19.3
The potential divider

195

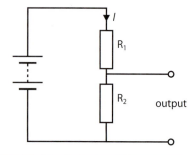

Figure 19.16
Fixed potential divider.

A fixed potential divider

In Figure 19.16 the potential drop across each of the resistors is IR_1 and IR_2 respectively. The larger R_2 is with respect to R_1, the larger the output potential.

If one of the resistors is replaced with an LDR, the output potential depends on the amount of light falling on it. If R_1 is replaced with the LDR then the more light that falls on it, the smaller its resistance and the larger the output potential. This could be used to trigger a circuit which turns on a light when it gets dark.

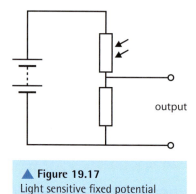

Figure 19.17
Light sensitive fixed potential divider.

The diode

Figure 19.18
The circuit diagram symbol for a diode

Diodes have a very high resistance in one direction and a very low resistance in the opposite direction. This means they allow currents to pass one way but not the other.

Diodes can be used to convert alternating currents into direct currents. We call this **rectification**.

Rectification

When the potential difference is in the forward direction (the direction in which the arrow in the diode symbol points) current is conducted through the diode. When the current is in the reverse direction, the diode does not conduct. This means that the current in the resistor is in one direction only, and so is a direct current. Likewise the potential difference across it is a direct voltage.

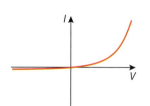

Figure 19.19
The current – potential difference curve for a diode.

With this simple circuit the direct current produced is very rough; it goes from zero to maximum, back to zero - where it remains for a time before going back to maximum again. In practical circuits the output is smoothed by using capacitors and more than one diode.

▶ **Figure 19.20**
The diode is being used to rectify the a.c. voltage. This is an example of half-wave rectification

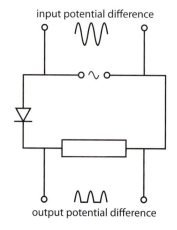

Activity 19.4
The diode

Electronics

Light-emitting diode (LED)
Light-emitting diodes are simply diodes that light up when there is a current passes through them. They require very much smaller currents than filament lamps and consequently are often used as indicator lights.

▲ Figure 19.21
Circuit diagram symbol for an LED.

The transistor
Transistors have three electrodes – known as the base, the emitter and the collector. Transistors can be used as current amplifiers or as switches. In this course, we will concentrate solely on their use as switches.

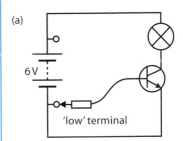
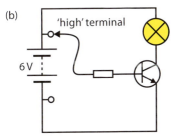

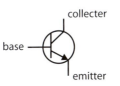

▲ Figure 19.22
Circuit diagram symbol for a transistor.

◀ Figure 19.23
The transistor as a switch.

When the base is connected to the 0 V (or the 'low' terminal), the transistor is off and the lamp does not light. When the base is connected to the 6 V (or 'high' terminal), the transistor is switched on and the lamp lights.

Activity 19.5
The transistor

Using a potential divider to supply the input to the base
The circuit in Figure 19.24 shows how a potentiometer can be used with a transistor to switch on a lamp. As the supply to the transistor base is increased from zero, it is found the lamp comes on when the input to the base is about 0.6 V.

In Figure 19.25, the lamp has been replaced by a milliammeter, and a voltmeter has been connected to measure the input voltage to the base (V_b). It will be seen that the current through the milliammeter rapidly increases to a maximum when V_b is about 0.6 V.

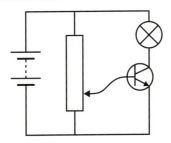

▲ Figure 19.24
Potentiometer and transistor as a switch.

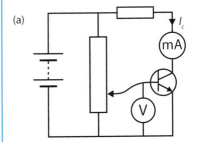
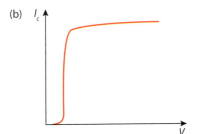

◀ Figure 19.25
Rapid current change seen in switch.

▼ Figure 19.26
Light sensitive switch.

A light operated switch
It is often useful to have a light switch on when the light level decreases.

When the light levels are high, the resistance of the LDR is low, so the input voltage to the base is low. When it gets darker, the resistance of the LDR increases. So the voltage to the base also increases, turning the light on. The variable resistor can be used to set the precise levels at which the light switches on.

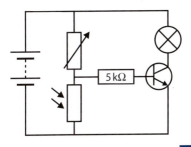

197

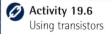

Activity 19.6
Using transistors

The advantage of using the transistor, rather than connecting the potential divider straight to the lamp is that the light switches fully on for a very small change in input voltage (light level), rather than being partly on over a range of input voltages or light levels.

A temperature controlled switch

In this circuit, a thermistor is used as the sensor. When the temperature falls, the resistance of the thermistor increases, so there is a greater potential difference across it. This increases the input voltage to the base. The transistor is switched on and this closes the **relay** switch.

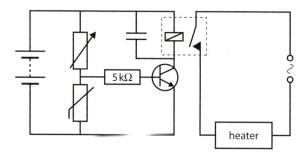

▶ Figure 19.27
Temperature controlled switch.

We use a relay in this circuit because a heater would require a much larger current than the transistor circuit could supply. The capacitor is required across the relay coil to avoid a large back e.m.f. being produced, which could destroy the transistor.

Transistors are often used where a low voltage circuit is used to control a high voltage circuit.

QUESTIONS

19.1 Figure 19.28 shows a potential divider. R_1 has a resistance of 18 Ω and R_2 has a resistance of 27 Ω.

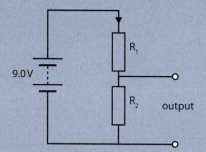

▶ Figure 19.28

a) Calculate the combined resistance of the two resistors.
b) Calculate the current in the circuit.
c) Calculate the potential difference across R_2.
d) Write down the output voltage.

Electronics

19.2 Figure 19.29 shows a circuit using a transistor to switch on a burglar alarm system.

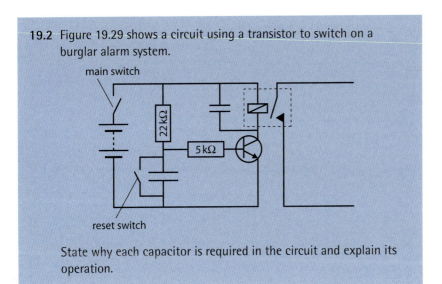

◀ **Figure 19.29**

State why each capacitor is required in the circuit and explain its operation.

19.2 Digital electronics
Digital and analogue signals

◀ **Figure 19.30**
Digital and analogue ammeters.

The digital meter's readout is in discrete steps, whereas the analogue meter has a needle that moves continuously across a scale.

▼ **Figure 19.31**
Digitally sampling a sound wave.

Consider the sound wave in Figure 19.31. To transmit this as a radio wave, an analogue system would make an exact electrical replica of the signal. A digital system samples the waves many times each second and breaks the wave down into a series of definite sized values, as shown by the vertical lines in Figure 19.31 These values are then converted into a binary number (a series of ones and zeros) which is then transmitted. At the receiver, the binary numbers are then reassembled back to reform the original wave.

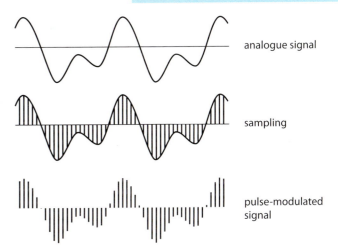

The advantages of digital systems are
- more information can be sent per second
- there is less distortion of the signal during transmission.

199

> **DID YOU KNOW?**
>
> Binary is a system of counting in which there are just two digits: 1 and 0. The table shows the normal numeral (base 10) and the binary equivalent.
>
> | Base 10 | Binary |
> |---|---|
> | 0 | 000 |
> | 1 | 001 |
> | 2 | 010 |
> | 3 | 011 |
> | 4 | 100 |
> | 5 | 101 |
> | 6 | 110 |
> | 7 | 111 |

Activity 19.7
Logic gates 1

Logic gates

Computers rule our modern world – minicomputers control car engines, washing machines, processes in factories and mobile phones. Computers are controlled by electronic switches called logic gates. Logic gates are electronic circuits that consist of transistors, resistors, and various other components. These circuits are generally deposited onto a small piece of silicon called a **chip** or **integrated circuit** (see Figure 19.3 on page 193).

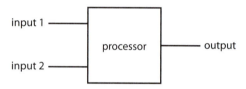

▶ Figure 19.32
Logic gate.

The gate has one or more inputs and an output. As with all digital electronics, the output is always in one of two states; on or off. 'On' is represented by the number 1, and 'off' is represented by the number 0.

The OR gate

We can make a mock-up of a logic gate using switches. Figure 19.32 shows a circuit with two switches in parallel. The lamp will light if switch S_1 is closed OR if S_2 is closed. It will also light if both S_1 and S_2 are closed.

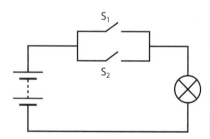

▲ Figure 19.33
A simple OR gate.

We can draw a table (known as a **truth table**) to summarise this.

▶ Table 19.1
Truth table for the simple OR gate.

Switch S_1	Switch S_2	Lamp
Open	Open	Off
Open	Closed	On
Closed	Open	On
Closed	Closed	On

This type of gate is known as an OR gate, because if either S_1 **OR** S_2 is closed, the lamp is lit.

A digital logic gate is simply an electronic version of this sort of circuit. There are various types of logic gate; the truth tables for some of them are shown on page 201. Note that the symbol 0 means 'off' and the symbol 1 means 'on'.

Electronics

▼ **Table 19.2**
Truth table for OR gate.

Input 1	Input 2	Output
0	0	0
0	1	1
1	0	1
1	1	1

The output is ON if either input 1 **OR** input 2 is ON

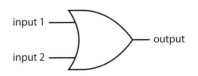

▲ **Figure 19.34**
The symbol for an OR gate.

The AND gate

▼ **Table 19.3**
AND truth table.

Input 1	Input 2	Output
0	0	0
0	1	0
1	0	0
1	1	1

The output is ON if input 1 **AND** input 2 is ON

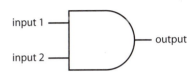

▲ **Figure 19.35**
The symbol for an AND gate.

The NOT gate

▼ **Table 19.4**
NOT truth table.

Input	Output
0	1
1	0

The output is ON if the input is **NOT** ON

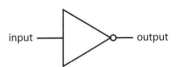

▲ **Figure 19.36**
The symbol for a NOT gate.

The NOT gate is often referred to as an **inverter**, as it swaps the signal from on to off, or from off to on.

Combining gates

The NAND gate

Gates can be combined to make new gates. A simple example is to add a NOT gate to an AND gate.

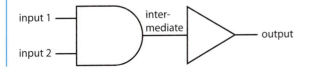

◀ **Figure 19.37**
Combining AND and NOT gates.

Activity 19.8
Logic gates 2

201

Table 19.5 shows the truth table for a NAND gate.

Input 1	Input 2	Intermediate	Output
0	0	0	1
0	1	0	1
1	0	0	1
1	1	1	0

▶ Table 19.5
NAND truth table.

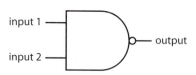

▲ Figure 19.38
The symbol for a NAND gate is made by adding a small circle after the symbol for an AND gate.

This is a 'NEGATIVE AND' gate, which is shortened to a NAND gate.

QUESTIONS

19.3 How would you make a NOR gate from the gates you have already met?

Activity 19.9
Logic gates 3

The NOR gate

Table 19.6 shows the truth table for a NOR gate.

▶ Table 19.6
NOR truth table.

Input 1	Input 2	Output
0	0	1
0	1	0
1	0	0
1	1	0

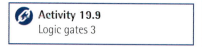

▲ Figure 19.39
The symbol for a NOR gate is made in a similar way to the symbol for a NAND gate. This time a small circle is added after the symbol for an OR gate.

Using logic gates in control systems

Figure 19.39 shows a system that could be used to turn on a heater in a greenhouse, if the temperature drops below a certain level.

At first glance it looks very complicated; however if we split it up into stages, it becomes much clearer.

▶ Figure 19.40
System for turning on a heater.

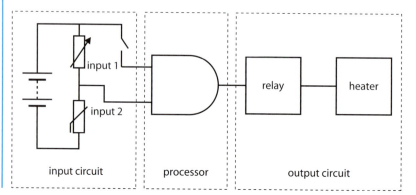

Electronics

Stage 1 is the input circuit. This is simply a potential divider. Input 1 is connected to the positive terminal of the battery (the high line). The gardener can open the switch if there are no plants in the greenhouse, making that input low (0).

Input 2 is connected so that when the temperature falls and the thermistor's resistance increases, it goes high (1).

Stage 2 is the processor. This is an AND gate. Both inputs must be high for the output to be high. This means that the gardener must have switched on the switch to input 1 and the temperature must have dropped to a low level.

Stage 3 is the output circuit. The relay is required because the heater requires far more power than the logic circuit can provide.

Activity 19.10
Logic gates in control

QUESTIONS

19.4 Draw a circuit similar to the one in Figure 19.32 to show how two switches could be used to make a mock-up of an AND gate.

19.5 Figure 19.41 shows a combination of different gates.

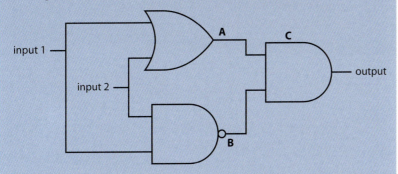

◀ Figure 19.41

a) Identify the three gates.
b) Copy and complete the truth table for this combination of gates.

Input 1	Input 2	A	B	Output
0	0			
0	1			
1	0			
1	1			

◀ Table 19.7

▼ Figure 19.42

19.6 Figure 19.42 shows a potential divider.
a) Name component Y.
b) Explain how the output voltage changes as the light conditions change.
c) Draw a circuit diagram showing how you would connect a potential divider so that the output potential increases when the temperature decreases.

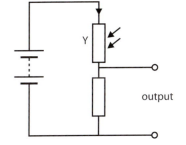

203

Figure 19.43

19.7 Use Figure 19.30 to explain the difference between digital and analogue instruments.

19.8 Fig 19.43 shows a circuit in which a warning indicator comes on when the temperature falls.

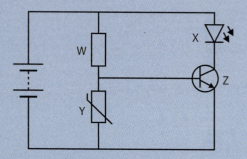

a) Name the components W, X, Y and Z.

b) X acts as the warning indicator.
   Explain why it comes on when the temperature falls.

19.9 a) Explain what is meant by a *logic gate*.

b) (i) Identify the logic gate in Figure 19.44.

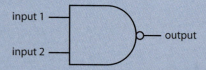

Figure 19.44

(ii) Explain the operation of this gate. You will find it helpful to draw a truth table.

19.10 A control circuit is required so that a light will come on when
   (i) it gets dark and
   (ii) the temperature drops below freezing.

a) Name the sensors you would use to trigger the processor.

b) Name the type of gate you would use in the system.

c) A high-powered floodlight is to be operated by the system. Explain why a relay must be used between the output from the control circuit and the circuit for the floodlight.

Summary

Now that you have completed this chapter, you should be able to:

- describe the use of the thermistor and the LDR as input sensors
- describe the action of capacitors in timing circuits
- describe the use of a potential divider
- describe the use of a diode in rectification
- describe the use of a transistor as an electronic switch
- show an understanding of light- and temperature-controlled circuits
- understand the difference between digital and analogue systems
- understand what is meant by a *logic gate*
- recognise the symbols for basic logic gates
- write out truth tables for each of the gates and for combinations of gates
- design simple control circuits using two or more logic gates
- understand how sensors may be used to control logic gates.

Chapter 20

The atom

Welcome to a great detective story – the search for an understanding of the atom.

The Ancient Greeks developed theories about atoms as long ago as the 5th century BCE, but it was not until the early part of the nineteenth century that modern atomic theory began to take shape. Developments in chemistry led to the identification of increasing numbers of elements. The basic building block of matter was considered to be the atom, and each element was made from its own unique atom.

The discovery of the electron gave the first hint that the atom was *not* the fundamental building block of matter. Its existence suggested that atoms must have a structure of their own. This led to the model of the atom which we will discuss in this chapter, and it also led to the question, 'Do the particles that make up the atom have structure?'

The current model says that sub-atomic particles, such as the proton and neutron, are made up of even smaller particles, called quarks.

The study of matter on this very small scale has contributed to our model of the universe and its beginnings. It is widely accepted that the universe started from a very hot, dense initial state, which rapidly cooled and expanded. This is known as the Big Bang theory.

▶ Figure 20.1
An artist's impression of the Big Bang.

The atom

What happens next? It depends on how much matter there is in the universe – it may continue to expand and cool, it may approach a maximum size without ever quite reaching it, or it might collapse under its own gravitational pull.

What was there before the Big Bang? Physics cannot fully answer this question, but according to Einstein's Theory of Relativity, there was nothing – neither space nor time.

20.1 An exciting time in the development of physics

The years from about 1890 to 1930 saw the most exciting development of the ideas of atomic structure in the history of science.

Developments in the uses of electricity and in particular the discovery of the mysterious rays known as cathode rays, triggered the advance. It was in 1897 that J. J. Thomson, whilst studying the nature of cathode rays, recognised that the rays were made up of particles smaller than the atom. He called the particles *electrons* because they conduct electricity through gases and even a vacuum. Thomson's discovery showed that the atom had an internal structure. The model of the atom as being indivisible, of being like a tiny unbreakable billiard ball, was consigned to history.

DID YOU KNOW?

J. J. Thomson was one of the greats of the scientific world at the turn of the nineteenth century. His discovery of the **electron**, and his subsequent model of the atom were defining points in a brilliant career. He held the prestigious post of Cavendish Professor of Experimental Physics at the University of Cambridge from 1884 to 1918.

By deflecting electron beams in electric and magnetic fields, he was able to measure the 'charge to mass ratio' of the electron.

He went on to do similar work with ionised gases and discovered the existence of isotopes of neon.

He won the Nobel Prize for physics in 1906 for his work on the electron.

▲ Figure 20.2
J. J. Thomson.

Deflection of charged particles

In Chapter 17 we looked at the deflection of cathode rays in electric and magnetic fields. Thomson used this deflection to measure the charge to mass ratio of the electron (q/m). The amount of deflection of a moving particle in an electric field depends on

- the speed of the particles – this can be determined from the accelerating potential
- the mass of the particle – the more massive the particle, the less the deflection
- the charge carried by the particle – the more charge, the greater the deflection.

▼ Figure 20.3
Deflection of electrons in an electric field.

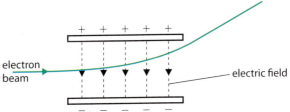

From his results, Thomson was able to show that q/m for the electron $= 1.8 \times 10^{11}$ C/kg. In a separate experiment, the American physicist Robert Millikan showed the charge on the electron $= 1.6 \times 10^{-19}$ C. From these figures we can calculate the mass of the electron $= 9.1 \times 10^{-31}$ kg.

Thomson went on to use a similar method to determine the masses of different ionised gases.

Thomson's model of the atom

Following the discovery of the electron, Thomson proposed a new model of the atom. He knew that the atom must be neutral, so he suggested that the electrons were embedded in a positively charged background cloud. This model is often described as the plum pudding model, the electrons being the plums or currants embedded in the positively charged dough.

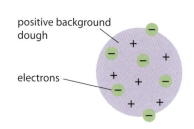

▲ Figure 20.4
The plum pudding model of the atom.

Rutherford's alpha-particle scattering experiment

In the years following Thomson's discovery of the electron and the new theory of atomic structure, many experiments were done to try and probe further into the nature of the atom. A single atom was much too small to be seen with even the most powerful microscopes of the day, so other techniques had to be used. One such way was to fire other particles at high speeds into the atom (a technique which is still used today!).

Ernest Rutherford suggested firing **alpha particles** (α-particles) at a very thin gold foil. Alpha particles were relatively newly discovered, positively charged particles with a mass some 8000 times larger than an electron (see Chapter 21).

Activity 20.1
Rutherford scattering model

Rutherford believed that the α-particles would pass straight through the atom with no significant deflection. The only things that could deflect them would be the electrons, and the huge difference in the masses made this impossible.

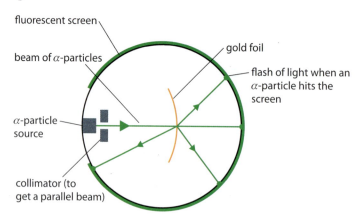

▶ Figure 20.5
Plan view of the apparatus used to study α-particle scattering.

Imagine Rutherford's surprise when a few days later, his research assistant (Marsden) told him that a few α-particles were scattered at large angles, some even appearing to bounce back towards the source. Rutherford himself said, 'It was quite the most incredible event of my life, it was as though I had fired a six-inch naval shell at a piece of tissue paper and the shell had bounced back and hit me.'

The atom

Rutherford's solar system model of the atom

Rutherford recognised that the plum pudding model of the atom did not satisfy the experimental results. He proposed a **nuclear model**: virtually all the mass of the atom and all of the positive charge being concentrated in a small **nucleus**, with the electrons orbiting the nucleus rather like the planets orbit the sun.

The existence of different elements could now be explained. The atoms of the different elements had different charges on their nuclei and different numbers of electrons orbiting the nucleus. Niels Bohr took this further in 1915 in which he postulated that electrons could only exist in definite orbits (or **orbitals**), and the number of electrons in each orbital was strictly limited, thus explaining much about the chemistry of matter.

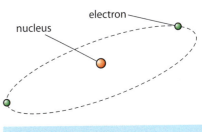

▲ **Figure 20.6** Rutherford's model of the atom.

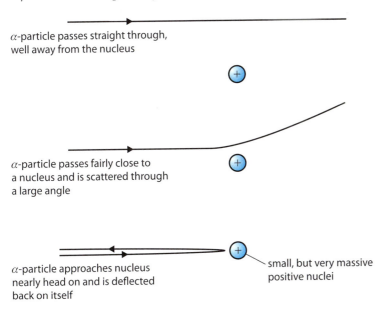

◀ **Figure 20.7** How Rutherford's model explains α-particle scattering.

Very few α-particles were scattered through large angles, which told Rutherford that the nucleus had a very small diameter. By a detailed study of the numbers of α-particles scattered at different angles, he was able to estimate the size of the nucleus.

Diameter of the atom	Diameter of the nucleus
10^{-9} m	10^{-14} m

◀ **Table 20.1** Relative sizes of the atom and its nucleus.

This means that if we could project a magnified image of the atom onto a screen so that it was 1 metre in diameter, the nucleus would be in the region of $\frac{1}{100}$ of a millimetre in diameter!

20.2 Nuclear structure

The story does not end with the nuclear model of the atom. Physicists then asked the question, 'Does the nucleus have structure?' Did the nuclei of different elements consist of different numbers of the same positive particle? If so, what held them together against the huge electrostatic repulsions between them? (They are all positively charged.) Why are the atomic masses of different elements not proportional to their number in the periodic table?

In 1919, Rutherford, whilst working with Bohr, proposed that the nucleus was made up of two different types of particle:
- the **proton**, which has the same size charge as the electron but is positive, and also a much greater mass than the electron
- the **neutron**, which has the same mass as a proton but no charge.

DID YOU KNOW?

Ernest Rutherford was one of the great experimental physicists; he became known as the father of nuclear physics. He was born in Nelson, New Zealand, where he was educated at Nelson College and Canterbury College (University of New Zealand) from where he won a scholarship to study at the Cavendish Laboratory at Cambridge.

He identified the nature of alpha and beta radiation and discovered that the radiation from a radioactive isotope decreased by equal fractions in equal time intervals (half-life). He won the Nobel Prize for chemistry, for work on the transmutation of elements (see Chapter 21). In 1919 he succeeded J. J. Thomson as Professor at the Cavendish Laboratory. He was knighted in 1914 and created a baron in 1931.

◀ Figure 20.8
Ernest Rutherford.

The three fundamental particles

▶ Table 20.2
The fundamental particles.

Particle	Relative mass	Relative charge	Location
Electron	$\frac{1}{2000}$	-1	Orbiting the nucleus
Proton	1	1	In the nucleus
Neutron	1	0	In the nucleus

DID YOU KNOW?

Atomic and nuclear masses are often measured in atomic mass units (symbol u). The mass of a proton is approximately 1 u, as is the neutron. The electron has a much smaller mass.

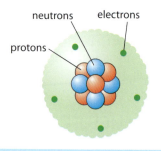

▲ Figure 20.9
The nuclear atom showing electrons surrounding the nucleus, which is made up of protons and neutrons. (Note that this is not drawn to scale; with this diameter of atom, the nucleus would be too tiny to see!)

The atom

Representation of nuclides

A **nuclide** is the term given to describe a particular nucleus, with given numbers of protons and neutrons.

The **proton number** is the number of protons in the nucleus. It gives the element its number in the periodic table.

The **nucleon number** is the number of protons plus the number of neutrons in the nucleus of the nuclide.

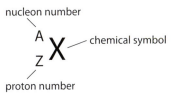

▲ Figure 20.10
The symbol for a nuclide of element X.

WORKED EXAMPLE

Identify the element and state the number of protons and neutrons in a nuclide with the symbol $^{40}_{18}\text{Ar}$.

State how many electrons there would be in the neutral atom.

The chemical symbol is that of the noble gas argon.
There are 18 protons (since Z = 18).
There are (40 − 18) = 22 neutrons.
There will be the same number of electrons as protons (= 18) in the neutral atom.

QUESTIONS

20.1 Identify the element and state the number of protons and neutrons in the nuclides with the following symbols.
a) $^{23}_{11}\text{Na}$ b) $^{197}_{79}\text{Au}$ c) $^{24}_{12}\text{Mg}$ d) $^{96}_{42}\text{Mo}$

Isotopes

When Thomson was investigating the deflection of beams of ionised gases in electric fields, he observed that there seemed to be two definite masses of neon ion: $^{20}_{10}\text{Ne}$ (the majority) and $^{22}_{10}\text{Ne}$.

Thomson had made a startling discovery and had contributed to the debate over the existence of the neutron. The two types of neon have the same number of protons, so are chemically identical. However, the nuclei of the two types differ in that the $^{20}_{10}\text{Ne}$ has 10 neutrons whilst $^{22}_{10}\text{Ne}$ has 12 neutrons. The term **isotope** is used to describe elements that have the same number of protons but different numbers of neutrons. This means that isotopes are chemically identical but their physical properties (like mass) are different.

◀ Figure 20.11
Hydrogen has three isotopes.

$^{1}_{1}\text{H}$
the most common form has a single proton

$^{2}_{1}\text{H}$
deuterium has one proton and one neutron

$^{3}_{1}\text{H}$
tritium has one proton and two neutrons

QUESTIONS

20.2 Outline the experimental evidence that led to the development of the plum pudding model of the atom.

20.3 Outline the experimental evidence that led to the development of the nuclear model of the atom.

20.4 State how many protons and neutrons there are in the following nuclides.

a) $^{16}_{7}N$ b) $^{14}_{7}N$ c) $^{12}_{6}C$ d) $^{90}_{39}Sr$ e) $^{235}_{92}U$

20.5 Copy and complete Table 20.3. The first line is done for you.

▶ Table 20.3

Number of protons	Number of neutrons	Nuclide representation
20	20	$^{40}_{20}Ca$
28	31	
88		$^{228}_{88}Ra$
	30	$^{56}_{26}Fe$
82	127	

Summary

Now that you have completed this chapter, you should be able to:

- understand that an electron has a very small mass and a negative charge

- understand that a proton has a mass of 1 atomic mass unit and a positive charge

- understand that a neutron has a mass of 1 atomic mass unit but no charge

- understand that an atom consists of a nucleus that contains protons and neutrons surrounded by electrons

- understand the experimental evidence that led to the nuclear model of the atom

- recognise and use the nuclide representations

- understand that isotopes have the same number of protons but different numbers of neutrons.

Chapter 21

Radioactivity

In 1896, the French physicist Henri Becquerel was looking for a link between the newly discovered X-rays and the natural phosphorescence of uranium salts that occurs when sunlight falls on them. He was surprised to find that uranium salts caused a photographic plate to go cloudy, even without being exposed to sunlight. He investigated the rays given off from the uranium and showed they were quite different from X-rays. Becquerel had discovered the phenomenon of radioactivity.

Marie and Pierre Curie also investigated the rays Becquerel had discovered and showed that not only uranium but also thorium gave off these rays. To aid their research they were given several tonnes of pitchblende, the ore of uranium. They distilled it down and discovered a new radioactive element, which they named polonium, after Marie's home country, Poland. They then discovered that the residue was also radioactive. Further separations led to the discovery of a second very highly radioactive element, which they called radium.

The work they did was painstaking and slow – they isolated only a few milligrams of radium from the tonnes of pitchblende. It is this type of determination, as well as the occasional bit of luck or an inspired guess, which leads to progress in science

▲ Figure 21.1
Marie Curie works as her husband Pierre looks on.

21.1 Background radiation

Background radiation is the radioactivity that is around us all the time, mostly from naturally occurring sources, such as rocks in the Earth's crust and cosmic rays. There are traces of a radioactive isotope of carbon in living tissue, uranium is naturally present in stones and cement, and the gas radon is produced by the decay of radium in the ground.

The amount of background radiation varies from area to area, according to the local environment, so parts of Namibia or Australia, which have a high content of uranium in the rocks, will have a significantly higher count rate than areas such as Ireland or Denmark that have less uranium in the bedrock.

 **DID YOU KNOW?**

We can measure the level of radioactivity as count rate – that is, the number of radioactive emissions per second.

213

Activity 21.1
Radiation around us

When we are measuring the radiation from a source, we must always take account of the background radiation.

Figure 21.2
Background radiation is all around us.

Safety precautions

If we are handling radioactive materials, there is a real chance of contamination and great care must be taken.

Many of the early researchers into radioactivity died from the disease leukaemia, cancer of the blood. Both Marie and her husband, Pierre Curie, complained of sores on their hands and faces from handling the radioactive isotopes. Pure radium is so radioactive that a phial of it will glow in the dark and Marie Curie liked to keep a sample of radium salts on her bedside table. It was not until many years later that the dangers from radiation were recognised.

Radioactive emissions have sufficient energy to ionise molecules, so that if they collide with living tissue they can alter the cell structure causing them to mutate into cancer cells. Beta and gamma radiation can penetrate deep into the body whereas alpha radiation tends to be absorbed by the dead layer of skin on the surface of our bodies. However, if the source of alpha radiation is ingested, for example radon gas is breathed in, it is highly dangerous. Alpha particles cause so much ionisation that the likelihood of causing mutations of the cells in the linings of the lungs is very high.

By far the majority of radiation we absorb is from background radiation. If a person works in a situation where they may be exposed to extra radiation, very careful checks are made as to the extra radiation they absorb.

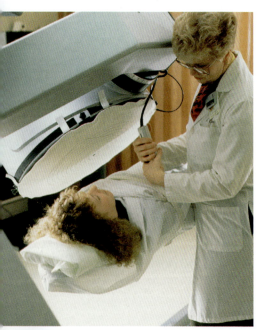

Figure 21.3
A radiographer in a hospital wears a badge to measure the amount of radiation they are exposed to. When the gamma rays are being produced they will stand and observe from behind a lead glass screen.

Radioactivity

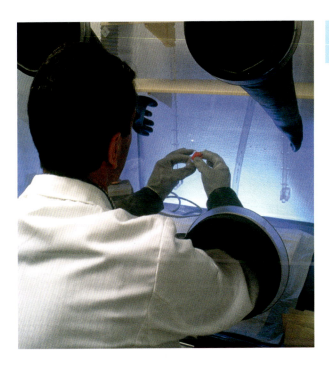

◀ Figure 21.4
Handling radioactive sources.

In the laboratory, we always handle radioactive sources with forceps and never put them near our bodies or faces. When not in use they are stored in locked cupboards in lead-lined boxes.

21.2 Types of radiation

▲ Figure 21.5
Storage for radioactive sources.

There are three different types of radiation – **alpha** (α), **beta** (β) and **gamma** (γ).

All three types cause ionisation of the air as they pass through. In the early years of research, this ionisation was detected by photographic film or an electroscope. Today there are many more types of detector, but generally we shall use the Geiger-Muller (GM) tube.

Penetration of different radiations

Activity 21.2
Penetration of radiations

The different types of radiation have quite different penetrations through matter.

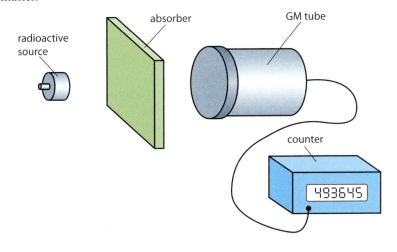

◀ Figure 21.6
An experiment to investigate the penetration of different radiations.

215

Such experiments show that alpha particles are the least penetrating of the three types of radiation. Alpha radiation is entirely absorbed by a few centimetres of air or by a thin sheet of paper.

Beta radiation is not affected by paper but is stopped by a few millimetres of aluminium.

Gamma radiation is the most penetrating of the three. It is not significantly affected by either paper or aluminium and is not even totally absorbed by several centimetres of lead.

> ▶ **Figure 21.7**
> The penetration of different radiations.

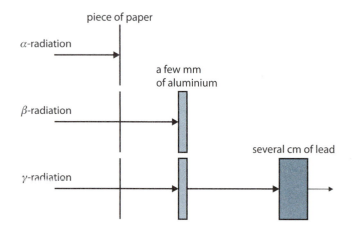

The cloud chamber

> **Activity 21.3**
> The cloud chamber

The cloud chamber such as in Figure 21.8 is a very powerful tool for studying radioactive emissions. Tracks are left showing the actual paths of individual particles.

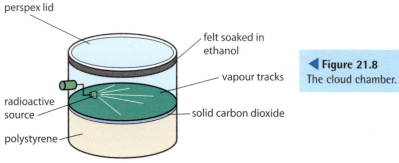

◀ **Figure 21.8**
The cloud chamber.

> ▼ **Figure 21.9**
> Alpha particles cause a lot of ionisation and leave thick tracks. The tracks are all the same length, which shows that the particles are all emitted with the same energy. The very long track is probably caused by an alpha particle hitting an ethanol molecule and knocking out a proton, which is less massive than the alpha particle, has a higher speed and travels further.

The ethanol evaporates in the upper half of the cloud chamber. The solid carbon dioxide cools the air, forming a supersaturated vapour. As radioactive particles travel through air, they knock electrons off the atoms causing ionisation. The vapour condenses on the ions leaving a track showing the path of the particles.

> ▶ **Figure 21.10**
> Beta particles cause much less ionisation and the tracks are much thinner. The ends of the tracks tend to be irregular, as the particle loses energy and slows down. Beta tracks are very hard to detect in a cloud chamber. These tracks are taken from its close relative, the bubble chamber.

Gamma radiation causes so little ionisation that they cannot be detected in the cloud chamber.

Identification of radiations

Rutherford identified the nature of alpha and beta radiation by deflecting them in magnetic fields.

Beta particles have a relatively small mass and their deflection can be demonstrated in the laboratory.

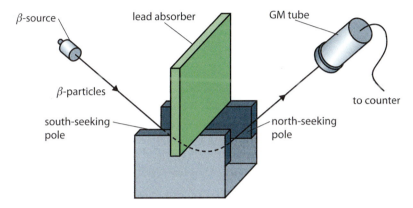

◀ Figure 21.11
Deflection of β-particles by a magnetic field.

Activity 21.4
Deflection of beta particles

Results from deflection experiments show that beta particles carry a negative charge and that they are very, very fast moving electrons. To understand how much energy the electrons in beta particles have, we can compare them with the electrons in cathode rays. The electrons in a cathode ray tube are accelerated by a few hundred volts. Beta particles have energies as though they had been accelerated through several hundred thousand volts!

It is not easy to show the deflection of alpha particles, as they are very much more massive than beta particles and require much stronger magnetic fields to deflect them. In addition, any experiment must be done in a vacuum so that the particles are not absorbed as they travel through the air.

Rutherford showed them to be positively charged particles and he eventually identified them as very fast moving helium nuclei (He^{2+}).

Gamma rays cannot be deflected by a magnetic field and they were first identified from their speed, 3×10^8 m/s. They are electromagnetic waves of very short wavelength.

Electric and magnetic fields will deflect alpha and beta particles. Note that the alpha particles are deflected towards a negative plate showing their positive charge, whilst beta particles are deflected towards a positive plate, showing their negative charge.

It should also be noted that the electric field needed to show the deflection of alpha particles must be very much stronger than that for the beta particles.

Gamma rays, being electromagnetic waves and therefore uncharged, are not deflected by either electric or magnetic fields.

▼ Figure 21.12
Deflection of the three types of radiation.

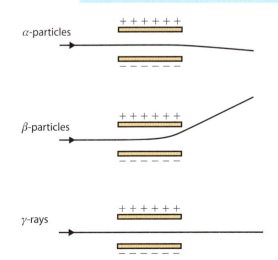

21.3 Radioactive disintegration

Radioactivity is a nuclear not an atomic phenomenon. It occurs when an unstable nucleus spontaneously emits an alpha, beta or gamma ray.

Alpha decay

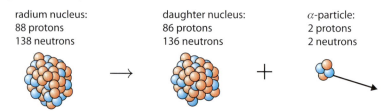

Figure 21.13 Examples of alpha emission.

Alpha emission tends to occur with the larger nuclei, which are unstable owing to their size. The unstable radium nucleus contains 88 protons and 138 neutrons. It spits out an alpha particle, which is made up of two protons and two neutrons. This leaves a **daughter** nucleus containing 86 protons and 136 neutrons. An inspection of the periodic table tells us that the daughter nucleus is an isotope of the gas radon.

We can write an equation of this decay, using nuclide representation.

Nuclide representation of radium — $^{226}_{88}Ra$
radon — $^{222}_{86}Rn$
alpha particle — $^{4}_{2}\alpha$

$$^{226}_{88}Ra \rightarrow {}^{222}_{86}Rn + {}^{4}_{2}\alpha$$

Note that the **nucleon** numbers on the right-hand side of the equation add up to those on the left-hand side. Similarly the proton numbers also balance.

Beta decay

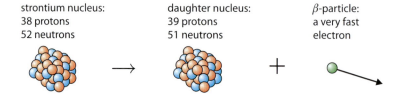

Figure 21.14 Example of beta emission.

The strontium nucleus contains 38 protons and 52 neutrons; it has too many neutrons to be stable. This causes an imbalance between neutrons and protons and a neutron decays into a proton and an electron. This is illustrated by the equation

$$^{1}_{0}n \rightarrow {}^{1}_{1}p + {}^{0}_{-1}\beta$$

n represents the neutron, which has a nucleon number 1 and zero charge or proton number.

p represents the proton, which has a nucleon number 1 and has a charge or proton number of 1.

β represents the electron, which has a nucleon number 0 and a charge of -1, so can be considered to have a proton number of -1.

Radioactivity

The nuclide equation for the beta decay of strontium is

$$^{90}_{38}\text{Sr} \rightarrow\ ^{90}_{39}\text{Y} +\ ^{0}_{-1}\beta$$

Again we see that the proton numbers and the neutron numbers balance on each side of the equation. The daughter element (yttrium) has 39 protons and 51 neutrons.

Gamma decay

radon nucleus which has just been formed following the α-decay of radium

the nucleons in the radon nucleus rearrange themselves into a more stable, lower energy configuration

energy emitted as a pulse of electromagnetic waves

 →   +

◀ Figure 21.15
Example of gamma emission.

Gamma decay occurs in conjunction with alpha or beta decay. After the original decay, the remaining nucleons are left in an unstable, high-energy arrangement. They will rearrange themselves into a more stable, lower energy state and the spare energy is emitted as a gamma ray.

 QUESTIONS

21.1 State what is meant by a) an alpha particle, b) a beta particle and c) a gamma ray.

21.2 State and explain two precautions that should be taken when using radioactive materials.

21.3 Write equations to show the decays of a) $^{222}_{86}$Rn by alpha emission b) $^{14}_{6}$C by beta emission.

Radioactive decay and half-life

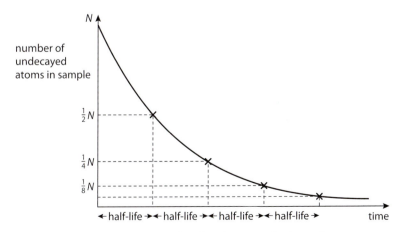

◀ Figure 21.16
Half-life of a radioactive sample.

Activity 21.5
Radioactive decay model

Radioactive emissions occur randomly. If a GM tube is used to measure the background count rate, it will be observed that the count does not go up steadily. It will go up in maybe two or three in quick succession, then

219

a gap before there is another count, then another gap before one or two more and so on.

For a particular nucleus there is a fixed chance that it will decay in the next minute. It is rather like throwing dice. If you throw a die there is 1 in 6 chance that it will show up a six. It may show a six on the very first throw or it may take many throws before the six shows, but on each throw the chances remain 1 in 6.

Because there are many millions of atoms in a sample then a fixed proportion will decay each second. If we start with a sample of isotope containing N atoms, then after a certain time half the atoms will have decayed, leaving $\frac{1}{2}N$ atoms. After an equal interval of time, half the remaining atoms will decay, so that the number of atoms now remaining will be $\frac{1}{4}N$, and so on.

Activity 21.6
Half-life of radon

The time taken for the number of atoms in a sample to halve is called the **half-life** of the isotope.

Half-lives of different isotopes vary from less than a microsecond to millions of years. The half-life of the isotope of radium, $^{226}_{88}$Ra, is 1600 years, yet that of the gas radon ($^{222}_{86}$Rn) is just under a minute.

As the number of atoms left undecayed decreases, so does the **activity** of the sample. The activity is defined as the number of atoms decaying per unit time. It is measured in units called the becquerel (Bq). 1 Bq is equal to 1 count per second.

> **WORKED EXAMPLE**
>
> A scientist finds that the count rate from a sample of a radioactive isotope of potassium is 960 Bq. He takes the count rate again 48 hours later and finds the count rate to be 60 Bq.
>
> Calculate the half-life of the isotope.
>
> $\frac{60}{960} = \frac{1}{16}$
>
> After 1 half-life the count rate falls to $\frac{1}{2}$ the original.
> After 2 half-lives the count rate falls to $\frac{1}{4}$ the original.
> After 3 half-lives the count rate falls to $\frac{1}{8}$ the original.
> After 4 half-lives the count rate falls to $\frac{1}{16}$ the original.
> Therefore four half-lives have passed. The half-life is $\frac{48}{4}$ = **12 hours**.

21.4 Uses of radioactivity

Medical uses

Cancer cells can be destroyed by intense gamma rays. Figure 21.17 shows how a beam of gamma rays is focussed on a tumour. The source is then rotated so that the rays still fall on the tumour but the surrounding healthy tissue receives smaller doses.

Some cancers can be treated with radiation from inside the body. The thyroid gland readily absorbs iodine. If a radioactive isotope of iodine is injected into the bloodstream, it finds its way to the thyroid and destroys the tumour.

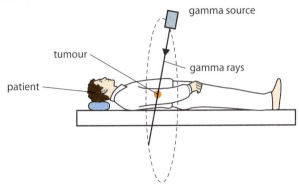

◀ Figure 21.17
Treating tumours with gamma radiation.

Radioactive isotopes are also used as tracers in the diagnosis of a variety of internal conditions. The patient swallows, or is injected with, a small amount of a radioactive isotope. Images of the internal organs can be made from the radiation given off.

Radioactive tracers

Radioactive tracers can be used in many other branches of science. The uptake of phosphates (fertilisers) by plants can be studied by introducing a radioactive isotope of phosphorous.

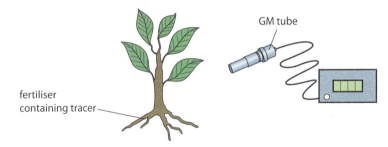

◀ Figure 21.18
The GM tube is used to detect the path of the phosphate through the plant.

The currents in seas or rivers can be studied by using a small amount of radioactive tracer.

Radiocarbon dating

Living tissue contains the radioactive isotope of carbon, $^{14}_{6}C$, formed by the cosmic ray bombardment of nitrogen nuclei in the upper atmosphere. Carbon-14 combines with oxygen to form carbon dioxide, which spreads through the atmosphere, down to ground level, where it is fixed in plants during photosynthesis and then fixed in the animals that eat them. Once the organism dies, the $^{14}_{6}C$ is no longer renewed and it decays with a half-life of 5570 years. By measuring the proportion of $^{14}_{6}C$ to $^{12}_{6}C$ in a sample of tissue, its age can be determined.

▶ Figure 21.19
Carbon dating has been used to date the Turin shroud (the cloth that is claimed to have wrapped the body of Christ) but the results remain controversial.

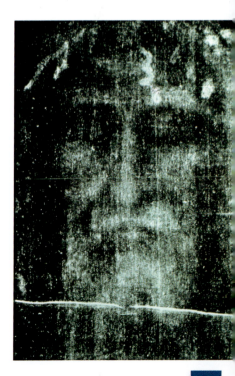

21.5 Nuclear fission

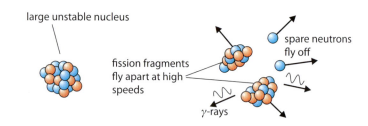

▶ **Figure 21.20** Nuclear fission.

Some of the largest nuclides are so unstable that they spontaneously break apart into two more or less equal halves. This releases large amounts of energy, mostly in the form of kinetic energy of the **fission fragments,** but also gamma rays and kinetic energy of the released neutrons. The process is known as **nuclear fission**.

▼ **Figure 21.21** Are nuclear power stations the energy providers for the future?

Fission is rare in nature, as **fissile** nuclides are rare. One that does exist is the isotope of uranium, $^{236}_{92}U$, but it makes up a tiny percentage of any uranium deposit. However, just less than 1% of natural uranium is the isotope $^{235}_{92}U$, which is capable of absorbing slow-moving neutrons to produce $^{236}_{92}U$. A nuclear reactor uses this to produce energy. The neutrons from one fission reaction are slowed down, enabling them to be captured by $^{235}_{92}U$ to produce more fission reactions. The kinetic energy of the fission fragments is converted to internal energy and used to heat water to produce steam to drive the turbines.

▶ **Figure 21.22** Reactor core of a nuclear power station.

Radioactivity

Advantages and disadvantages of nuclear energy

In a world in which there is a severe shortage of fossil fuels, nuclear energy offers an attractive alternative. There are advantages of using nuclear energy as well as disadvantages. These must be weighed up as decisions are made.

Advantages of nuclear energy
- plentiful supply of suitable fuels
- clean; only small quantities of 'greenhouse gases' emitted

Disadvantages of nuclear energy
- dangers of leaks of radioactive materials
- dangers of meltdown leading to large-scale release of radioactive materials
- the fission fragments are usually radioactive themselves, some with very long half-lives – these need to be stored safely for thousands of years
- the danger that rogue states could use research on nuclear energy as a front for developing nuclear weapons
- the cost of building, and eventually dismantling, a nuclear power station

Myths

If we are making a decision about whether to use nuclear energy and build nuclear power stations, we must beware of the myths and the facts which are often used to argue for or against nuclear energy.

▼ **Table 21.1**
Myths and facts about nuclear energy.

Myth	Fact
A nuclear reactor could run so fast that it becomes a nuclear bomb.	The percentage of $^{235}_{92}U$ in a reactor is not high enough for this to happen. The worst case is that the reactor core would get so hot that there could be a fire or meltdown, releasing radioactive isotopes into the atmosphere.
Terrorists could get hold of enough uranium to build a nuclear bomb.	The percentage of $^{235}_{92}U$ in a reactor is not high enough for them to be able to do this. The fuel would have to be further enriched. They are highly unlikely to have the technology to do this.
No greenhouse gases are emitted in the production of nuclear energy.	In purifying or enriching the fuel with $^{235}_{92}U$ some greenhouse gases are emitted, but less per unit of energy than burning fossil fuels.

21.6 Nuclear fusion

Nuclear fusion is the opposite of nuclear fission. Fission is the splitting of large nuclei into two halves, whereas fusion is the joining together of small nuclei to form larger nuclei.

A helium nucleus (^4_2He) has less potential energy than two separate deuterium nuclei (^2_1H). So if two deuterium nuclei are combined, a large amount of energy is released. The difficulty is actually doing it, as the deuterium atoms need to collide together with speeds large enough to overcome the electrostatic repulsions.

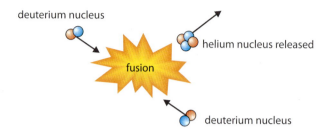

▶ Figure 21.23
Nuclear fusion.

To reach the speeds necessary for fusion to occur, the gas has to be at incredibly high temperatures, in the order of 10 million degrees Celsius! This is so hot that the electrons are ripped off the atoms and it becomes a soup of positive (nuclei) and negative (electrons) particles, known as a **plasma**. In these conditions, the deuterium nuclei can fuse to form helium nuclei with the release of huge amounts of energy. It is fusion reactions that fuel the Sun.

Nuclear fusion has been achieved on Earth, in the H-bomb. The aim is to achieve controlled fusion in which the reaction keeps running at a steady pace rather than running out of control as in the bomb. One of the problems in harnessing fusion power is containing the plasma. If fusion could be controlled it would be an important source of energy – but the problems involved make it highly unlikely that it will be achieved in the near future.

QUESTIONS

21.4 Table 21.2 shows the readings from an experiment to measure the half-life of $^{222}_{86}$Rn.
The background count is negligible.

▶ Table 21.2

Time (s)	Count rate (Bq)
0	348
10	304
20	266
30	233
40	204
50	179
60	157
70	137
80	120
90	105

a) Use the figures to plot a graph of activity against time.
b) Use the graph to find the half-life of $^{222}_{86}$Rn.

Radioactivity

21.5 Describe one medical and one non-medical use of radioactive isotopes.

21.6 Give three advantages of using nuclear fuel to generate electricity compared with using fossil fuels.

21.7 Complete the equations showing the decay of radioactive isotopes.
a) $^{138}_{57}\text{La} \rightarrow \text{Ce} + \beta$
b) $^{192}_{78}\text{Pt} \rightarrow \text{Os} + \alpha$

21.8 The equation gives one form of fusion reaction.
$$^2_1\text{H} + ^3_1\text{H} \rightarrow ^4_2\text{He} + ^1_0\text{n} + \text{energy}$$
a) Give a description of each particle in the reaction.
b) Explain where the energy comes from in the reaction.

21.9 a) Experiments show that α-particles have a shorter range than β-particles and that they both have a shorter range than γ-rays. They also show that α-particles cause most ionisation and γ-rays the least.
Explain how these facts are linked and explain what information they give us about the nature of the different radiations.
b) Experiments with different radiations in electric fields show:
γ-rays cannot be deflected.
β-particles are easily deflected towards the positive plate.
α-particles, though difficult to deflect, can be deflected towards the negative plate.
Explain what these facts tell us about the nature of α, β and γ.

Summary

Now that you have completed this chapter, you should be able to:

- recognise the existence of background radiation
- describe the detection of α-particles, β-particles and γ-rays
- recognise that γ-rays are the most penetrating radiation, followed by β-particles and that α-particles are the least penetrating
- recognise that γ-rays cause the least ionisation, followed by β-particles, and that α-particles cause the most ionisation
- understand the meaning of radioactive decay
- write equations showing changes in the nucleus with alpha and beta decay
- understand the term *half-life* and use it in simple examples
- be aware of safe practice when using or storing radioactive material
- understand what is meant by nuclear fission
- describe the deflection of α-particles, β-particles and γ-rays in electric and magnetic fields
- understand what is meant by nuclear fusion.

Appendix: Circuit diagrams

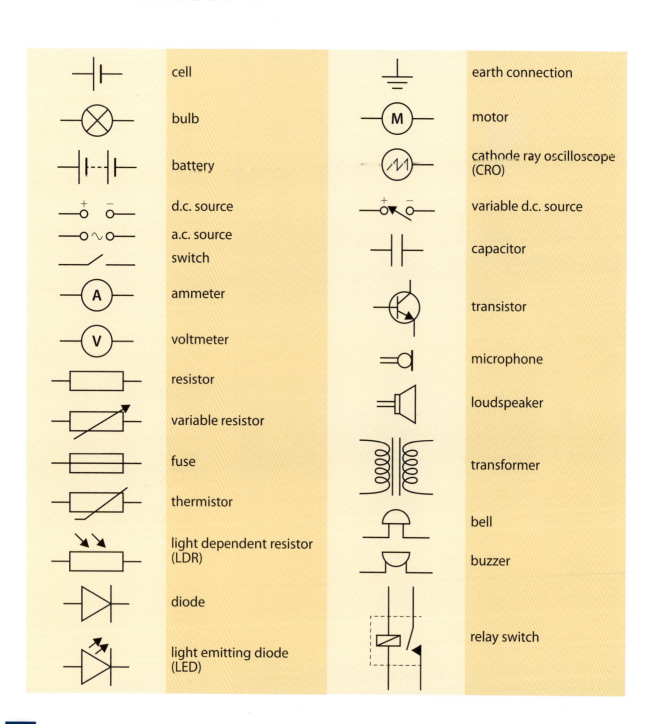

Index

Page numbers in *italics* refer to illustrations.

A

acceleration 13, 16–18, 28, 29, 31
acetate 150
activity (nuclear decay) 220
air resistance 29–30
alpha particles 208, 214, 215, 216, 217, 218
alternating currents 137, 176, 196
alternating emfs 176
ammeters 143–4, 145
ampere (unit) 143, 158
amplitude, waves 98
analogue systems 199
AND gates 201, 203
angles of incidence 112, 116, 117, 118, 119
angles of reflection 112
angles of refraction 116, 117, 118, 119
Antarctica 70
atmospheric pressure 47–9
atomic mass units 210
atoms 62, 150, 206, 207, 209

B

background radiation 213–14
Baird, John Logie 185
barometers 48–9
batteries 155
beam balances 39, 41
becquerel (unit) 220
Becquerel, Henri 213
beta radiation 214, 215, 216, 217, 218–19
Big Bang theory 206–7
bimetal strips 73
binary numbers 199, 200
biofuels 58
Bohr, Niels 209, 210
boiling 87
boiling points 83
Boyle, Robert 67
Boyle's law 67
Brown, Robert 63
Brownian motion 63

C

cancer 214, 220–1
capacitors 194, 195
carbon 221
carbon brushes 173, 174, 176
carbon dioxide 57, 92
cathode ray oscilloscopes (CROs) 186–8
cathode ray tubes 217
cathode rays 207
Celsius scale 75, 81
centres of mass 39–40, 41
centripetal force 31–2
charges (*see* electric charges)
chemical potential energy 53, 54, 55
circuit breakers 166
circuit diagrams 142–3, 144, 226
circular motion 30–2
cirrus clouds 79
clinical thermometers 75
cloud chambers 216–17
compressions (waves) 99, 104
computers 192–3, 200
condensation 84
conductors, electricity 142, 151, 160
conductors, heat 88–90
conservation of energy 56, 178
control systems 202–3
convection 90–1
convection currents 91
converging lenses 121–3
copper 88–9
copper sulfate 90
corkscrew rule 135
coulomb (unit) 151, 156, 157, 167
critical angles (refraction) 118–19
cumulus clouds 79
Curie, Marie & Pierre 213, 214
currents (*see* electric currents)

D

daughter nuclei (atoms) 218
Davy, Humphrey 89
Davy Safety Lamp 89

density 7–9
deuterium *211*, 223–4
diamonds *61*, 118
diffraction 102, 128
diffuse reflection *112*
digital systems 199
diminished images 120
diodes 196
direct currents 137, 176, 196
dispersion, light 127
distance–time graphs 14

E

Earth 134
echo sounding 106
echoes 106
Edison, Thomas 141
Einstein's Theory of Relativity 207
elasticity 24
electric cars 155
electric charges 149–52
electric currents 135–6, 143–5, 155–68, 172–3
electric fields 150, 207
electric forces 149
electric motors 173–4
electrical hazards 165
electrical potential energy 53, 155, 167–8, 178, 195
electricity 181
electromagnetic induction 175
electromagnetic spectrum 92, 126–30, 217
electromagnets 137–8
electron beams 186–7, 207
electron microscopes *61*
electrons 150, 151, 152, 186, 189, 207–8, 209, 210, 217, 218
e.m.f.s 157, 175, 176
endoscopes 120
energy 51, 52–7, 59
equilibrium 38, 41
errors 3
evaporation 87

227

expansion 71–4
eyes, humans 113, 130

F

Faraday, Michael 176
Faraday's law of electromagnetism 175
ferromagnetic materials 132, 136
fissile nuclides 222
fission fragments 222
fixed points, temperature scales 75
fixed potential dividers 196
Fleming's Left Hand Rule *173*
focal lengths 121
force fields (*see* electric fields, magnetic fields)
forces (*see also* electric forces) 21–32, 56
fossil fuels 51, 57, 92
Franklin, Benjamin 148
free electrons 90, 151
frequency, waves 98, 99
fuses (electricity) 166

G

gamma radiation 130, 214, 215, 216, 217, 219
    uses 220
gases 62, 65, 74
Geiger-Muller (GM) tubes 215, 219
geothermal energy 58
gradients, graphs 17
graphs 14–18
gravitational potential energy 53, 56
gravity 22, 29, 32, 133
Greeks 206
greenhouse effect 57, 92–3, 223

H

H-bombs 224
half-lives 220, 221
helium 223
Hooke's law 24
hydroelectricity 58
hydrogen *211*

I

infrared radiation 55, 92–3, 128, 130
insulators, electricity 142, 151
insulators, heat 90
integrated circuits 192, 200
internal energy 54, 55, 80
inverse relationships 66
inverted images 120
iodine 221
isotopes 211, 221

J

Joint European Torus 131
joule (unit) 51, 52, 156, 167

K

kinetic energy 53, 54, 57, 83, 84
kinetic model of matter 64, 83, 84

L

laminas 40
latent heats of fusion 83, 85
latent heats of vaporisation 83, 86
lateral inversion 114
length 3
lenses 111, 120–3
Lenz, Heinrich 178
Lenz's law 178
leukaemia 214
light 112–23, 127–8
light dependent resistors (LDRs) 193, 196
light-emitting diodes 197
light operated switches 197
lightning conductors 148
limits of proportionality 24
linear scales 74
lines of magnetic force 133
liquid-in-glass thermometers 74, 76
liquids 62, 64, 73
logic gates 200–3
longitudinal waves 103–4
Lovell Radio Telescope *126*

M

maglev trains 171
magnetic fields 133–6, 172, 188–9, 207
magnetic induction (*see also* electromagnetic induction) 132
magnets 131–7, 171, 172–3
magnifying glasses 123
manometers 48
mass 5–6, 22
measuring cylinders 4
melting points 83
menisci (*singular* meniscus) 4
mercury 48
metals 71, 90, 151
metre 2, 3
microwaves 129
Millikan, Robert 208
mirrors 113–14
models (theories) 65
molecules 62–7
moments 35–7
motor effect 173

N

NAND gates 202
negative charges 149, 150
neon 211
neutrons 150, 210, 211, 218
newton (unit) 21, 22, 28
Newton, Isaac 25, 129
newton metre (unit) 36

Newton's First Law of Motion 25
nimbocumulus clouds *79*
north-seeking poles 131
NOR gates 203
NOT gates 201
nuclear energy 223
nuclear fission 58, 222, 223
nuclear fusion 131, 223–4
nuclear model (atoms) 209
nuclear potential energy 53
nuclei (atoms) 150, 209–11, 218–19
nucleon numbers 211, 218
nuclides 211, 218, 220, 222

O

ohm (unit) 158
optical fibres 120
OR gates 200–1
oscilloscopes 107

P

parallax error 3
parallel circuits 144–5, 163–4, 165
pendulums 5
periods (pendulums) 5
periscopes 114, 119
pivots 38
plasmas 224
poles, magnets 131
pollutants 57
polythene 150, 152
positive charges 149, 150
potential differences 156–7, 158, 163, 164, 165, 167–8, 194
potential dividers 195–6, 197, 203
power 58–9
prefixes (units) 2
pressure 43–9
    gases 66–7
pressure waves 104
primary coils (transformers) 179
principal foci (lenses) 121
prisms 119, 127
proportionality 23, 24
proton numbers 211
protons 150, 210, 211, 218

Q

quarks 206

R

radiation (heat) 55, 92–3
radio waves 102, 129
radioactive tracers 221
radioactivity 213–21
radiocarbon dating 221
radium 218
radon 218, *219*
range, thermometers 74

Index

range of hearing 108
rarefactions (waves) 99, 104
real images 120
rectification (electric currents) 196
reflection 101, 112
refraction 101, 115–17, 118
refractive indices 116–17, 118, 119
relay switches 138, 198
resistance 158–64, 194
resistors 162–4, 194
ring commutators 173, 174
ripple tanks 100
riveting 72
Röntgen, Wilhelm *126*
Royal Society 67
Rutherford, Ernest 208–9, 210, 217

S

scalars 16
scattering, light *112*
secondary coils (transformers) 179
sensitivity, thermometers 74
sensors (electronics) 193
series circuits 143, 162–3, 165
SI units 2
silicon chips (*see* integrated circuits)
slip rings 176
soft iron 137, 174, 178, 179
solar energy 58
solenoids 136, 138, 177–9
solids 62, 64
sound 103–8
sound energy 54
south-seeking poles 131
specific densities 81
specific heat capacities 80

specific latent heats of fusion 85
specific latent heats of vaporisation 86
speed 12–13
speed of sound 105
speed–time graphs 15, 17, 18
spring balances 23
stability 41
standard form 3
step-down transformers 179, 181
step-up transformers 179, 180–1
strain energy 53
stratus clouds *79*
strontium 218–19
supernovas *70*

T

television 185
temperature 65–7 , 70, 74–6
temperature controlled switches 198
terminal velocities 30
thermal capacities 80–2
thermal conduction 88
thermionic emission 185
thermistors 193, 198
thermochromic strips 74
thermocouples 75–6
thermometers 74–6
Thomson, J.J. 207–8, 211
thunderstorms *148*
tidal energy 58
time 4–5
time delay circuits 195
total internal reflection 118, 119, 120
transformers 179–81
transistors 197, 198
transmission lines (electricity) 181

transverse waves 99
tritium *211*
truth tables 200

U

ultraviolet radiation 129, 130
uncertainty 2–3
uranium 213, 222

V

variable potential dividers 195
variable resistors 197
vector diagrams 26
vectors 16, 26
velocity 16
virtual images 113
volt (unit) 156, 158, 167
Volta, Alessandro 155
voltmeters 156
volume 4

W

water 8
watt (unit) 58, 59
wave energy 58
wavefronts 100, 101
wavelengths 98, 99, 101, 102
waves 97–102, 128
weight 6, 22
winds 91
work 51–2, 54–5

X

X-rays *61*, *126*, 130, 213